THE NO-LAWSUIT GUIDE TO REAL ESTATE TRANSACTIONS

Dear Greg,
Best wishes and
No Lawsuits.
Barbara Nichols
5-23-14

THE NO-LAWSUIT GUIDE TO REAL ESTATE TRANSACTIONS

Barbara Nichols

McGraw-Hill

New York   Chicago   San Francisco   Lisbon
London   Madrid   Mexico City   Milan   New Delhi
San Juan   Seoul   Singapore   Sydney   Toronto

1 2 3 4 5 6 7 8 9 10   DIG/DIG   15 14 13 12

ISBN 13: 978–0–07–147759–8
ISBN 10: 0–07–147759–4

This publication is designed to provide accurate and authoritative information in regard to the subject matter covered. It is sold with the understanding that neither the author nor the publisher is engaged in rendering legal, accounting, real estate, futures/securities trading, or other professional service. If legal advice or other expert assistance is required, the services of a competent professional person should be sought.

> —*From a Declaration of Principles jointly adopted by a Committee*
> *of the American Bar Association and a Committee of Publishers*

REALTOR® is a federally registered collective membership mark which identifies a real estate professional who is a member of the NATIONAL ASSOCIATION OF REALTORS® and subscribes to its strict code of ethics.

McGraw-Hill books are available at special quantity discounts to use as premiums and sales promotions, or for use in corporate training programs. For more information, please write to the Director of Special Sales, Professional Publishing, McGraw-Hill, Two Penn Plaza, New York, NY 10121–2298. Or contact your local bookstore.

This book is printed on acid-free paper.

CONTENTS

Chapter 3

Chapter 4

Chapter 5

Chapter 8

Mold, Mildew, Lead Paint, and Other Environmental Hazards   91

Chapter 9

Material Facts   113

Chapter 10

Property Stigmas   117

Chapter 11

Standard of Care   123

Chapter 14

Seller Repairs and Credits   155

Chapter 15

Building Permits   167

Chapter 31

Home Warranties, Seller Protection Plans, and General Property Inspector Warranty Plans   271

Chapter 32

Select Your Real Estate Agent the Way You Would Select Your Brain Surgeon!   277

Chapter 33

Summary   289

ACKNOWLEDGMENTS

I would like to extend my sincere thanks to the following individuals and organizations for their review and contribution of ideas presented in this book.

Many of the topics covered in this book were drawn from articles I wrote over the past six years for *REALTOR Magazine,* a publication of the National Association of Realtors. *REALTOR Magazine* law articles that served as the basis for chapters in this book are cited in the references. I am grateful to *REALTOR Magazine* and particularly to Sara Geimer, formally senior editor and now a consultant for NAR *REALTOR Magazine,* and to Mariwyn Evans, senior editor; both worked with me on these articles. I would also like to thank Robert Freedman, senior editor, who motivated me to write this book.

Thanks to: Paul Deffenbaugh, editorial director, *Professional Builder* magazine, Oak Brook, Illinois; Robert T. Bancroft, MAI, RM, certified appraiser, Oregon, Washington, Idaho, and California, Bancroft Appraisal Company, 27 years of experience, Eugene, Oregon; Lee Wilson, chief title officer, First American Title, Los Angeles, California; Michael Merlo, senior title officer, title operations manager, United Title Company, Glendale, California; J. Robert Eckley, managing attorney, Eckley & Associates, Phoenix, Sedona, Tucson, Arizona, and Portland, Oregon; Greg Pyfrom, managing attorney, Blatz, Pyfrom & Associates, Agoura Hills, California; Coleman Greenberg, certified property inspector, certified member ASHI, Dominion Risk Management, Sedona, Arizona; John St. George, 25 years as a general property inspector, member ASHI, NAHI, licensed general contractor, expert witness for property inspections; Stacey Gross, regional vice president, Old Republic Home Protection, Phoenix, Arizona; Jo Gaerlan, vice president, American Home Shield, Santa Rosa, California; Nate Seward, P.E., BCMC, CIEC, CRMI, president, Criterion Environmental, mold, asbestos, lead, vocs (volatile organic compounds), and radon testing, Ventura, California; David Hedman, president, Precision Environmental, CMR, AMRT, CMRS, mold, asbestos, lead, termites, bacteria, viruses, and odor remediators, Ventura, California; Cece and Lew Rubin, Realtors, GRI, MEA, 30 years of experience, New Port Ritchey, Florida; Manel Touvinen, Ph.D., Realtor, 25 years of experience, Columbus, Ohio; Karen Edgers,

Realtor, ABR, CRS, GRI, 27 years of experience, Brookline and Newton, Massachusetts; Rob Paterkiewicz, CAE, IOM, executive director, ASHI, Des Plaines, Illinois; Mary Bension, president, MB Escrow, Inc., Beverly Hills, California; Wendy Keller, literary agent, Keller Media, Inc., Malibu, California; Miguel A. Rosa, graphic designer, Miguelángelo Design, Alameda, California.

I would also like to thank my father, Charles M. Nichols, a licensed general contractor and expert witness, from whom I learned so much and who always believed in me.

Barbara Nichols

INTRODUCTION

Lawsuits: The Overlooked Subject in Real Estate

So you are buying or selling a property, or representing a buyer or seller as the real estate agent. Maybe you are a general property inspector, a builder, a developer, or a property manager. Are you thinking about the transaction leading to a lawsuit? You may not be considering the potentially costly and nerve-racking situation of a lawsuit, but you should be thinking about it—and you should be prepared to avoid it.

> This book covers the importance of understanding the risk of liability in any real estate transaction, to all parties involved, and how liability can be prevented.

Most purchase and sale lawsuits are brought by disgruntled buyers against everyone else involved. However, sellers sue as well and will often sue their agent, the buyer's agent, and the property inspector in a cross complaint, when they are sued by the buyer.

There were over 7 million existing home sales and over 1.4 million new-home sales in the United States in 2005. Millions more apartments and homes are rented each year. Existing properties usually have a history, good or bad, regarding their neighborhood and condition. New-home sales have no history and rely heavily on the integrity and attention to quality of the builder and developer.

Countless books and infomercials tout the potential for making money in purchasing real estate as a homeowner or investor. Yet none warns about the potential pitfalls of these huge financial decisions. How can you be sure you are getting what you think you are getting? How do you properly investigate your potential purchase? What role can real estate agents play in helping to prevent lawsuits? What is the role of the general property inspector and of other inspectors in assessing property condition? How can builders and developers more effectively avoid being sued by unhappy buyers? All these parties play interactive roles, each relying on the other, and each requiring an understanding of his or her duties and the legal minefield that awaits them. It is not enough to deny responsibility, deflect the blame to others, or claim ignorance. Prevention is the best policy. It is, after all, the desire of all involved that a transaction, once completed, does not have to be revisited in an attorney's office or courtroom.

Construction and housing are our nation's largest industry and the engine of our economy. Purchasing a home or investment property is typically the largest financial decision of a person's life. It has sometimes amazed me how little the average buyer and seller truly understands about the ramifications of their decisions throughout the entire purchase process. Some real estate agents have received very little training in risk management, although this is changing. Individuals and companies jump into the inspection business, sometimes untrained and unprepared for the consequences of their actions. Builders and developers are sometimes uncertain of what they should disclose and face price pressures that may lead to regrettable quality decisions.

Even if buyers or sellers are not losing sleep over fear of a lawsuit in their real estate transactions, handling a transaction in a way that will most effectively reveal a property's true condition will, in the end, result in a more satisfied client. All buyers want to know what they are buying and hate surprise revelations of problems after the close. All sellers want to say goodbye to their property and not deal with it again in a lawsuit.

Thousands of real estate–related lawsuits are filed each year. Many more buyers or sellers arbitrate or mediate their disputes, and still many more would like to sue and cannot because of the cost of initiating a lawsuit. This book is written by an active real estate broker who has consulted on hundreds of real estate–related lawsuits. I am not an attorney and, therefore, cannot give legal advice. The content of this book is based on my many years of practical experience as an expert witness and real estate broker.

It is easy enough to blame lawsuits on lawyers. I have frequently heard those who are sued talk about "frivolous" lawsuits. My experience has been that lawyers are reluctant to take on lawsuits that do not appear to have merit. It is the "merit" or situation of dissatisfaction that needs to be eliminated to eliminate the lawsuits, and that is the subject of this book.

> *Avoid lawsuits beyond all things; they pervert your conscience,*
> *impair your health, and dissipate your property.*
>
> —Jean de la Bruyere

1
CHAPTER

The Liability Problem

ESCALATING NUMBER OF LAWSUITS

No one wants to become involved in a lawsuit! Real estate agents, their brokers, buyers, sellers, and general property inspectors, these key participants in resale real estate transactions are, however, being sued in record numbers—by one another. In new construction sales, the builder and developer are also involved in the lawsuit. Property managers are sued by tenants, and tenants are sued by property managers and owners.

Statistics show that one in five real estate agents will be involved in a lawsuit. The legal environment in recent years, especially since the mid-eighties, has shifted from "buyer beware" to "agents and sellers take care." The burden to disclose information that might affect the value of the property, which buyers could not reasonably be expected to know or discover, has been placed on the sellers and real estate agents. The general property inspector's role has become much more prominent in the past 20 years than it used to be, and some of the disclosure duty has shifted to the general property inspector. Buyers and sellers need to understand their role in preventing lawsuits, and the roles of their agents, inspectors, and builders in protecting their interests.

> Lawsuit claims most often involve property condition, personal injury, fair housing, property management, neighborhood issues, environmental hazards, and agent misconduct.

All the participants in a real estate transaction unwittingly find themselves in a lawsuit because of a lack of knowledge or faulty knowledge on how to avoid the problems that lead to a lawsuit. Rarely, in my experience, do these lawsuits result from intentional malice on the part of any one participant. The participants either underestimate the significance of a property defect or do not believe that it is their responsibility to see it, know it, research it, disclose it, or repair it.

As property prices are rising, potential losses to disgruntled buyers and sellers are rising. Real estate is now a significant part of an individual's or family's investment and retirement portfolio. Higher values generally translate into higher losses when problems are discovered, and these losses make even high-cost lawsuits viable.

To solve a problem it is necessary to think. It is necessary to think even to decide what facts to collect.

—Robert Maynard Hutchins

COST OF LAWSUITS TO ALL PARTIES

Lawsuits result in a high financial cost to all involved. Our legal process moves slowly, and lawsuits can take years to resolve. Few attorneys today will undertake the expense of a real estate lawsuit on contingency. Buyers and sellers are usually on a "pay as they bill" status with their attorneys and experts. The sellers may have to take back the property, or pay out huge claims. Real estate agents may not be covered by errors and omissions (E&O) insurance, or if covered, their insurance may have a high deductible or not cover all of their costs. Buyers have to pay large sums to hire lawyers and experts on their case with no assurance they will win. If the buyers lose the case, the defendants may ask the court to award them their legal expenses, which the buyers would then have to pay. General property inspectors often have no E&O insurance and limited assets.

Those inspectors with E&O insurance have deductibles and, in some cases, may have claims their insurance does not cover. Builders and developers may or may not have insurance coverage and also face legal expenses to defend their case, sometimes against a class action lawsuit brought by many buyers.

The property management company, manager, or property owners will also have expenses for defending themselves if sued, even if insured, and unlikely will recover all of the costs, even if they win in a lawsuit brought by a tenant. Few real estate lawsuits actually go to trial, and most are settled out of court. Civil court cases with a jury are very expensive to litigate and defend. Even a bench trial with a judge and no jury involves a tremendous amount of time and preparation by the parties involved and their attorneys. Sometimes the plaintiff who wins in court may be astonished at the low court award for damages. Winners in real estate lawsuits seldom believe they receive adequate funds to pay their attorneys and make necessary property repairs; let alone compensate them for their stress, inconvenience, and sometimes related health issues.

> *I was never ruined but twice: once when I lost a lawsuit, and once when I won one.*
>
> —Voltaire

ERRORS AND OMISSIONS AND LIABILITY INSURANCE

Real estate agents, general property inspectors, builders, and developers are spending more every year on their E&O insurance. The National Association of Realtors' monthly publication, *REALTOR Magazine,* published an article in January 2005 that reported that although estimates varied by carrier and by state, typical basic premiums for real estate E&O insurance range from $200 to $400 per associate per month. Rates are increasing annually as lawsuits and claims paid increase. Even though real estate agents may not be found at fault in a lawsuit, the costs of defense are still high, representing 40 to 60 percent of the cost of a claim. Some insurance carriers have withdrawn from the market, or from states with high numbers of lawsuits and claims paid. Real estate agents also need liability insurance to cover possible damage they, or prospective buyers or other agents, may do to a property and to cover possible injury to prospective buyers or real estate agents at the property.

General property inspectors are almost always drawn into a real estate lawsuit. Liability coverage is necessary in case the inspector damages the property being inspected. Some inspectors are bonded for claims of theft. Builders and developers need worker's comp insurance, liability insurance, bonding insurance, and E&O insurance. Sellers need fire, theft, and liability insurance.

As with any insurance coverage, there are always exclusions. Fraud is never covered by insurers. The accused may have his legal defense covered by his insurance, because the charge of fraud is as yet unproven. However, if the accused is found to have committed a fraud, the insurer will not pay any court award to the injured party. Mold and mildew claims have increased so much in recent years that E&O insurers are no longer covering this claim in lawsuits. The accused may be defended under his policy, but any agreed-to settlement or court award will not be paid by the insurer. Insurers have also excluded other situations that they foresee as possible conflicts of interest. For example, the real estate agent who is a dual agent, representing both the sellers and buyers, who also elects to become one of the buyers, will probably not be covered under her E&O insurance for either the cost of defense or the pay out of a claim if she is successfully sued by the sellers. Parties found at fault can find themselves in debt for many years paying a claim.

STRESS OF A LAWSUIT

The stress of a lawsuit can be incredible. Initially, the party sued receives a complaint for damages, with charges of misrepresentation and/or fraud. The complaint is usually delivered by a process server to the unsuspecting recipient. Upon opening the envelope and starting to read the complaint, the recipient may experience sweating palms, an increased heart rate, a rise in blood pressure, weak knees, and wobbly legs. All are typical signs of acute panic and anticipation of the ordeal to come. As the reader advances through the 20 to 40 pages of charges and complaints, the symptoms intensify. This scenario is only the beginning of what is usually a two- to three-year misery that hangs over his head night and day. Yet to come are the endless meetings with attorneys. The interrogatories, the search for documents and records, the depositions, the revised complaints, and the countersuits that are part of the lawsuit process are exhausting to those who sue and those being sued.

Nothing in life is to be feared. It is only to be understood.

—Marie Curie

AVENUES FOR MAKING A COMPLAINT PRIOR TO A LAWSUIT

The unhappy buyers, sellers, or tenants may first file a complaint with the real estate agent's local chapter of the National Association of Realtors for review by its grievance committee and possibly its professional standards committee. An impartial panel of real estate agents will then hear all sides, and if the real estate agent is found at fault, fines may be levied. In addition, the agent may be required to take courses, such as an ethics course. I currently serve on the professional standards committee of my chapter association of Realtors, so I can attest to the fact that real estate agents sincerely want their peers to act professionally and appropriately with the public they serve. These professional panels, however, cannot award money to the complaining member of the public. This process of professional review is available to any client or customer of a real estate agent who is a member of the National Association of Realtors. Many real estate agents also serve on arbitration panels, which assist the parties in a dispute in attempting to settle their complaint before it becomes a lawsuit. Many real estate contracts now have an arbitration clause included, which, when signed by the parties, requires arbitration prior to a lawsuit being filed. There are currently over 1.2 million members of the National Association of Realtors. It is the largest trade association in the world. However, not all real estate agents belong to the National Association of Realtors, whose members can refer to themselves as Realtors as well as real estate agents.

The party with a real estate transaction complaint can also appeal to her state department of real estate, board of registration, and so on. Each state has its own procedures for filing complaints and investigating lenders, real estate agents, property inspectors, builders, and developers whom they license and whose activities they monitor. It is usually when these avenues of complaint are exhausted that disgruntled buyers or sellers will turn to the court system. Some complaints can be dealt with in small claims court for amounts usually under $10,000. Claims of over $10,000, or the request for some kind of equitable remedy such as rescission of the transaction, are usually brought to the attention of an attorney. Most attorneys are reluctant to undertake a case for a plaintiff if damages fall under $25,000, because of the time and expense of lawsuits.

FREQUENT COMPLAINTS BY BUYERS AND SELLERS

Complaints may be brought before the department of real estate and the contractor's state license board. The most frequent complaints about real estate licensees, or those acting as real estate licensees who do not have a real estate license, that are brought by buyers and sellers are:

- Making any substantial misrepresentation
- Fraud or dishonest dealing in a licensed capacity
- Violation of real estate law or regulations
- Conduct that would have warranted denial of a license
- Negligence or incompetence in performing licensed acts
- Failure of real estate brokerages to supervise their real estate salespeople
- Fraud or dishonest dealing as a principal
- Secret profit or undisclosed compensation
- Failure of a developer to give a public report to the buyer
- Sale of subdivision lots without a public report
- False subdivision advertising

Builders may be the subject of a complaint to the state contractor's licensing board. These licensing agencies of state governments have the capacity to pursue and initiate prosecution of unlicensed builders as well as of those who have obtained licenses. Frequent complaints about builders and developers in new construction are:

- Failure to complete the project in a good and professional manner
- Willful disregard of plans and specifications
- Willful disregard and violation of building laws
- Failure to complete a project for the price stated in the contract
- Committing a fraudulent act
- Failure to complete a project in a timely fashion
- Failure to comply with contract requirements
- False advertising

Many other complaints can be brought in individual or class action lawsuits, depending on the specific circumstances of the transaction.

IMPACT OF LAWSUITS

Lawsuits can have a devastating effect on the people being sued.

Damage to Reputations

The increase in the number of lawsuits being brought affects the reputation of real estate agents and licensed contractors. As I am both a licensed real estate broker and a licensed general contractor, I want the reputation of my profession to be well regarded by the general public. In writing this book, I hope to make all parties to the real estate transaction more aware of how they can act to reduce consumer complaints and lawsuits and improve the public image of their professions.

It is also my hope to educate the buying and selling public in their responsibilities to protect their interests in a real estate transaction. The public's selection of the most qualified providers of real estate and building services will eventually reduce or eliminate those who are not providing an acceptable standard of care.

> *A man's reputation is the opinion people have of him; his character is what he really is.*
>
> —Jack Miner

Possible Loss of a License

Real estate agents and builders risk having their licenses suspended or revoked if they are found at fault in a civil lawsuit. A serious mistake can cost them their career and reputation. Careful attention to detail and risk management procedures can significantly reduce the likelihood of their ever having to face their client in court or defend their right to practice their profession.

THE GROWING COMPLEXITY OF THE REAL ESTATE MARKET

Participants in any capacity in today's real estate market know how complex the typical transaction has become. It seems that every day another document is added to the contract or the disclosures. Average buyers need treatment for writer's cramp after signing volumes of transaction documents. It is usually at this point that the buyers start to feel panic. Have we done the right thing? Did we buy (or rent) the right property? Do we know enough about what we're buying? What are all these documents? Have we just signed our lives away? The sellers may be experiencing another kind of panic. Have we sold for enough money? Should we have told the buyers about something else? Did we forget to mention something? Did we decide not to mention something and now wish we had? Will this transaction come back to haunt us later? Can we really escape to another state?

There has never been a time when more was demanded of real estate agents to meet the requirements of their profession and the needs of their clients and customers. Nor has there ever been more required of buyers and sellers to understand the roles of those they hire to represent their interests as well as their duties and obligations to protect their own interests. To deal with this complexity, real estate departments have been incorporated into the curriculum of many colleges and universities to teach the complexities not only of large commercial developments but also of residential and smaller investment properties as well.

THE ROLE OF THE REAL ESTATE BROKERAGE

Frequent complaints in lawsuits against real estate agents and real estate brokers often result from a lack of adequate training and supervision provided by their office. Office training should include proper completion of all transaction documents and disclosures, information on how to refer and work with property inspectors, handling deposits and escrow funds, dealing with other real estate offices and service providers, fair housing policies, ethics, and the content of this book, which covers risk management and contributing to the professionalism of the real estate community.

Real estate brokerages should have procedures in place to carefully review agent files in a timely fashion and make necessary corrections in how a transaction is progressing. All complaints should be handled promptly by management and should not be left to evolve into a dreaded lawsuit.

THE ROLE OF THE PROPERTY INSURER

Many buyers, sellers, real estate agents, and tenants have mistaken beliefs concerning what property insurers will cover in the event of a problem. Property insurers consist of general insurers that cover fire, theft, and liability, and they sometimes have special coverage, such as for earthquake or flood. Property warranty companies offer policies that warranty repair of certain systems of the property under certain conditions. Umbrella policies may cover certain claims over and above those covered by the other policies of the insured. I have consulted on many legal cases in which the insurer was involved, and I have concluded that few policyholders actually read their policies. They assume more coverage for more circumstances than are actually covered. Buyers need to be aware that their homeowners insurance will probably not cover any preexisting defects in the property. If the prior owners failed to repair leaking pipes that resulted in a mold problem, the insurer might cover repair of the ceiling that was damaged by the leaking pipe. However, leaking pipes are a maintenance issue and would not be covered. Mold resulting from leaking pipes, or any other cause, has been eliminated from most policies, or the coverage has been limited to a maximum of, for example, $5,000.

Making a claim against the sellers and expecting that their insurance carrier would cover latent defects found after the close of the transaction is also unlikely to be productive. The insurer may well deny the claim, saying that it could not be determined when the actual defect occurred. In some circumstances, the sellers' insurer may defend them in a claim made by the buyers, but it would be unlikely that this insurer would pay any resulting settlement or court award.

Insurance umbrella policies are quite specific in what they will and will not cover. They usually provide for additional coverage beyond the coverage of existing policies. They do not cover defects or problems not covered already by an existing policy, and they do not add coverage protection to property warranty policy limits.

NEIGHBOR-TO-NEIGHBOR LAWSUITS

Neighbor-to-neighbor lawsuits are definitely on the rise. Seldom do buyers, who are preoccupied with their property purchase, take the time or even consider their soon-to-be new neighbors as a potential liability. The real estate agents involved in the transaction may also overlook this issue or simply not know of some existing problem. The sellers would know of most relevant neighbor issues that would be important to buyers but may not realize the importance or the necessity of disclosing them. Some sellers may choose to not disclose a neighbor problem for fear of affecting their property value or becoming unable to sell at all. Any sellers who knowingly fail to disclose an important neighbor issue known to them are setting themselves up for a lawsuit later. Within days or hours the new buyers will become aware of the problem by some action of the neighbor or will be told of the problem by another neighbor. If you are the offending neighbor, in some cases your property insurer may defend you in a lawsuit brought by the neighbor you have possibly harmed. Examples of such situations might be:

- The neighbor accuses you of cutting down trees on her property to improve your view
- The neighbor below the rear of your property sues for damages as a result of a portion of your rear, down-sloping yard sliding onto his property
- The neighbor accuses your dog of having bitten her child
- The neighbor accuses you of encroaching on his property with your fence

Dog attacks or bites have now become so common that many insurers will no longer cover dog liability. Some will cover dogs, but exclude certain breeds that are very large or have a history of frequent biting and attacks. Buyers should consult with their property insurer to be sure that their pet is covered under their policy. Neighbor issues, such as loud parties, vicious dogs, barking dogs, frequent loud motorcycles, and so on, are off-site issues. They are not covered by general property inspectors. The buyers will justifiably rely on the sellers to disclose these facts. Other neighbor-related issues may be disputes with the neighbors in a condominium building or the condo association management or board of directors. Examples of these issues might be:

- The neighbor who plays loud music late at night
- The neighbor with an illegal pet (according to the association rules)
- The neighbor who picks fights with others in the building
- The neighbor who refuses to comply with exterior decor requirements of the association, such as hanging noisy wind chimes or painting his balcony blue

The resulting animosity of neighbor-to-neighbor lawsuits can linger long after the issue is resolved.

1 PART

ISSUES RAISED IN LAWSUITS

2 CHAPTER

Misrepresentation and Fraud

WHAT IS MISREPRESENTATION?

Typical time frames for buyers or sellers to file a lawsuit claiming misrepresentation against a real estate agent or broker are two years from the date the transaction closes. For a claim of fraud, the time frame is up to three years after the fraud is discovered. The time frame to file for misrepresentation or fraud may vary somewhat from state to state.

Misrepresentation is categorized in three forms:

1. *Negligent misrepresentation.* Making a false statement about a material fact that the broker (or party) did not know but should have known was false.
2. *Negligent nondisclosure.* Failure to disclose a material fact for lack of exercising adequate care in obtaining information about the property.
3. *Negligent advice.* Giving incorrect professional advice when the agent should have known the advice was wrong.[1]

Only misstatements of facts are actionable, not statements of opinion. However, opinion statements may be interpreted as actionable if they are

---

[1] Robert de Heer, *Realty Blue Book* (Chicago: Real Estate Education Company, a division of Dearborn Publishing, Inc., 1998) edition 32, misrepresentation and nondisclosure, c–7.

stated as if they are fact by someone in a position to know the truth. A real estate agent who points to a fence and says that in her opinion that fence is on the property boundary may have this representation regarded as fact, unless stated as merely an opinion.

FRAUD CAN BE ACTIVE OR PASSIVE

There are two types of fraud claims that can be made—active fraud or passive:

1. *Intentional misrepresentation (active fraud).* Knowingly making a false statement about a material fact.
2. *Intentional concealment (constructive fraud or passive fraud).* Knowingly failing to disclose a material fact.[2]

In a claim of intentional misrepresentation or active fraud, the plaintiff must prove:

a. a false representation
b. of a material fact (rather than opinion)
c. which the speaker knows to be false or makes in culpable ignorance of its truth or falsity
d. upon which the speaker intends the (party) to rely
e. which is justifiably relied upon by the (party), and
f. which leads to injury to the (party).[3]

Misrepresentation and fraud can be claimed through oral or written representations of the party being sued. The property owner may be vicariously liable for damages for the real estate agent's misrepresentation, even where the property owner was not the source of the erroneous information conveyed to the buyer by the agent. The real estate agent can be liable for the misrepresentations of the seller if she repeats those misrepresentations to the buyer and has reason to believe those representations may not be true. The seller's agent may also be liable if she repeats representations of the seller and has made no effort to either verify the truth or claim that the representations have not been verified by the agent.

---

[2] Ibid.

[3] From *Buyer Beware to Broker Take Care*, Legal Liability Series (Chicago: National Association of Realtors, 1988), reprinted with permission.

LOAN FRAUD

Most real estate lenders will give a better loan rate to a property that is to be owner-occupied than to one that will not be owner-occupied. Some lenders will not loan at all on non-owner-occupied or investment properties. When the real estate agent for the buyers or the buyers themselves represent to the buyers' lender that the property will be owner-occupied, knowing that it will not be, they can later be accused of loan fraud.

Another form of loan fraud is a real estate agent or a buyer asking an appraiser to inflate the value of the property to allow the buyer a higher loan amount on the property in excess of what the lender would have otherwise provided.

From the errors of others a wise man corrects his own.

—Publilius Syrus

ADVERTISING AND MISREPRESENTATION

Nothing modernizes a home so completely as an ad offering it for sale.

—Jerome K. Jerome

Real estate advertising descriptions, sometimes referred to as "puffing," are generally all right, as long as they are stated as opinions and not representations of fact. For example:

- This property has a lovely yard.
- This is a wonderful home for entertaining.
- The living room and family room are spacious.

Advertising should be carefully reviewed to ensure that it is not misleading or incorrect. For example:

- This property has over 4,000 square feet (when the square footage has not been verified).
- This property is in the Beverly Hills school district (when it is not).
- This property has been totally remodeled (when the real estate agent has not asked in detail what the seller did that constitutes a total remodel).

Completely remodeled! Ocean view!

Real estate agents must be very careful about what they claim in their advertising, MLS (multiple listing service) listings, and ad brochures. Lawsuit claims frequently reference literature prepared by the agent upon which the buyer relied. The agent should verify any information provided in her advertising, MLS listings, and brochures or not include it. The seller should be asked to read and approve all advertising, MLS listings, and brochures.

3

C H A P T E R

Red Flags

In real estate we refer to red flags all the time, but do all the participants to the real estate transaction really understand what red flags are and why they are so important?

> A red flag can be anything that alerts you to a potential problem or that just doesn't seem quite right.

Noting red flags in a transaction may result in the buyer's request for repairs, but it is far better than overlooking them, which can leave the buyer and seller vulnerable to a lawsuit, as well as the real estate agents, their brokers, and the general property inspector.

Red flags can be divided into three major categories: visual or sensory, written, and situational.

VISUAL OR SENSORY RED FLAGS

A *visual red flag* is one that can be seen, such as a stain on a ceiling, a retaining wall that is leaning, or floors that aren't level. A *sensory red flag* might be a strange, musty odor or a feeling of dampness. Even in states where real estate agents are not required to provide a written disclosure of observed property defects, it is a good policy for the buyer's or seller's agent to disclose what he or she knows, or can reasonably observe, concerning the physical defects of a property.

> The agent's observation of a property's possible defect, or a condition that might lead to a defect, should be completely separate from either the seller's disclosures or the report of the general property inspector, even if these disclosures overlap.

In one legal case, the listing agent represented a bank, which had taken a property in a foreclosure. He observed and photographed cracks on exterior walls at the foundation. However, he failed to provide the photo or disclose his observation to the buyers or the buyers' agent after the bank's workers repainted the property, concealing the cracks. The property cracks began to reappear shortly after the buyers' purchase. Further investigation by the buyers revealed that the property had significant land movement and required major repairs. The agents, general property inspector, and bank were sued by the buyers. The bank had to take back the property. The key fact in this case was the red flag observation by the listing agent of foundation cracks, which was not disclosed, and once concealed, was not within the observation of the buyers to investigate further.

Repair work can also raise red flags. For example, wide cracks in a patio deck that have been filled with cement and floor tile in the adjoining interior that appears new may indicate a repair that is masking an underlying problem. Did the cracks outside also extend inside? Is the new tile covering interior cracks in the cement slab below? The sellers in one case knew of these defects when they purchased the property, but they failed to disclose the engineer's reports describing the extent of the problem. The sellers claimed to have fixed a foundation problem, but they provided no permits or receipts. The house was repainted and the floor tile was replaced before the property was listed for sale. The buyer preferred hardwood flooring. When the new tile was pulled up, the large cracks were revealed. The entire foundation of the house needed to be rebuilt, and the subsoil had to be amended and compacted. The sellers, agents, and general property inspector were sued.

The agents, buyer, and general property inspector should document the sellers' answers to these types of questions and recommend appropriate further inspections. The listing agent should strongly advise her seller clients to disclose anything that may have been "covered" by recent repairs. Sellers should be advised that paint and carpet may temporarily cover a problem but that buyers will eventually find the defect, and the sellers will be liable.

> *Conceal a flaw and the world will imagine the worst.*
>
> —Marcus Valerius Martialis

WRITTEN RED FLAGS

Red flags can also appear in writing in any transaction document such as the listing in the multiple listing service (MLS), the listing agent's advertising, or the preliminary title report. In a transaction several years ago, I represented the buyer of a property for which the preliminary title report indicated that the owner of record for the property was not the individual who signed the contract of sale. The listing agent was contacted, and she questioned her seller client. The client explained that his brother had quitclaimed the property to him, but apparently he had failed to properly record the quitclaim. The title officer was then contacted and was able to correct the problem by having the quitclaim properly recorded. The appropriate action of the agents, in noting and investigating this red flag, cleared the title issue and allowed the transaction to proceed.

In a mold case where the dual agent represented his mother-in-law, the seller, the agent overlooked an obvious red flag in his mother-in-law's property disclosure. She claimed that after living 54 years on the subject property, there were absolutely no defects to document. Unfortunately, there is no such perfect property.

Beware the seller who claims a perfect property in any written disclosure.

Another written red flag is when the seller admits in the disclosure to constructing an addition without a permit, but says that it was built to code. That claim is highly unlikely, as reputable builders do not build without permits, and if the seller is willing to violate local permit ordinances, why not also the building codes?

SITUATIONAL RED FLAGS

A *situational red flag* is indicated by circumstances of sale or area issues. For example, a foreclosure sale by a bank might be regarded as a situational red flag. The bank may have no information on the history of the property and is usually exempt from providing a written disclosure, even in states requiring a seller's written disclosure of property defects. The bank must still disclose what it knows about property condition, but this is usually minimal information. Banks or anyone taking back a property in foreclosure and then making cosmetic repairs must be careful not to inadvertently cover defects the cause of which has not been analyzed. All repairs made should be disclosed. States may vary in their requirements for disclosures on foreclosed properties.

Problems prevalent in the area can also be situational red flags. Does a particular development have a reputation for having houses with faulty chimneys? The real estate agents for the buyer and seller should recommend that the buyer have a chimney inspection to ensure that the chimney on the property being purchased does not have a problem. Is the property in an area known to have poor soil conditions that result in foundation problems? The agents for the buyers and sellers should recommend to the buyer that a structural engineer examine the foundation. Knowing that there are situational red flags in the area will further alert the buyer to investigate thoroughly, in relation to the specific purchase. The agents who omit this type of red flag disclosure are left open to a lawsuit. It will probably take only a few days or weeks until a neighbor informs the new buyer about these issues, which the buyer will justifiably believe the seller and agents should have disclosed.

Environmental issues, such as the potential presence of lead paint, asbestos, mold, or radon gas, might also be situational red flags in certain areas and in properties built before certain dates. Real estate agents should be aware of the existence of these issues in their area. Each of these environmental hazards may be present but may not be observable to either the buyers or the agents. Few general property inspectors are properly

Note visual red flags!

certified or licensed to test for the presence of environmental hazards. Buyers should be told by the sellers and agents if these environmental hazards may be present in the area, and the buyers should be advised to hire the appropriate environmental experts to test for them.

Builders and developers can face many of these same situational and environmental red flags. As land becomes scarce for development, builders sometimes take huge risks to develop properties near former waste dumps, industrial sites, polluted waterways, or on poor and unstable soils. Situational red flags must be thoroughly disclosed to prospective buyers, and the buyers should be encouraged to investigate them.

4
C H A P T E R

The Real Estate Agents' Visual Inspection and Disclosures

In a transaction, what real estate agents don't see, if it's something they should have seen, can result later in a lawsuit. Real estate agents are required to disclose any known or readily observable property defects to buyers and sellers.

A real estate agent could be held liable for negligent misrepresentation by providing a material fact to a buyer without actually knowing if the material fact is true. For example, does the seller's real estate agent actually know that the roof was replaced three years ago or that the only area of the building constructed without a permit is a downstairs bathroom? Is the agent just repeating what the seller told her? In acting as a conduit of information between the buyer and the seller, the seller's and buyer's agents need to make clear to the buyer what information provided has been verified and what has not been verified. All disclosures of observed or known facts should be put in writing to the buyer.

Ignorance is no defense for a real estate agent, representing either the buyer or the seller, if the real estate professional *should* have known about a material defect. The real estate agent may still be liable for innocent misrepresentation. The National Association of Realtors (NAR) code of ethics obligates Realtors to discover and disclose adverse factors reasonably apparent to someone with expertise in the areas authorized by

their real estate licensing authority. Real estate agents are not expected to
have the expertise of a general contactor or a general property inspector.
Real estate agents are not expected to climb into attics or crawl under
houses. However, real estate agents do have a duty to use their powers of
observation in a reasonable and orderly way to spot flaws or potential
flaws that are clearly visible.

Nothing is so firmly believed as that which is least known.

—Michel de Montaigne

The real estate agents for both the buyer and the seller have this
independent duty of disclosure. In some states a written visual disclosure
by the real estate agents is required only in sales of one- to four-unit properties. In other states, no written disclosure is required at all. Real estate
agents can still be held liable if it is later discovered that they knew of
property defects and did not disclose them, whether the property is one to
four units or more. Many state associations of Realtors recommend that
real estate agents provide written disclosure whether mandated by the
state or not.

> All real estate agents representing buyers or sellers should conduct a
> visual inspection of the property and note all material facts, observed
> or known, in written form, to be delivered to the buyers and copied to
> the sellers and other agents. This recommendation is applicable to all
> property types.

CONDUCTING A VISUAL PROPERTY INSPECTION

I would recommend that the buyer's and seller's real estate agents independently do their own inspection. Each should start on the outside of the
building, with paper and pen. Does the rear yard slope down toward the
house? Is the cement or tile around the pool cracked or lifting? Is the brick
cracked on an exterior chimney? Now the real estate agents should look
inside the structure. Is there any sign of mold or mildew on walls or
floors? Is there a musty odor? Are there cracks in the walls?

Some real estate offices and real estate associations have developed forms to help guide the real estate agents through their inspection process, in much the same way that general property inspectors follow a prescribed format in viewing the property. However, this form is designed for real estate agents and their more limited visual inspection. A column on the left lists those areas of the property the agent would be expected to look at and note any defects. The area to the right of each observed area has lines where the agent can note any observation of a defect. This form can be attached to the seller's disclosure form or retyped for separate delivery.

What we see depends mainly on what we look for.

—John Lubbock

After the seller's agent has completed his visual inspection, he should question the seller regarding defects he has observed. If the buyer's agent sees inconsistencies in the seller's disclosures concerning his observations or knowledge of property defects, these should be discussed with the seller's agent and confirmed in writing. Explanations from the seller concerning these defects should then be noted in a disclosure to the buyer.

The agents recording their observations should sign and date the document. The buyer and seller should also have a place to sign and date, indicating that they have received a copy of the document. A statement in bold type, above where the seller and buyer are to sign and date should state, **"By signing below, I indicate receipt of a copy of this document, at the time of signing."**

Oral representations are often remembered quite differently by the party speaking the representation and the one hearing it. What is written and signed is a factual and indisputable record.

RECORDING OBSERVATIONS PROPERLY

The real estate agents should record what they see as clearly as possible, without analyzing the possible cause of the problem or defect, unless that cause is absolutely known to the agent. What may appear obvious as a cause of a defect may not turn out to be the cause at all. For example:

Agents should note and disclose any defects known or observed.

Incorrect description: There are cracks in the driveway caused by the roots of the adjacent oak tree.

Correct description: There are cracks in the driveway, adjacent to the oak tree. The buyer should investigate the cause, if this is of concern to him or her.

It may be that the tree roots are not the problem at all, but rather faulty soil conditions, some other type of geologic problem, or a poorly constructed driveway. By analyzing the cause of the problem, the real estate agent is putting herself in the position of an arborist, for which she is unqualified.

Another example of describing a property defect might be:

Incorrect description (by the seller's agent): The stain on the living room ceiling is from a roof leak this past winter. The seller has repaired the roof leak.

Correct description (by the seller's agent): The seller has stated that the stain on the living room ceiling is from a roof leak this past winter. The seller had a licensed roofing contractor repair the leak, which he believes is repaired. However, it has not rained since the repair was made. The buyer is advised to conduct her own inspection with a licensed roofing contractor to satisfy herself about the condition of the roof.

In the correct description the real estate agent is confirming *the source* of the information. He is also saying that the agent and seller *do not warrant the repair which was made,* and the buyer is *encouraged to conduct her own inspection.*

Good elements in the description of a defect are:

- Site the source of the information.
- Attach a receipt supporting the repair, if it is available.
- Indicate that the real estate agent and seller do not know that the defect has in fact been repaired, unless this is known for sure, such as the faucet no longer drips.
- Encourage buyers to make their own investigation before the close of the transaction.

The real estate agents should remember to never call a crack "minor" or refer to an unlevel floor as "normal settling." I have had those phrases quoted to me by unhappy buyers who are suing the real estate agents.

RECOMMENDING A PARTICULAR TYPE OF INSPECTION

Should the real estate agent recommend a particular type of inspection? The answer to this frequently asked question is yes and no. In the real estate agent's disclosure statement, if the agent doesn't know what the cause or causes of a problem might be, the best approach would be for the agent to recommend that the buyer "investigate further" as in the example for cracks in the driveway. Of course, the buyer's next question to the agent would be, "Whom should I call to investigate further?" In this case, it might be a good idea to ask the general property inspector to recommend the appropriate follow-up inspection. However, it is appropriate and a good idea for the real estate agent of the sellers or the buyers to make a recommendation to the buyers for a particular type of inspection, if the defect suggests an obvious choice. For example:

- There are horizontal cracks at the foundation on the south and west sides of the house. I recommend the buyer have a structural engineer inspect this condition.
- I observe a black stain at the vent holes of the attic, under the eave on the north side of the house. I recommend that the buyer have a mold inspection.

Horizontal cracks at the foundation would usually require a structural engineer's analysis. If the agent said that he recommends "further investigation," the buyers would once again turn to their agent and say, "What type of inspector should we call?" Black stains at the vent holes of the attic could just be dirt, but in one recent lawsuit it was mold, which resulted from a shower venting into the attic rather than through the roof as it should have. Any suspicion or red flag for mold should be followed by a recommendation for a mold inspection.

I know what you are thinking: shouldn't the general property inspector be the one to make these recommendations, not the sellers or the real estate agents? It is certainly the duty of the general property inspector to make recommendations for further inspections based on his findings or observations. However, the repetition of these recommendations by the sellers and the agents lends further weight to their importance. It also eliminates the later potential accusation by the buyers that their agent told them, "Not to do the follow-up inspection(s) recommended by the general property inspector." Now the agents have something in writing, signed by the buyers, as proof that they did make the same recommendation as the general property inspector.

WHAT NOT TO SAY IN A PROPERTY DISCLOSURE

Real estate agents should never write statements such as the following on their property condition disclosures:

- I don't see any defects.
- This property is totally redone.
- This house is remodeled to the studs.
- The property is in excellent condition.
- This property is meticulously maintained.
- I'm not a contractor. The buyers should get a property inspection.

There is no defect-free property. Real estate agents making such an observation are indicating that they made no serious effort whatsoever to walk the property and make any observation of defects. Even a newly constructed building is not defect-free. What does "totally redone" mean? What do "redone to the studs" or "excellent condition" really mean? These descriptions may be interpreted differently by the real estate agent and the buyer. A better way to describe remodeling is, "The seller added the family room," or "The house has recently been painted inside and out." The seller's agent should be specific as to what was done by the seller.

The agents conducting a property inspection should focus on the major areas of buyer concern, namely roofs, foundations, heat and air, plumbing, electrical, drainage, chimneys, pools and spas, mold and mildew.

IS THE PROPERTY INSPECTION LIMITED TO THE FORM USED?

In some states, real estate agents are required to record their observations on a prescribed form. The amount of space on the form will vary by state. If the form has four to five lines of space for each agent's visual observations or other disclosures, this should in no way limit the agent's observations and commentary. In California, where a seller's transfer disclosure form is mandated, the buyer's and seller's agents each have a space of four lines on that form to record their observations of property defects. The agents should write on those four lines "see attached" and then write or type their observations and information clearly on as many pages as needed.

ADDRESSING PROBLEMS IN THE NEIGHBORHOOD

The agent's property disclosure should also address prevalent problems in the neighborhood. For example:

- Residents typically get water in their basements on rainy days.
- The developer of this community has a reputation for building houses with faulty chimneys. The buyer is advised to have a chimney inspection by a licensed and qualified chimney inspection company.
- The next-door neighbor leaves the dog outside frequently. The buyer should assess whether dog barking is a concern.

- There is known gang activity in this area, and the buyer is advised to check with the local police department for further information.
- Square footage was provided by (the seller, MLS data source, etc.), and the buyer is advised to verify the square footage with an appraiser.

Even though some of these disclosures are mentioned in the boiler-plate of the standard contract, it is a good idea to repeat those that are applicable to this particular property transaction. Any reasonable buyer would want to know these facts. Yet many of these facts cannot be determined by the general property inspector or other inspectors because they are beyond their scope.

RELAYING INFORMATION PROVIDED BY THE SELLER

In a recent lawsuit the seller's real estate agent attended the buyer's property inspection but the seller did not attend. The agent incorrectly provided oral representations in response to questions by the buyer and the buyer's inspector. When the buyer's geologist noted moisture stains inside an entry closet against an outside wall, the agent replied, "That was from an exterior planter that has been removed." The implication was that the problem was solved. When cupping of the hardwood floor was noticed in the kitchen, the agent replied, "The seller experienced minor water intrusion caused by a clogged exterior drain which has been cleared." The implication again was that the problem no longer existed. She added that, "There was a roof leak in one area, and that section of roof was replaced along with leaking skylights." Again, she assured the buyer that the repairs were made and that the water intrusion issues were resolved.

This agent made a number of fatal errors that led to a three-week trial:

- The agent's disclosures should have been in writing, or confirmed in writing after the inspection, citing the source and whether she had or had not verified the information provided.
- She never questioned the seller in more detail concerning the repairs that were made.
- She never asked the seller if the seller had investigated whether the water intrusion from the exterior planter had caused mold or other water damage inside the wall.

- She didn't ask if the seller's contractor also believed that the cause of the water intrusion into the kitchen was caused solely by the clogged drain.
- She never asked the seller for the name of the roofing contractor and for a warranty on his work.
- She didn't ask the seller if there was a permit for replacing the skylights or the new section of roof.

The buyer moved into the house during the dry season, and several months later during heavy rains the house experienced flooding and moisture intrusion through the roof, walls, and floors. The seller's agent provided information that was "mistaken" or "false" or "misstated" and omitted information thus making her statements half-truths. For example, the exterior planter was removed, but the wall framing had extensive damage which was not repaired by the seller. The one drain was clogged, but the seller's contractor had told her that he believed the drain was not the sole cause of the kitchen flood. The roof replacement had a permit; however, the skylight replacement did not. The new section of roof did not fix the leak, and there was no warranty on the roofer's work.

A representation made with an honest belief in its truth may still be negligent because of lack of reasonable care in ascertaining the facts or in the manner of expression. However, when someone conveys a false impression by disclosing some facts and not others, there is a false representation that what is disclosed is the whole truth.

Nothing is at last sacred but the integrity of your own mind.

—Ralph Waldo Emerson

5 CHAPTER

The Seller's Property Disclosure

All real estate agents should ask their seller clients to disclose any flaws they may know about their property, all repair or remodeling work they have had done, and information about the immediate area of which they are aware that reasonable and prudent buyers would want to know. However, just asking sellers questions about the property may not jog their memories as well as we might hope. The seller's agent should take the seller for a walk around the property, starting outside and then room by room inside. The agent should point out anything that catches his eye as a possible flaw, such as cracks in the walls or a stain on the ceiling. The agent should ask the seller what he believes may have caused these problems and what, if anything, has been done to correct the source of the problem. He should ask for receipts, permits, and so forth and take notes about what the seller says.

Sellers can get themselves in trouble, and their real estate agent with them, when they have the usually unspoken thought that, "The buyers will find the problem with their inspection"; "It was fixed, so it isn't worth mentioning"; or "It's just something to do as maintenance, not really a flaw." Real estate agents, on the other hand, should never say to sellers, "You don't have to disclose that defect (situation, etc.)." Real estate agents should remind sellers that they are required to reveal any issue that is not within the reasonable observation or investigation of the buyers.

The sellers may have forgotten to answer a question on the prescribed form, such as, "Does this property have any nonpermitted structures?" Maybe the question was accidentally skipped, or was it skipped intentionally? The agents need to hand the disclosure back to the sellers and request that the skipped question(s) be answered. Some forms will ask the sellers to explain what has been checked as a defect or problem. If what is written by the sellers either cannot be read or does not fully explain the issue, such as, "Some areas of this property do not have permits," it should also be given back to the sellers to be written more clearly and explained more completely.

Latent defects known by the sellers must be disclosed. *Latent defects* are defects that are concealed or not visually apparent. The concealment and nondisclosure of known defects are representations that such defects do not exist.

Where is there dignity unless there is honesty?

—Cicero

IF THERE IS NO STATE-MANDATED WRITTEN DISCLOSURE DOCUMENT

Some state associations of Realtors strongly recommend the use of seller disclosure forms for their state and have developed forms for agents to present to sellers, even if the forms are not mandated by the state department of real estate.

All real estate agents should recommend the use of a seller disclosure form when representing sellers in a transaction, and buyers' agents should require the sellers to complete a seller disclosure form in the contract offer, even when these forms are not required by the state.

WHAT SHOULD THE DISCLOSURE CONTAIN?

If there is a requirement within the state for use of a specified form on which sellers are to make disclosures, that form would typically include:

Don't forget to disclose repairs or defects not within the buyers' visual observation.

- A checklist of property features, such as burglar alarm, pool, garage, central air-conditioning, public sewer system, sprinklers, dishwasher, and so on
- A request to the seller to check those features that are applicable to the property and if any are not in good working order, describe what is not operative
- Questions concerning any defects in the systems of the property, such as electrical, roof, and foundation, and to describe what is wrong with any item checked as defective
- Questions concerning seller awareness of such items as additions without permits, property line encroachments, and flooding or drainage problems with an explanation of each situation
- Questions relating to whether the property is insulated (walls and ceiling), since many properties built prior to the 1970s may have no insulation

- Questions about insurability for earthquake, hurricane, flood, fire, landslide, or other conditions
- Real estate agents' disclosure of any defects they have visually observed and any other known facts that reasonable buyers would want to know

An example of a seller's and agents' property disclosure form is one used by the California Association of Realtors (Figure 5.1). This form is required in California on all one- to four-unit transactions. Although this form is not required on transactions of over four units in California, the seller is still required to disclose all known defects to the buyer in written form.

WRITING THE SELLER'S DISCLOSURE

Sellers should type the disclosure comments if their handwriting is not totally legible. The disclosure cannot protect the sellers if it cannot be read by the buyers, the agents, and possibly an attorney. Sellers should be clear in describing what defects exist, what may have recently been repaired, and why. If sellers have done any remodeling or made modifications to the property during their term of ownership, they need to fully describe what they did. Sellers should never use words to describe remodeling like "such as" or "etc." They must be specific and all inclusive. An agent who sees this type of comment must question the seller further. For example:

> *Incorrect description:* Some areas of the structure were added without permits.
>
> *Correct description:* The bathroom adjacent to the kitchen was added without a permit by the prior owner. The third, rear bedroom was added by the present seller with a permit and was built by a licensed general contractor.

It is always better for the seller to answer a question with "I don't know" rather than to guess at an answer. However, beware of too many "I don't knows." Some sellers may think that this insulates them from liability for matters they do know. When sellers walk the property with their real estate agent, sellers should write down issues addressed that should be noted on the seller's disclosure. The sellers should be given the disclosure form when the listing is taken and have enough time to complete it. Everything about their property may not come to mind the first time they look at

FIGURE 5.1

Real estate transfer disclosure statement

CALIFORNIA
ASSOCIATION
OF REALTORS®

REAL ESTATE TRANSFER DISCLOSURE STATEMENT
(CALIFORNIA CIVIL CODE §1102, ET SEQ.)
(C.A.R. Form TDS, Revised 10/03)

THIS DISCLOSURE STATEMENT CONCERNS THE REAL PROPERTY SITUATED IN THE CITY OF _____
_____, COUNTY OF _____, STATE OF CALIFORNIA,
DESCRIBED AS _____.
THIS STATEMENT IS A DISCLOSURE OF THE CONDITION OF THE ABOVE DESCRIBED PROPERTY IN COMPLIANCE
WITH SECTION 1102 OF THE CIVIL CODE AS OF (date) _____. IT IS NOT A WARRANTY OF ANY
KIND BY THE SELLER(S) OR ANY AGENT(S) REPRESENTING ANY PRINCIPAL(S) IN THIS TRANSACTION, AND IS
NOT A SUBSTITUTE FOR ANY INSPECTIONS OR WARRANTIES THE PRINCIPAL(S) MAY WISH TO OBTAIN.

I. COORDINATION WITH OTHER DISCLOSURE FORMS

This Real Estate Transfer Disclosure Statement is made pursuant to Section 1102 of the Civil Code. Other statutes require disclosures,
depending upon the details of the particular real estate transaction (for example: special study zone and purchase-money liens on
residential property).

Substituted Disclosures: The following disclosures and other disclosures required by law, including the Natural Hazard Disclosure
Report/Statement that may include airport annoyances, earthquake, fire, flood, or special assessment information, have or will be made
in connection with this real estate transfer, and are intended to satisfy the disclosure obligations on this form, where the subject matter
is the same:

☐ Inspection reports completed pursuant to the contract of sale or receipt for deposit.
☐ Additional inspection reports or disclosures: _____
_____

II. SELLER'S INFORMATION

The Seller discloses the following information with the knowledge that even though this is not a warranty, prospective
Buyers may rely on this information in deciding whether and on what terms to purchase the subject property. Seller hereby
authorizes any agent(s) representing any principal(s) in this transaction to provide a copy of this statement to any person or
entity in connection with any actual or anticipated sale of the property.
THE FOLLOWING ARE REPRESENTATIONS MADE BY THE SELLER(S) AND ARE NOT THE
REPRESENTATIONS OF THE AGENT(S), IF ANY. THIS INFORMATION IS A DISCLOSURE AND IS NOT
INTENDED TO BE PART OF ANY CONTRACT BETWEEN THE BUYER AND SELLER.

Seller ☐ is ☐ is not occupying the property.

A. The subject property has the items checked below (read across):

☐ Range	☐ Oven	☐ Microwave
☐ Dishwasher	☐ Trash Compactor	☐ Garbage Disposal
☐ Washer/Dryer Hookups		☐ Rain Gutters
☐ Burglar Alarms	☐ Smoke Detector(s)	☐ Fire Alarm
☐ TV Antenna	☐ Satellite Dish	☐ Intercom
☐ Central Heating	☐ Central Air Conditioning	☐ Evaporator Cooler(s)
☐ Wall/Window Air Conditioning	☐ Sprinklers	☐ Public Sewer System
☐ Septic Tank	☐ Sump Pump	☐ Water Softener
☐ Patio/Decking	☐ Built-in Barbecue	☐ Gazebo
☐ Sauna		
☐ Hot Tub	☐ Pool	☐ Spa
☐ Locking Safety Cover*	☐ Child Resistant Barrier*	☐ Locking Safety Cover*
☐ Security Gate(s)	☐ Automatic Garage Door Opener(s)*	☐ Number Remote Controls ____
Garage: ☐ Attached	☐ Not Attached	☐ Carport
Pool/Spa Heater: ☐ Gas	☐ Solar	☐ Electric
Water Heater: ☐ Gas	☐ Water Heater Anchored, Braced, or Strapped*	
Water Supply: ☐ City	☐ Well	☐ Private Utility or
Gas Supply: ☐ Utility	☐ Bottled	Other _____
☐ Window Screens	☐ Window Security Bars ☐ Quick Release Mechanism on Bedroom Windows*	

Exhaust Fan(s) in _____ 220 Volt Wiring in _____ Fireplace(s) in _____
☐ Gas Starter _____ ☐ Roof(s): Type: _____ Age: _____ (approx.)
☐ Other: _____
Are there, to the best of your (Seller's) knowledge, any of the above that are not in operating condition? ☐ Yes ☐ No. If yes, then
describe. (Attach additional sheets if necessary): _____

(*see footnote on page 2)

TDS REVISED 10/03 (PAGE 1 OF 3) Print Date

Buyer's Initials (_____)(_____)
Seller's Initials (_____)(_____)

Reviewed by _____ Date _____

EQUAL HOUSING
OPPORTUNITY

REAL ESTATE TRANSFER DISCLOSURE STATEMENT (TDS PAGE 1 OF 3)

(continued)

F I G U R E   5.1

Real estate transfer disclosure statement (*continued*)

Property Address: _____   Date: _____

B. Are you (Seller) aware of any significant defects/malfunctions in any of the following? ☐ Yes ☐ No. If yes, check appropriate space(s) below.
  ☐ Interior Walls ☐ Ceilings ☐ Floors ☐ Exterior Walls ☐ Insulation ☐ Roof(s) ☐ Windows ☐ Doors ☐ Foundation ☐ Slab(s)
  ☐ Driveways ☐ Sidewalks ☐ Walls/Fences ☐ Electrical Systems ☐ Plumbing/Sewers/Septics ☐ Other Structural Components
(Describe: _____
_____
_____
_____)

If any of the above is checked, explain. (Attach additional sheets if necessary.): _____
_____
_____
_____
_____

*This garage door opener or child resistant pool barrier may not be in compliance with the safety standards relating to automatic reversing devices as set forth in Chapter 12.5 (commencing with Section 19890) of Part 3 of Division 13 of, or with the pool safety standards of Article 2.5 (commencing with Section 115920) of Chapter 5 of Part 10 of Division 104 of, the Health and Safety Code. The water heater may not be anchored, braced, or strapped in accordance with Section 19211 of the Health and Safety Code. Window security bars may not have quick release mechanisms in compliance with the 1995 edition of the California Building Standards Code.

C. Are you (Seller) aware of any of the following:
  1. Substances, materials, or products which may be an environmental hazard such as, but not limited to, asbestos, formaldehyde, radon gas, lead-based paint, mold, fuel or chemical storage tanks, and contaminated soil or water on the subject property .... ☐ Yes ☐ No
  2. Features of the property shared in common with adjoining landowners, such as walls, fences, and driveways, whose use or responsibility for maintenance may have an effect on the subject property .... ☐ Yes ☐ No
  3. Any encroachments, easements or similar matters that may affect your interest in the subject property .... ☐ Yes ☐ No
  4. Room additions, structural modifications, or other alterations or repairs made without necessary permits .... ☐ Yes ☐ No
  5. Room additions, structural modifications, or other alterations or repairs not in compliance with building codes .... ☐ Yes ☐ No
  6. Fill (compacted or otherwise) on the property or any portion thereof .... ☐ Yes ☐ No
  7. Any settling from any cause, or slippage, sliding, or other soil problems .... ☐ Yes ☐ No
  8. Flooding, drainage or grading problems .... ☐ Yes ☐ No
  9. Major damage to the property or any of the structures from fire, earthquake, floods, or landslides .... ☐ Yes ☐ No
  10. Any zoning violations, nonconforming uses, violations of "setback" requirements .... ☐ Yes ☐ No
  11. Neighborhood noise problems or other nuisances .... ☐ Yes ☐ No
  12. CC&R's or other deed restrictions or obligations .... ☐ Yes ☐ No
  13. Homeowners' Association which has any authority over the subject property .... ☐ Yes ☐ No
  14. Any "common area" (facilities such as pools, tennis courts, walkways, or other areas co-owned in undivided interest with others) .... ☐ Yes ☐ No
  15. Any notices of abatement or citations against the property .... ☐ Yes ☐ No
  16. Any lawsuits by or against the Seller threatening to or affecting this real property, including any lawsuits alleging a defect or deficiency in this real property or "common areas" (facilities such as pools, tennis courts, walkways, or other areas co-owned in undivided interest with others) .... ☐ Yes ☐ No

If the answer to any of these is yes, explain. (Attach additional sheets if necessary.): _____
_____
_____
_____

Seller certifies that the information herein is true and correct to the best of the Seller's knowledge as of the date signed by the Seller.

Seller_____   Date _____

Seller_____   Date _____

Buyer's Initials (_____)(_____)
Seller's Initials (_____)(_____)

TDS REVISED 10/03 (PAGE 2 OF 3)

Reviewed by _____ Date _____

EQUAL HOUSING OPPORTUNITY

REAL ESTATE TRANSFER DISCLOSURE STATEMENT (TDS PAGE 2 OF 3)

Property Address: _____   Date: _____

III. AGENT'S INSPECTION DISCLOSURE
(To be completed only if the Seller is represented by an agent in this transaction.)

THE UNDERSIGNED, BASED ON THE ABOVE INQUIRY OF THE SELLER(S) AS TO THE CONDITION OF THE PROPERTY AND BASED ON A REASONABLY COMPETENT AND DILIGENT VISUAL INSPECTION OF THE ACCESSIBLE AREAS OF THE PROPERTY IN CONJUNCTION WITH THAT INQUIRY, STATES THE FOLLOWING:

☐ Agent notes no items for disclosure.

☐ Agent notes the following items: _____
_____
_____
_____
_____

Agent (Broker Representing Seller) _____ By _____ Date _____
                    (Please Print)   (Associate Licensee or Broker Signature)

IV. AGENT'S INSPECTION DISCLOSURE
(To be completed only if the agent who has obtained the offer is other than the agent above.)

THE UNDERSIGNED, BASED ON A REASONABLY COMPETENT AND DILIGENT VISUAL INSPECTION OF THE ACCESSIBLE AREAS OF THE PROPERTY, STATES THE FOLLOWING:

☐ Agent notes no items for disclosure.

☐ Agent notes the following items: _____
_____
_____
_____

Agent (Broker Obtaining the Offer) _____ By _____ Date _____
                    (Please Print)   (Associate Licensee or Broker Signature)

V. BUYER(S) AND SELLER(S) MAY WISH TO OBTAIN PROFESSIONAL ADVICE AND/OR INSPECTIONS OF THE PROPERTY AND TO PROVIDE FOR APPROPRIATE PROVISIONS IN A CONTRACT BETWEEN BUYER AND SELLER(S) WITH RESPECT TO ANY ADVICE/INSPECTIONS/DEFECTS.

I/WE ACKNOWLEDGE RECEIPT OF A COPY OF THIS STATEMENT.

Seller _____ Date _____ Buyer _____ Date _____
Seller _____ Date _____ Buyer _____ Date _____
Agent (Broker Representing Seller) _____ By _____ Date _____
                    (Please Print)   (Associate Licensee or Broker Signature)
Agent (Broker Obtaining the Offer) _____ By _____ Date _____
                    (Please Print)   (Associate Licensee or Broker Signature)

SECTION 1102.3 OF THE CIVIL CODE PROVIDES A BUYER WITH THE RIGHT TO RESCIND A PURCHASE CONTRACT FOR AT LEAST THREE DAYS AFTER THE DELIVERY OF THIS DISCLOSURE IF DELIVERY OCCURS AFTER THE SIGNING OF AN OFFER TO PURCHASE. IF YOU WISH TO RESCIND THE CONTRACT, YOU MUST ACT WITHIN THE PRESCRIBED PERIOD.

A REAL ESTATE BROKER IS QUALIFIED TO ADVISE ON REAL ESTATE. IF YOU DESIRE LEGAL ADVICE, CONSULT YOUR ATTORNEY.

SURE•TRAC   Published and Distributed by:
The System for Success®   REAL ESTATE BUSINESS SERVICES, INC.
                a subsidiary of the California Association of REALTORS®
                525 South Virgil Avenue, Los Angeles, California 90020

TDS REVISED 10/03 (PAGE 3 OF 3)

Reviewed by _____ Date _____

EQUAL HOUSING OPPORTUNITY

REAL ESTATE TRANSFER DISCLOSURE STATEMENT (TDS PAGE 3 OF 3)

a disclosure form or start to write a listing of disclosures. For this reason, the sellers should not date the disclosure document until it is given to the buyers. Should something be remembered even after an offer is accepted and the disclosure form given to the buyers, the sellers should not hesitate to inform their agent and the buyers of this newly remembered fact. A defect that has only just surfaced should also be reported.

WHAT SELLERS SHOULD PROVIDE WITH THE DISCLOSURE

Sellers should provide the following documentation concerning their property with their disclosure document:

- Permits for work that was done by them or permits given to them by the prior owner when they purchased the property.
- Any disclosure documents given to the present sellers by the prior owner, such as a land survey, geologic report, or structural engineering report, should be provided to the new buyers along with any of these kinds of reports done by the present sellers. Sometimes the buyers may choose to rehire the same experts to update the reports they did previously.
- Plans and receipts for any remodeling or additions done by the sellers.
- Quotes the sellers may have received on repairs they deferred making.
- Any conflicting information on the property, such as two land surveys with somewhat different boundaries indicated.
- Any receipts for major repairs or work done, such as a new roof, a new sewer line from the house to the street, or the addition of a new heat and air system.
- Any warranties in effect on work done by the sellers, such as on the roof, which might be passed along to the newer buyers.
- Any information on insurance claims made by the sellers for damage to the property, including money received and receipts for the subsequent repairs made.
- Any information on a class action lawsuit by property owners in the development or condo building, describing the problems with this property, and information on any money received and repairs made, even if these relate to a prior seller.

- All reports generated by the sellers including a prelisting general property inspection and termite report.
- Information they have received from homeowners associations regarding recent changes in regulations, building code changes, road repairs, or other issues that may affect the property.
- Insurance information, including current insurer and policy coverage, since this may be transferable.
- Neighbor issues that could affect the property, such as major nearby construction that will continue for several years.
- The possible upcoming installation of city sewers to replace septic systems.
- Rental property restrictions.
- Home warranty claims made.

This information should be copied, and copies should be provided to the buyers and the agents. In addition, the sellers should keep a copy for their files. The items provided should be listed by the sellers, and the buyers should sign a receipt for the package of documents.

REVIEWING THE SELLER'S DISCLOSURES

The seller's real estate agent should carefully review the seller's disclosure statement and attached documentation. In addition to the seller's disclosure, the agent should thoroughly question the seller on additional areas of possible concern to the buyer. For example:

- Property modifications resulting from home warranty claims
- Repaired past defects in major systems, including septic, well, crawl spaces, drainage, soil, grading, and retaining walls
- Disaster relief, insurance or civil settlements received by the past or the present owners, and whether these funds were used to make the relevant repairs
- Water and mold issues
- Problems with animals on the property, pet stains or odors, damage caused, and repairs made

- Easement issues and encroachments
- Tree infestations, sprinkler operation, pool and spa operation
- Common interest condominiums and developments; any pending or proposed dues increases, assessments, insurance issues, or litigation
- Title and ownership issues or claims, past or pending lawsuits, bankruptcy, tax liens, or foreclosures affecting the property
- Neighborhood issues including noise, traffic, agricultural operations, parties, wildlife, airplanes, building restrictions, and so on
- Governmental issues such as condemnation, annexation, rent control, building or use moratoria, proposed bonds or assessments, proposed construction of roadways, public transit, required brush clearing, restricted tree removal, protected habitat, historical designation, and the like

The California Association of Realtors has developed an excellent form titled the "seller property questionnaire" that covers these issues (see Figure 5.2). It is advised that every real estate agent representing a seller request the seller complete this form in California, or one similar applicable in your area, and then review the completed form with the seller. If the seller's agent has not requested the seller to complete this or a similar form, the buyer's agent should request that the seller complete the form.

The disclosure documents should be signed by the seller and provided to the buyer according to the specified terms of the contract. The earlier in the transaction these documents can be provided to the buyer, the better. They should be brought to the general property inspection to be reviewed by the general property inspector, assisting him in answering questions he may have and directing his investigation. In some areas it is customary to provide disclosure forms to prospective buyers before they complete and submit their offer. Real estate agents and sellers who do not use seller disclosure forms and documentation are taking a huge liability risk. A property is what it is, and regardless of whether disclosure will reduce the sale price, *the seller must disclose fully and completely.* Believe me, the buyer will find out what is not disclosed, and a lawsuit will cost you far more than truthful disclosure at the outset.

F I G U R E 5.2

Seller property questionnaire

CALIFORNIA ASSOCIATION OF REALTORS®

SELLER PROPERTY QUESTIONNAIRE
(C.A.R. Form SPQ, 04/05)

This form is not a substitute for the Real Estate Transfer Disclosure Statement (TDS). It is used by the Seller to provide additional information when a TDS is completed or when no TDS is required.

I. Seller makes the following disclosures with regard to the real property or manufactured home described as _____, Assessor's Parcel No. _____, situated in _____, County of _____, California ("Property").

II. **The following are representations made by the Seller. Unless otherwise specified in writing, Broker and any real estate licensee or other person working with or through Broker has not verified information provided by Seller. A real estate broker is qualified to advise on real estate transactions. If Seller or Buyer desire legal advice, they should consult an attorney.**

III. **Note to Seller:** PURPOSE: To tell the Buyer about known material or significant items affecting the value or desirability of the Property and help to eliminate misunderstandings about the condition of the Property.
  • Answer based on actual knowledge and recollection at this time.
  • Something that you do not consider material or significant may be perceived differently by a Buyer.
  • Think about what you would want to know if you were buying the Property today.
  • Read the questions carefully and take your time.

IV. **Note to Buyer:** PURPOSE: To give you more information about known material or significant items affecting the value or desirability of the Property and help to eliminate misunderstandings about the condition of the Property.
  • Something that may be material or significant to you, may not be perceived the same way by the Seller.
  • If something is important to you, be sure to put your concerns and questions in writing (C.A.R. form BMI).
  • Sellers can only disclose what they actually know. Seller may not know about all material or significant items.
  • Seller's disclosures are not a substitute for your own investigations, personal judgments and common sense.

V. **SELLER AWARENESS: For each statement below, answer the question "Are you (Seller) aware of..." by checking either "Yes" or "No." Provide explanations to answers in the space provided or attach additional comments and check section VI.**

REPAIRS AND ALTERATIONS: ARE YOU (SELLER) AWARE OF...
  1. Any alterations, modifications, remodeling, replacements or material repairs on the Property (including those resulting from Home Warranty claims) .... ☐ Yes ☐ No
  2. Ongoing or recurring maintenance on the Property (for example, drain or sewer clean-out, tree or pest control service) .... ☐ Yes ☐ No
  3. Any part of the Property being painted within the past 12 months. .... ☐ Yes ☐ No

Explanation: _____
_____
_____

STRUCTURAL, SYSTEMS AND APPLIANCES: ARE YOU (SELLER) AWARE OF...
  4. Defects in any of the following, (including past defects that have been repaired) heating, air conditioning, electrical, plumbing (including the presence of polybutelene pipes), water, sewer, waste disposal or septic system, sump pumps, roof, gutters, chimney, fireplace, foundation, crawl space, attic, soil, grading, drainage, retaining walls, interior or exterior doors, windows, walls, ceilings floors or appliances .... ☐ Yes ☐ No

Explanation: _____
_____
_____

DISASTER RELIEF, INSURANCE OR CIVIL SETTLEMENT: ARE YOU (SELLER) AWARE OF...
  5. Financial relief or assistance, insurance or settlement, sought or received, from any federal, state, local or private agency, insurer or private party, by past or present owners of the Property, due to any actual or alleged damage to the Property arising from a flood, earthquake, fire, other disaster, or occurrence or defect, whether or not any money received was actually used to make repairs ... ☐ Yes ☐ No

Explanation: _____

SPQ 04/05 (PAGE 1 OF 3) Print Date

Buyer's Initials (_____)(_____)
Seller's Initials (_____)(_____)

Reviewed by _____ Date _____

EQUAL HOUSING OPPORTUNITY

SELLER PROPERTY QUESTIONNAIRE (SPQ PAGE 1 OF 3)

(continued)

F I G U R E   5.2

Seller property questionnaire (*continued*)

Property Address: _____   Date: _____

WATER-RELATED AND MOLD ISSUES: **ARE YOU (SELLER) AWARE OF...**
  6. Water intrusion into any part of any physical structure on the Property; leaks from or in any
     appliance, pipe, slab or roof; standing water, drainage, flooding, underground water,
     moisture, water-related soil settling or slippage on or affecting the Property. .... □ Yes □ No
  7. Any problem with or infestation of mold, mildew, fungus or spores, past or present, on or
     affecting the Property. . . . . □ Yes □ No
  8. Rivers, streams, flood channels, underground springs, high water table, floods, or tides on
     or affecting the Property or neighborhood . . . . □ Yes □ No
Explanation: _____
_____
_____

PETS, ANIMALS AND PESTS: **ARE YOU (SELLER) AWARE OF...**
  9. Pets on or in the Property. . . . . □ Yes □ No
 10. Problems with livestock, wildlife, insects or pests on or in the Property . . . . □ Yes □ No
 11. Past or present odors, urine, feces, discoloration, stains, spots or damage in the Property, due
     to any of the above . . . . □ Yes □ No
 12. Past or present treatment or eradication of pests or odors, or repair of damage due to any of
     the above. . . . . □ Yes □ No
     If so, when and by whom _____
Explanation: _____
_____

BOUNDARIES, ACCESS AND PROPERTY USE BY OTHERS: **ARE YOU (SELLER) AWARE OF...**
 13. Surveys, easements, encroachments or boundary disputes . . . . □ Yes □ No
 14. Use of the Property, or any part of it, by anyone other than you, with or without permission,
     for any purpose, including but not limited to, using or maintaining roads, driveways or other
     forms of ingress or egress or other travel or drainage . . . . □ Yes □ No
 15. Use of any neighboring property by you . . . . □ Yes □ No
Explanation: _____
_____

LANDSCAPING, POOL AND SPA: **ARE YOU (SELLER) AWARE OF...**
 16. Diseases or infestations affecting trees, plants or vegetation on or near the Property. . . . . □ Yes □ No
 17. Operational sprinklers on the Property . . . . □ Yes □ No
     (a) If yes, are they □ automatic or □ manually operated.
     (b) If yes, are there any areas with trees, plants or vegetation not covered by the sprinkler system . . □ Yes □ No
 18. An operational pool heater on the Property . . . . □ Yes □ No
 19. An operational spa heater on the Property . . . . □ Yes □ No
 20. Past or present defects, leaks, cracks, repairs or other problems with the sprinklers, pool, spa,
     waterfall, pond, stream, drainage or other water-related decor including any ancillary
     equipment, including pumps, filters, heaters and cleaning systems, even if repaired . . . . □ Yes □ No
Explanation: _____
_____

COMMON INTEREST CONDOMINIUMS AND DEVELOPMENTS: **ARE YOU (SELLER) AWARE OF...**
 21. Any pending or proposed dues increases, special assessments, rules changes, insurance
     availability issues or litigation by or against the Homeowner Association affecting the Property . □ Yes □ No
Explanation: _____
_____

TITLE, OWNERSHIP AND LEGAL CLAIMS: **ARE YOU (SELLER) AWARE OF...**
 22. Any other person or entity on title other than Seller(s) signing this form . . . . □ Yes □ No
 23. Leases, options or claims affecting or relating to title or use of the Property. . . . . □ Yes □ No
 24. Past, present, pending or threatened lawsuits, mediations, arbitrations, tax liens, mechanics'
     liens, notice of default, bankruptcy or other court filings, or government hearings affecting or
     relating to the Property, Homeowner Association or neighborhood . . . . □ Yes □ No
Explanation: _____
_____

Buyer's Initials (_____)(_____)
Seller's Initials (_____)(_____)

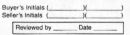

Reviewed by _____ Date _____

SELLER PROPERTY QUESTIONNAIRE (SPQ PAGE 2 OF 3)

Property Address: _____ Date: _____

NEIGHBORHOOD: **ARE YOU (SELLER) AWARE OF...**

25. Neighborhood noise, nuisance or other problems from sources such as, but not limited to, the following: neighbors, traffic, parking congestion, airplanes, trains, light rail, subway, trucks, freeways, buses, schools, parks, refuse storage or landfill processing, agricultural operations, business, odor, recreational facilities, restaurants, entertainment complexes or facilities, parades, sporting events, fairs, neighborhood parties, litter, construction, air conditioning equipment, air compressors, generators, pool equipment or appliances, or wildlife . . . . ☐ Yes ☐ No

Explanation: _____

GOVERNMENTAL: **ARE YOU (SELLER) AWARE OF...**

26. Ongoing or contemplated eminent domain, condemnation, annexation or change in zoning or general plan that apply to or could affect the Property . . . . ☐ Yes ☐ No
27. Existence or pendency of any rent control, occupancy restrictions or retrofit requirements that apply to or could affect the Property . . . . ☐ Yes ☐ No
28. Existing or contemplated building or use moratoria that apply to or could affect the Property . . . . . ☐ Yes ☐ No
29. Current or proposed bonds, assessments, or fees that do not appear on the Property tax bill that apply to or could affect the Property . . . . ☐ Yes ☐ No
30. Proposed construction, reconfiguration, or closure of nearby government facilities or amenities such as schools, parks, roadways and traffic signals . . . . ☐ Yes ☐ No
31. Existing or proposed Government requirements affecting the Property (i) that tall grass, brush or other vegetation be cleared; (ii) that restrict tree (or other landscaping) planting, removal or cutting or (iii) that flammable materials be removed. . . . . ☐ Yes ☐ No
32. Any protected habitat for plants, trees, animals or insects that apply to or could affect the Property. . . . . ☐ Yes ☐ No
33. Whether the Property is historically designated or falls within an existing or proposed Historic District . . . . ☐ Yes ☐ No

Explanation: _____

OTHER: **ARE YOU (SELLER) AWARE OF....**

34. Reports, inspections, disclosures, warranties, maintenance recommendations, estimates, studies, surveys or other documents, pertaining to (i) the condition or repair of the Property or any improvement on this Property in the past, now or proposed; or (ii) easements, encroachments or boundary disputes affecting the Property . . . . ☐ Yes ☐ No
   (If yes, provide any such documents in your possession to Buyer)
35. Any past or present known material facts or other significant items affecting the value or desireability of the Property not otherwise disclosed to Buyer . . . . ☐ Yes ☐ No

Explanation: _____
_____
_____
_____

VI. ☐ (IF CHECKED) ADDITIONAL COMMENTS: The attached addendum contains an explanation or additional comments in response to specific questions answered "yes" above. Refer to line and question number in explanation.

Seller represents that Seller has provided the answers and, if any, explanations and comments on this form and any attached addenda and that such information is true and correct to the best of Seller's knowledge as of the date signed by Seller. Seller acknowledges (i) Seller's obligation to disclose information requested by this form is independent from any duty of disclosure that a real estate licensee may have in this transaction and (ii) Nothing that any such real estate licensee does or says to Seller relieves Seller from his/her own duty of disclosure.

Seller _____ Date _____
Seller _____ Date _____

By signing below, Buyer acknowledges that Buyer has read, understands and has received a copy of this Seller Property Questionnaire form.

Buyer _____ Date _____
Buyer _____ Date _____

Published and Distributed by:
REAL ESTATE BUSINESS SERVICES. INC.
a subsidiary of the California Association of REALTORS®
525 South Virgil Avenue, Los Angeles, California 90020

Reviewed by _____ Date _____

SPQ 04/05 (PAGE 3 OF 3)

SELLER PROPERTY QUESTIONNAIRE (SPQ PAGE 3 OF 3)

REDUCING THE REAL ESTATE AGENTS' AND SELLER'S LIABILITY IN THEIR DISCLOSURE DUTIES

There are many forms, pamphlets, and addenda to the contract available to real estate agents and sellers that can be given to buyers to help inform them of potential problems. Each area has its own issues that should be disclosed. Some forms and addenda include:

- Warnings about lead paint
- Warnings about an unsafe brand of furnace that has been pulled from the market
- Warnings to be alert to mold issues or radon gas
- Letter to the buyer who refuses inspections
- Buyer's request for repairs
- Homeowner insurance alert to apply for insurance immediately, or limitations on available types of coverage
- Homeowner association information request
- Notice to seller to perform
- Notice to buyer to perform
- Buyer's final walk-through inspection
- Recommendations about property inspections
- Advice about getting building permits
- Neighborhood concerns to investigate
- Supplements to the contract listing inspections recommended
- Contingency for sale or purchase of another property
- Extension of time for inspections or removal of contingencies
- Receipt and delivery of notices to perform
- "13 seer rating" disclosure for central air-conditioning systems and heat pumps, according to the U.S. Department of Energy new regulations
- Buyer and seller advisories
- Seller's protection plan coverage endorsement, offered by some E&O companies through the agents they insure
- Importance of a land survey
- Megan's law addendum
- Natural hazard disclosure statement

- Smoke detector and/or carbon monoxide detector installation
- Receipt for reports and contingency removal

Some pamphlets may include:

- *You Must Have Inspection Protection*
- Pamphlets produced by the national property inspection associations, American Society of Home Inspectors (ASHI) and National Association of Home Inspectors (NAHI), and state associations of inspectors
- *A Consumer Guide to Asbestos,* from the Contractors State License Board, California
- *Protect Your Family from Lead in Your Home,* from the Environmental Protection Agency (EPA)
- *A Brief Guide to Mold, Moisture and Your Home,* from the EPA
- *A Combined Hazards Book (Toxic Mold, Lead and Earthquake Safety),* from the California Association of Realtors

There are many other possible forms, addenda, and pamphlets produced in each area to cover local issues. All these forms can be very useful when used in a timely fashion to inform and protect the buyers and sellers. All forms, addenda, and pamphlets should be signed as received by the buyers.

OVERRELIANCE ON WARNING FORMS AND ADVISORIES

The California Association of Realtors has produced a seller's advisory" (see Figure 5.3) advising sellers to fully disclose all property defects and information reasonable buyers would want to know. It also covers issues related to contract terms, legal requirements, and marketing conditions. Real estate agents rely on this advisory, other advisories, and warning forms to reduce liability for themselves and the sellers.

I have consulted on lawsuits in which the buyer has been given a "warning about mold" form. The buyer's agent is amazed when he is sued, believing that the buyer was told in the warning that a property might have mold, and if the buyer was concerned about mold, to inspect for mold. The buyer chose not to inspect for mold. Mold was later found by the buyer, and the agents were sued. The buyer's lawsuit might be justified in spite of the warning.

FIGURE 5.3

Seller's advisory

CALIFORNIA ASSOCIATION OF REALTORS®

SELLER'S ADVISORY
(C.A.R. Form SA, Revised 10/01)

Property Address: _____ ("Property")

1. **INTRODUCTION:** Selling property in California is a process that involves many steps. From start to finish, it could take anywhere from a few weeks to many months, depending upon the condition of your Property, local market conditions and other factors. You have already taken an important first step by listing your Property for sale with a licensed real estate broker. Your broker will help guide you through the process and may refer you to other professionals as needed. This advisory addresses many things you may need to think about and do as you market your Property. Some of these things are requirements imposed upon you, either by law or the listing or sale contract. Others are simply practical matters that may arise during the process. Please read this document carefully and, if you have any questions, ask your broker for help.

2. **DISCLOSURES:**

   A. **General Disclosure Duties:** You must affirmatively disclose to the buyer, in writing, any and all known facts that materially affect the value or desirability of your Property. You must disclose these facts whether or not asked about such matters by the buyer, any broker, or anyone else. This duty to disclose applies even if the buyer agrees to purchase your Property in its present condition without requiring you to make any repairs. If the Property you are selling is a residence with one to four units, your broker also has a duty to conduct a reasonably competent and diligent visual inspection of the accessible areas and to disclose to a buyer all adverse material facts that the inspection reveals. If your broker discovers something that could indicate a problem, your broker must advise the buyer.

   B. **Statutory Duties** (For one-to-four Residential Units):

      (1) You must timely prepare and deliver to the buyer, among other things, a Real Estate Transfer Disclosure Statement ("TDS"), and a Natural Hazard Disclosure Statement ("NHD"). You have a legal obligation to honestly and completely fill out the TDS form in its entirety. (Many local entities or organizations have their own supplement to the TDS that you may also be asked to complete.) The NHD is a statement indicating whether your Property is in certain designated flood, fire or earthquake/seismic hazard zones. Third-party professional companies can help you with this task.

      (2) Depending upon the age and type of construction of your Property, you may also be required to provide and, in certain cases you can receive limited legal protection by providing, the buyer with booklets titled "The Homeowner's Guide to Earthquake Safety," "The Commercial Property Owner's Guide to Earthquake Safety," "Protect Your Family From Lead in Your Home" and "Environmental Hazards: A Guide For Homeowners and Buyers." Some of these booklets may be packaged together for your convenience. The earthquake guides ask you to answer specific questions about your Property's structure and preparedness for an earthquake. If you are required to supply the booklet about lead, you will also be required to disclose to the buyer any known lead-based paint and lead-based paint hazards on a separate form. The environmental hazards guide informs the buyer of common environmental hazards that may be found in properties.

      (3) If you know that your property is: (i) located within one mile of a former military ordnance location; or (ii) in or affected by a zone or district allowing manufacturing, commercial or airport use, you must disclose this to the buyer. You are also required to make a good faith effort to obtain and deliver to the buyer a disclosure notice from the appropriate local agency(ies) about any special tax levied on your Property pursuant to the Mello-Roos Community Facilities Act.

      (4) If the TDS, NHD, or lead, military ordnance, commercial zone or Mello-Roos disclosures are provided to a buyer after you accept that buyer's offer, the buyer will have 3 days after delivery (or 5 days if mailed) to terminate the offer, which is why it is extremely important to complete these disclosures as soon as possible. There are certain exemptions from these statutory requirements. However, if you have actual knowledge of any of these items, you may still be required to make a disclosure as the items can be considered material facts.

   C. **Death and Other Disclosures:** Many buyers consider death on real property to be a material fact in the purchase of property. In some situations, it is advisable to disclose that a death occurred or the manner of death. However, California Civil Code Section 1710.2 provides that you have no disclosure duty "where the death has occurred more than three years prior to the date the transferee offers to purchase, lease, or rent the real property, or [regardless of the date of occurrence] that an occupant of that property was afflicted with, or died from, Human T-Lymphotropic Virus Type III/Lymphadenopathy-Associated Virus." This law does not "immunize an owner or his or her agent from making an intentional misrepresentation in response to a direct inquiry from a transferee or a prospective transferee of real property, concerning deaths on the real property."

   D. **Condominiums and Other Common Interest Subdivisions:** If the Property is a condominium, townhouse, or other property in a common interest subdivision, you must provide to the buyer copies of the governing documents, the most recent financial statements distributed, and other documents required by law or contract. If you do not have a current version of these documents, you can request them from the management of your homeowners' association. To avoid delays, you are encouraged to obtain these documents as soon as possible, even if you have not yet entered into a purchase agreement to sell your Property.

Seller's Initials (_____)(_____)

Reviewed by _____ Date _____

SA REVISED 10/01 (PAGE 1 OF 2) Print Date

SELLER'S ADVISORY (SA PAGE 1 OF 2)

Property Address: _____   Date: _____

3. CONTRACT TERMS AND LEGAL REQUIREMENTS:
  A. Contract Terms and Conditions: A buyer may request, as part of the contract for the sale of your Property, that you pay for repairs to the Property and other items. Your decision on whether or not to comply with a buyer's requests may affect your ability to sell your Property at a specified price.
  B. Withholding Taxes: Under federal and California tax laws, a buyer is required to withhold a portion of the purchase price from your sale proceeds for tax purposes unless you sign an affidavit of non-foreign status and California residency, or some other exemption applies and is documented.
  C. Prohibition Against Discrimination: Discriminatory conduct in the sale of real property against individuals belonging to legally protected classes is a violation of the law.
  D. Government Retrofit Standards: Unless exempt, you must comply with government retrofit standards, including, but not limited to, installing operable smoke detectors, bracing water heaters, and providing the buyer with corresponding written statements of compliance. Some city and county governments may impose additional retrofit standards, including, but not limited to, installing low-flow toilets and showerheads, gas shut-off valves, tempered glass, and barriers around swimming pools and spas. You should consult with the appropriate governmental agencies, inspectors, and other professionals to determine the retrofit standards for your Property, the extent to which your Property complies with such standards, and the costs, if any, of compliance.
  E. Legal, Tax and Other Implications: Selling your Property may have legal, tax, insurance, title or other implications. You should consult an appropriate professional for advice on these matters.

4. MARKETING CONSIDERATIONS:
  A. Pre-Sale Considerations: You should consider doing what you can to prepare your Property for sale, such as correcting any defects or other problems. Many people are not aware of defects in or problems with their own Property. One way to make yourself aware is to obtain professional home inspections prior to sale, both generally, and for wood destroying pests and organisms, such as termites. By doing this, you then have an opportunity to make repairs before your Property is offered for sale, which may enhance its marketability. Keep in mind, however, that any problems revealed by such inspection reports should be disclosed to the buyer (see "Disclosures" in paragraph 2 above). This is true even if the buyer gets his/her own inspections covering the same area. Obtaining inspection reports may also assist you during contract negotiations with the buyer. For example, if a pest control report has both a primary and secondary recommendation for clearance, you may want to specify in the purchase agreement those recommendations, if any, for which you are going to pay.
  B. Post-Sale Protections: It is often helpful to provide the buyer with, among other things, a home protection/warranty plan for the Property. These plans will generally cover problems, not deemed to be pre-existing, that occur after your sale is completed. In the event something does go wrong after the sale, and it is covered by the plan, the buyer may be able to resolve the concern by contacting the home protection company.
  C. Safety Precautions: Advertising and marketing your Property for sale, including, but not limited to, holding open houses, placing a keysafe/lockbox, erecting FOR SALE signs, and disseminating photographs, video tapes, and virtual tours of the premises, may jeopardize your personal safety and that of your Property. You are strongly encouraged to maintain insurance, and to take any and all possible precautions and safeguards to protect yourself, other occupants, visitors, your Property, and your belongings, including cash, jewelry, drugs, firearms and other valuables located on the Property against injury, theft, loss, vandalism, damage, and other harm.
  D. Expenses: You are advised that you, not the Broker, are responsible for the fees and costs, if any, to comply with your duties and obligations to the buyer of your Property.

5. OTHER ITEMS: _____
_____
_____
_____

Seller has read and understands this Advisory. By signing below, Seller acknowledges receipt of a copy of this document.

Seller _____   Date _____
Print Name _____

Seller _____   Date _____
Print Name _____

Real Estate Broker _____   By _____
                                                                                    (Agent)
Address _____   City _____   State _____   Zip _____
Telephone _____   Fax _____   E-mail _____

THIS FORM HAS BEEN APPROVED BY THE CALIFORNIA ASSOCIATION OF REALTORS® (C.A.R.). NO REPRESENTATION IS MADE AS TO THE LEGAL VALIDITY OR ADEQUACY OF ANY PROVISION IN ANY SPECIFIC TRANSACTION. A REAL ESTATE BROKER IS THE PERSON QUALIFIED TO ADVISE ON REAL ESTATE TRANSACTIONS. IF YOU DESIRE LEGAL OR TAX ADVICE, CONSULT AN APPROPRIATE PROFESSIONAL.

This form is available for use by the entire real estate industry. It is not intended to identify the user as a REALTOR®. REALTOR® is a registered collective membership mark which may be used only by members of the NATIONAL ASSOCIATION OF REALTORS® who subscribe to its Code of Ethics.

Published and Distributed by:
REAL ESTATE BUSINESS SERVICES, INC.
a subsidiary of the California Association of REALTORS®
525 South Virgil Avenue, Los Angeles, California 90020

SA REVISED 10/01 (PAGE 2 of 2)

Reviewed by _____ Date _____

In a current case, the seller did not disclose any problem that may have indicated a red flag for mold. The agents and the general property inspector did not observe or note any condition that would be a red flag for mold. The buyer had no basis to warrant an inspection for mold. However, the seller said he had a water leak in the utility room and filed an insurance claim. The seller said there was no mold on his disclosure form and that the insurance company had sent a contractor to repair the leak. The buyer later learned that the seller never filed an insurance claim and never had a contractor make repairs. In addition there was mold all over the wall under the wallpaper and behind the water heater and furnace. The agents did not ask the seller for supporting documentation on the insurance claim and repair. The unqualified general property inspector overlooked the red flags for mold and made no recommendation for a mold inspection. The agents were sued because their reliance on the "mold warning" was not a substitute for their thorough diligence in the interest of their client.

> Buyer warnings of any type do not substitute for real estate agents' investigation, questioning of sellers, and referral to competent inspectors.

SHOULD THE AGENT COMPLETE THE SELLER'S DISCLOSURE?

I once represented a seller in her eighties with Alzheimer's disease. She could no longer remember how to turn on her heat and air-conditioning. She certainly could not remember her property defects to fill out a disclosure form. One of her sons had power of attorney to act for his mother and completed the disclosure form for her. He had been responsible for maintaining his mother's home for some time and was familiar with its flaws. There are some instances when sellers simply cannot complete a disclosure form themselves.

Other examples of sellers who may have trouble with disclosure forms and, for that matter, other contract documents, are those who do not speak English, do not speak English well enough to understand what they are filling out and signing, or those who are ill or have poor eyesight. Request that a seller's attorney, an interpreter, designated family member, or friend undertake that task. Request some written authorization signed by the seller, giving that party the authority to fill out the disclosure form, interpret, or sign for the seller.

The listing agent should never fill out a disclosure form for a seller.

PROBATE, TRUST, AND FORECLOSURE SALES—DUTY OF THE SELLERS AND AGENTS TO DISCLOSE

Probate and foreclosure sales are usually exempt from property disclosures because the sellers may have no direct knowledge of property condition. However, if the heirs or lender has knowledge of property condition or neighborhood issues material to the transaction, these must be disclosed. The agents representing the sellers and buyers are still obligated to undertake an agent's disclosure of known or observed defects and neighborhood issues. Buyers of these properties do not have the benefit of seller disclosures and property history and must be vigilant to investigate all relevant issues.

6

CHAPTER

The Buyer's Property Inspections (Due Diligence)

WHAT SHOULD THE BUYER SEE?

The question always comes up in lawsuits, "Well, couldn't the buyers have seen that defect just as well as their agent?" Buyers have neither the experience nor the mindset to visually observe and note the significance of property defects. Sure, average buyers can see cracks in the driveway, a leaning retaining wall, and the stain on the living room ceiling, but they may not know the significance of what they are observing in terms of the underlying problem or the cost of repair. Buyers are justifiably wrapped up in the emotion and euphoria of the purchase, no matter how grounded they may appear. They are observing the floor plan, the lighting, how their family will function in the property, how their furniture will fit, and what their friends and family will think about this purchase.

It is the critical role of the real estate agents to focus their clients' attention on property condition, disclosures, investigation, and negotiation addressing these subjects. The real estate agents should not assume that the buyers can observe any defects.

IS THE BUYER'S VISUAL INSPECTION ADEQUATE PROTECTION?

Sometimes I hear an agent refer to the "buyer's inspection" when, in truth, the buyer is not inspecting the property at all. The buyer is "visiting" the property or "walking through" the property in an effort to assess if it is right for him and whether he should make an offer. Unless the buyer is a well-qualified general property inspector, he is not inspecting the property.

> *It isn't that they can't see the solution. It is that they can't see the problem.*
>
> —G. K. Chesterton

WHY ARE EXPERT INSPECTORS AND INSPECTIONS IMPORTANT?

Properties are complicated interconnected systems, with a defect in one system usually affecting another system. In most states real estate agents are limited in liability when they refer experts, such as geologists and structural engineers, to their clients, because these experts are in highly technical fields, licensed by the state, and assumed to have superior knowledge.

Experts, including licensed contractors, plumbers, electricians, heat and air companies, roofers, chimney inspectors, pool and spa companies, and land surveyors, can all have their license status checked, usually online through the state contractors licensing board. In lawsuits against real estate agents, the agents are frequently surprised to learn that the licensed contractor they were referring to the client was not licensed at all or has had his license suspended or revoked or has a history of claims or complaints. The real estate agents may then find themselves accused of a "negligent referral."

Some real estate agents and their companies have dealt with this "referral to experts" dilemma by not referring anyone at all, or by giving their clients lists of inspectors of different types and attempting to transfer all investigations of their credentials to the buyer. This seldom works to the benefit of the real estate agents, or the buyer or seller. A buyer will have a reasonable legal case against a buyer's agent who refuses to advise the buyer or refer inspectors to the buyer on the basis of "failure of fiduciary duty" and obligation to "advise and counsel the client." Merely listing three companies in each category of inspectors, without knowing the qualifications or licensing status of those referred, and providing this list to the buyer with, "Here, you pick one," is not an acceptable approach to reducing liability.

> There is no reasonable or prudent substitute for referring clients to "prequalified" inspectors.

Any list of inspectors should be prequalified by the brokerage office or the real estate agent and should not be based on any "purchased" placement by an inspector paying a fee to the brokerage. Only a prequalified list that is objective and based on qualifications should be given to the buyer, who can then be directed to select inspectors from that list. However, buyers must also be given some guidance from their real estate agents as to what to ask the inspectors to determine who is more qualified. Without this guidance, buyers will probably ask the inspector only two questions:

- Are you available on Tuesday? (or whatever day they have in mind)
- How much will the inspection cost?

When the buyer is given a list of prequalified inspectors who the real estate agent knows have similar credentials and insurance, the availability and pricing will no doubt be similar. The buyer is now comparing apples to apples, not apples to oranges!

Many real estate agents ask, "What if I believe that one general property inspector in my area is far superior to the others and I know her qualifications to support that belief? Is it okay for me to recommend that one inspector?" The answer to that question is yes, as long as the agent knows and has verified the inspector's credentials.

What if the buyer says he knows a general property inspector or other inspector he would like to use for the relevant inspections? If these are inspectors the buyer's agent knows are qualified, the agent is probably in no jeopardy of being accused by the buyer of negligent advice leading to poor inspections. However, if the inspectors are unknown to the buyer's agent, the agent should request of the buyer, in writing, verification of the credentials of the person(s) he wants to use, since they are unfamiliar to the agent and the agent wants to be sure that the buyer receives thorough inspections for his own protection. The buyer's agent should be sure to tell the buyer, in writing, what to ask the inspector regarding credentials, such as insurance coverage, experience, and confirmation of an active license, if a license is required by the state. Even buyers who select their own, incompetent inspectors can later sue their real estate agents for not adequately advising them that they may be making a poor choice and not recommending competent inspectors.

Sometimes the inspector desired by the buyer may be a longtime personal friend or relative. The buyer's agent should remind the buyer that if this inspector misses some critical defect, a lawsuit later will end the relationship. The better approach might be to work with both the buyer's choice, to avoid offending the inspector friend, and an inspector recommended by the buyer's agent.

What if the buyer absolutely insists on using an inspector his agent knows nothing about or believes is less competent than other inspectors the agent could refer to the buyer? The buyer's agent should prepare a memo to be signed by her buyer client, indicating:

> As your buyer's agent in the transaction to purchase the property at (blank, blank), I have provided you with the attached list of qualified general property inspectors. As it is the buyer's decision to hire an inspector unknown to this agent, this brokerage and agent cannot take any responsibility for the competency or completeness of the inspection to be performed.

Some people have advised buyers to avoid any inspectors recommended by their real estate agents, convinced that they are incompetent or recommended by the agent because they will minimize defects and not "mess up the deal." If buyers feel this way about their real estate agents, they are working with the wrong agents. Real estate agents have a duty to their clients to place their clients' interest first, and they will be left open to a lawsuit if their conduct is so unprofessional as to intentionally refer incompetent inspectors they know will minimize or omit property defects.

Qualifying inspectors referred to clients is not only a matter of ensuring a thorough inspection; it is a reflection of the expected professionalism of the real estate agent. The buyer's agent is the professional and will be viewed as such by a court. The buyer probably knows little to nothing about selecting inspectors to determine the condition of what he is buying. The buyer will say, with just cause in a lawsuit, "I relied on the advice and counsel of my agent."

> The more buyers can learn about what they are buying, the less likely they will have a basis for a lawsuit.
>
> The better qualified the inspectors of the property, the more likely the inspectors will be accurate and thorough.
>
> The more qualified the inspectors and the more thorough the inspection process, the less likely that the agents or the inspectors will be sued by the buyers.

THE BUYER'S DUTY TO INVESTIGATE

Buyers have a duty to investigate! Real estate contracts and disclosure documents advise the buyers to investigate. A buyer's inspection advisory (for example, Figure 6.1) lists many possible investigations buyers could make including:

- The general physical inspection
- Square footage
- Age
- Boundaries
- Wood destroying pests
- Soil stability
- Sewer and septic
- Water, utilities, and wells
- Environmental hazards, such as lead paint, asbestos, mold, mildew, and radon gas
- Earthquakes, flooding, hurricanes, tornadoes, and blizzards
- Fire hazards
- Zoning, building, permit requirements or limitations, and view ordinances
- On-site parking requirements
- Rental property restrictions
- Security and safety and crime statistics

FIGURE 6.1

Buyer's inspection advisory

CALIFORNIA
ASSOCIATION
OF REALTORS®

BUYER'S INSPECTION ADVISORY
(C.A.R. Form BIA, Revised 10/02)

Property Address: _____ ("Property").

A. IMPORTANCE OF PROPERTY INVESTIGATION: The physical condition of the land and improvements being purchased is not guaranteed by either Seller or Brokers. For this reason, you should conduct thorough investigations of the Property personally and with professionals who should provide written reports of their investigations. A general physical inspection typically does not cover all aspects of the Property nor items affecting the Property that are not physically located on the Property. If the professionals recommend further investigations, including a recommendation by a pest control operator to inspect inaccessible areas of the Property, you should contact qualified experts to conduct such additional investigations.

B. BUYER RIGHTS AND DUTIES: You have an affirmative duty to exercise reasonable care to protect yourself, including discovery of the legal, practical and technical implications of disclosed facts, and the investigation and verification of information and facts that you know or that are within your diligent attention and observation. The purchase agreement gives you the right to investigate the Property. If you exercise this right, and you should, you must do so in accordance with the terms of that agreement. This is the best way for you to protect yourself. It is extremely important for you to read all written reports provided by professionals and to discuss the results of inspections with the professional who conducted the inspection. You have the right to request that Seller make repairs, corrections or take other action based upon items discovered in your investigations or disclosed by Seller. If Seller is unwilling or unable to satisfy your requests, or you do not want to purchase the Property in its disclosed and discovered condition, you have the right to cancel the agreement if you act within specific time periods. If you do not cancel the agreement in a timely and proper manner, you may be in breach of contract.

C. SELLER RIGHTS AND DUTIES: Seller is required to disclose to you material facts known to him/her that affect the value or desirability of the Property. However, Seller may not be aware of some Property defects or conditions. Seller does not have an obligation to inspect the Property for your benefit nor is Seller obligated to repair, correct or otherwise cure known defects that are disclosed to you or previously unknown defects that are discovered by you or your inspectors during escrow. The purchase agreement obligates Seller to make the Property available to you for investigations.

D. BROKER OBLIGATIONS: Brokers do not have expertise in all areas and therefore cannot advise you on many items, such as soil stability, geologic or environmental conditions, hazardous or illegal controlled substances, structural conditions of the foundation or other improvements, or the condition of the roof, plumbing, heating, air conditioning, electrical, sewer, septic, waste disposal, or other system. The only way to accurately determine the condition of the Property is through an inspection by an appropriate professional selected by you. If Broker gives you referrals to such professionals, Broker does not guarantee their performance. You may select any professional of your choosing. In sales involving residential dwellings with no more than four units, Brokers have a duty to make a diligent visual inspection of the accessible areas of the Property and to disclose the results of that inspection. However, as some Property defects or conditions may not be discoverable from a visual inspection, it is possible Brokers are not aware of them. If you have entered into a written agreement with a Broker, the specific terms of that agreement will determine the nature and extent of that Broker's duty to you. **YOU ARE STRONGLY ADVISED TO INVESTIGATE THE CONDITION AND SUITABILITY OF ALL ASPECTS OF THE PROPERTY. IF YOU DO NOT DO SO, YOU ARE ACTING AGAINST THE ADVICE OF BROKERS.**

E. YOU ARE ADVISED TO CONDUCT INVESTIGATIONS OF THE ENTIRE PROPERTY, INCLUDING, BUT NOT LIMITED TO THE FOLLOWING:
1. **GENERAL CONDITION OF THE PROPERTY, ITS SYSTEMS AND COMPONENTS:** Foundation, roof, plumbing, heating, air conditioning, electrical, mechanical, security, pool/spa, other structural and non-structural systems and components, fixtures, built-in appliances, any personal property included in the sale, and energy efficiency of the Property. (Structural engineers are best suited to determine possible design or construction defects, and whether improvements are structurally sound.)
2. **SQUARE FOOTAGE, AGE, BOUNDARIES:** Square footage, room dimensions, lot size, age of improvements and boundaries. Any numerical statements regarding these items are APPROXIMATIONS ONLY and have not been verified by Seller and cannot be verified by Brokers. Fences, hedges, walls, retaining walls and other natural or constructed barriers or markers do not necessarily identify true Property boundaries. (Professionals such as appraisers, architects, surveyors and civil engineers are best suited to determine square footage, dimensions and boundaries of the Property.)
3. **WOOD DESTROYING PESTS:** Presence of, or conditions likely to lead to the presence of wood destroying pests and organisms and other infestation or infection. Inspection reports covering these items can be separated into two sections: Section 1 identifies areas where infestation or infection is evident. Section 2 identifies areas where there are conditions likely to lead to infestation or infection. A registered structural pest control company is best suited to perform these inspections.
4. **SOIL STABILITY:** Existence of fill or compacted soil, expansive or contracting soil, susceptibility to slippage, settling or movement, and the adequacy of drainage. (Geotechnical engineers are best suited to determine such conditions, causes and remedies.)

BIA REVISED 10/02 (PAGE 1 OF 2) Print Date

Buyer's Initials (_____)(_____)
Seller's Initials (_____)(_____)

Reviewed by _____ Date _____

EQUAL HOUSING
OPPORTUNITY

BUYER'S INSPECTION ADVISORY (BIA PAGE 1 OF 2)

Property Address: _____   Date: _____

5. **ROOF:** Present condition, age, leaks, and remaining useful life. (Roofing contractors are best suited to determine these conditions.)
6. **POOL/SPA:** Cracks, leaks or operational problems. (Pool contractors are best suited to determine these conditions.)
7. **WASTE DISPOSAL:** Type, size, adequacy, capacity and condition of sewer and septic systems and components, connection to sewer, and applicable fees.
8. **WATER AND UTILITIES; WELL SYSTEMS AND COMPONENTS:** Water and utility availability, use restrictions and costs. Water quality, adequacy, condition, and performance of well systems and components.
9. **ENVIRONMENTAL HAZARDS:** Potential environmental hazards, including, but not limited to, asbestos, lead-based paint and other lead contamination, radon, methane, other gases, fuel oil or chemical storage tanks, contaminated soil or water, hazardous waste, waste disposal sites, electromagnetic fields, nuclear sources, and other substances, materials, products, or conditions (including mold (airborne, toxic or otherwise), fungus or similar contaminants). (For more in formation on these items, you may consult an appropriate professional or read the booklets "Environmental Hazards: A Guide for Homeowners, Buyers, Landlords and Tenants," "Protect Your Family From Lead in Your Home" or both.)
10. **EARTHQUAKES AND FLOODING:** Susceptibility of the Property to earthquake/seismic hazards and propensity of the Property to flood. (A Geologist or Geotechnical Engineer is best suited to provide information on these conditions.)
11. **FIRE, HAZARD AND OTHER INSURANCE:** The availability and cost of necessary or desired insurance may vary. The location of the Property in a seismic, flood or fire hazard zone, and other conditions, such as the age of the Property and the claims history of the Property and Buyer, may affect the availability and need for certain types of insurance. Buyer should explore insurance options early as this information may affect other decisions, including the removal of loan and inspection contingencies. (An insurance agent is best suited to provide information on these conditions.)
12. **BUILDING PERMITS, ZONING AND GOVERNMENTAL REQUIREMENTS:** Permits, inspections, certificates, zoning, other governmental limitations, restrictions, and requirements affecting the current or future use of the Property, its development or size. (Such information is available from appropriate governmental agencies and private information providers. Brokers are not qualified to review or interpret any such information.)
13. **RENTAL PROPERTY RESTRICTIONS:** Some cities and counties impose restrictions that limit the amount of rent that can be charged, the maximum number of occupants; and the right of a landlord to terminate a tenancy. Deadbolt or other locks and security systems for doors and windows, including window bars, should be examined to determine whether they satisfy legal requirements. (Government agencies can provide information about these restrictions and other requirements.)
14. **SECURITY AND SAFETY:** State and local Law may require the installation of barriers, access alarms, self-latching mechanisms and/or other measures to decrease the risk to children and other persons of existing swimming pools and hot tubs, as well as various fire safety and other measures concerning other features of the Property. Compliance requirements differ from city to city and county to county. Unless specifically agreed, the Property may not be in compliance with these requirements. (Local government agencies can provide information about these restrictions and other requirements.)
15. **NEIGHBORHOOD, AREA, SUBDIVISION CONDITIONS; PERSONAL FACTORS:** Neighborhood or area conditions, including schools, proximity and adequacy of law enforcement, crime statistics, the proximity of registered felons or offenders, fire protection, other government services, availability, adequacy and cost of any speed-wired, wireless internet connections or other telecommunications or other technology services and installations, proximity to commercial, industrial or agricultural activities, existing and proposed transportation, construction and development that may affect noise, view, or traffic, airport noise, noise or odor from any source, wild and domestic animals, other nuisances, hazards, or circumstances, protected species, wetland properties, botanical diseases, historic or other governmentally protected sites or improvements, cemeteries, facilities and condition of common areas of common interest subdivisions, and possible lack of compliance with any governing documents or Homeowners' Association requirements, conditions and influences of significance to certain cultures and/or religions, and personal needs, requirements and preferences of Buyer.

Buyer and Seller acknowledge and agree that Broker: **(i)** Does not decide what price Buyer should pay or Seller should accept; **(ii)** Does not guarantee the condition of the Property; **(iii)** Does not guarantee the performance, adequacy or completeness of inspections, services, products or repairs provided or made by Seller or others; **(iv)** Does not have an obligation to conduct an inspection of common areas or areas off the site of the Property; **(v)** Shall not be responsible for identifying defects on the Property, in common areas, or offsite unless such defects are visually observable by an inspection of reasonably accessible areas of the Property or are known to Broker; **(vi)** Shall not be responsible for inspecting public records or permits concerning the title or use of Property; **(vii)** Shall not be responsible for identifying the location of boundary lines or other items affecting title; **(viii)** Shall not be responsible for verifying square footage, representations of others or information contained in Investigation reports, Multiple Listing Service, advertisements, flyers or other promotional material; **(ix)** Shall not be responsible for providing legal or tax advice regarding any aspect of a transaction entered into by Buyer or Seller; and **(x)** Shall not be responsible for providing other advice or information that exceeds the knowledge, education and experience required to perform real estate licensed activity. Buyer and Seller agree to seek legal, tax, insurance, title and other desired assistance from appropriate professionals.

By signing below, Buyer and Seller each acknowledge that they have read, understand, accept and have received a Copy of this Advisory. Buyer is encouraged to read it carefully.

_____   Date _____   _____   Date _____
Buyer Signature   Buyer Signature

_____   Date _____   _____   Date _____
Seller Signature   Seller Signature

Published and Distributed by:
REAL ESTATE BUSINESS SERVICES, INC.
a subsidiary of the California Association of REALTORS®
525 South Virgil Avenue, Los Angeles, California 90020

Reviewed by _____ Date _____

The System for Success®

BIA REVISED 10/02 (PAGE 2 OF 2)

BUYER'S INSPECTION ADVISORY (BIA PAGE 2 OF 2)

- Neighborhood issues, such as noise, lighting, street parking, traffic, proximity of registered sex offenders, telecommunications availability, and existing and proposed transportation
- Requirements or limitations on owners from homeowners associations
- Issues of lawsuits, reserve funds, dues assessments, maintenance of common areas, construction defects of planned developments and condo buildings
- Proximity and quality of schools
- Proposed nearby development or highway expansions
- Proximity to former waste disposal sites
- Locations in the flight path of airports or their planned expansion
- History of insurance claims [Comprehensive Loss Underwriting Exchange (CLUE) report]

The buyers rely on the following to guide themselves regarding which inspections and investigations to conduct:

- The representations and disclosures of the seller
- The representations and disclosures of the real estate agents
- The guidance of the general property inspector
- Their own intended use of the property

Can buyers investigate everything on the list above? Were buyers to tackle all of these investigations, they would probably need six months and likely would not have adequate funds remaining for their down payment. Clearly, *all* items recommended for further inspection by the general property inspector should be inspected, such as electrical or the roof or property drainage. The agent representing the buyers should recommend in writing to her clients that they conduct all inspections recommended by the general property inspector.

Buyers should focus on the "big ticket" expense items in their inspections. These include roofing, electrical, plumbing, heat and air, mold, drainage, foundation, pool and spa, chimneys, and septic systems. These are expensive items to repair, if problems are found later. Real estate agents should make sure, regardless of whether they represent the sellers or the buyers, that these major systems are inspected to the buyers' satisfaction.

WHO SHOULD ATTEND THE INSPECTIONS?

If at least one buyer cannot be present at the general property inspection, it should be rescheduled by the real estate agents.

> It is of critical importance that buyers attend the general property inspection so that they can have direct one-on-one contact with the general property inspector.

When the property inspector points out a problem, he can describe its nature and significance directly to the buyers. The buyers can then ask questions of the inspector.

> The buyers' agent must avoid becoming a conduit of information from the general property inspector to absent buyers. No matter how conscientiously the agent tries to relate the conditions orally described or pointed out by the inspector, the buyers can always claim later that the significance of these issues was minimized by their agent. Even if buyers must fly from across the country to attend the general property inspection, they should attend.

Both the real estate agents for the buyers and the sellers should attend the general property inspection. They should be present for the whole inspection. When the buyers ask questions of the inspector or the sellers and the inspector or sellers answer those questions, the real estate agents should take notes. Questions raised by the buyers that cannot be answered by the inspector should also be noted. In a lawsuit it is not always what the agent said to the buyers or sellers, but what the buyers or sellers believe the agent said that is the issue, and those two things may not be the same. Therefore, all important conversations should be confirmed in writing.

At least one seller should also be present at the buyers' general property inspection, preferably the most knowledgeable seller regarding property maintenance and condition. I know some real estate agents may not agree with this advice, but I have never seen buyers and sellers have an unpleasant confrontation at a property inspection. Both buyers and sellers can be counseled by their agents not to ask too many personal questions, make unnecessary negative remarks, or speak in a foreign language in front of one another. The purpose of having the sellers at this inspection is to answer questions raised by the general property inspector or the buyers regarding property condition, maintenance, additions, and location and operation of systems.

Sometimes the sellers have forgotten to mention certain maintenance issues or defects in their written disclosure, and the buyers' or their inspector's questions might jog the sellers' memories. With all parties present, I have often seen questions or issues resolved on the spot. All parties are also witnesses to the inspection and what is said and done. The real estate agents, however, should not inspect with the inspector. They are there to observe, ask questions, and take notes. A follow-up letter to the buyers might start with, "This is to confirm what was said at the general property inspection . . ."

Is it better to try to have all inspectors the buyers want at the property at the same time or at different times or days? Start with the general property inspector. Ask the general property inspector to note in her report other inspections she would recommend. Sometimes the general property inspector may want to have another inspector present at the same time, such as a geologist or structural engineer. It is a good idea to discuss this issue with the general property inspector at the time the buyers' agent or the buyers are setting up the appointment with the general property inspector.

If subsequent inspections are needed, be sure that all parties attend if possible. Nonattendance at crucial inspections can be pointed to in lawsuits as falling below the standard of care by agents. Real estate agents should remind clients of the importance of their attendance. Subsequent inspections, after the general property inspection, can usually be grouped at one time or sequentially. Buyers should be present to hear what structural engineers, geologists, soils engineers, and mold inspectors have to say. These are important inspections, and buyers should hear firsthand the initial evaluation of these inspectors, even if their final reports may not be available for several days.

If the buyers must come from out of town, the buyers' agent can attend for them at inspections by an electrician, plumber, heat and air company, pool and spa company, chimney company, or land surveyor. These people can provide their reports and can be called with questions.

These inspections can be scheduled close to one another in time, since each inspector is looking at a different part of the property.

THE MOST PRODUCTIVE INSPECTION

Following is advice to sellers for the most productive inspection:

- Try to leave young children and pets with a friend or relative, since they are distracting to both the buyers and sellers. All areas need to be inspected, including the dog's territory in the backyard and the sleeping child's bedroom.
- Do not have other family members or friends present, unless one person is necessary as an aid to an older person or as a translator, since a crowd starts to offer advice or gets in the way.

Following is advice to buyers for the most productive inspection:

- Only the buyers should be present; this is not the time to bring friends and relatives to show them the property. You need to focus your attention on the inspection since this is your opportunity to find out what you are buying.
- Leave small children and pets with others during the inspection, since they can also distract from your attention to the inspection.

INSPECTIONS IN ADDITION TO THE GENERAL PROPERTY INSPECTION

The Chimney Inspection

All chimneys should be inspected. The general property inspector cannot inspect the interior chimney flue from the floor to the roof, and this is a normal exclusion in most general property inspection reports. A licensed chimney company that conducts inspections and has a chimney scope, which is used to inspect the interior of the chimney flue, is the correct inspector for this inspection.

A chimney flue that has developed cracks from land settlement, earthquake, wind, or other causes may allow smoke or flames to enter the structure and cause a fire that can burn down the building. The replacement cost for a chimney flue is $5,000 to $10,000, or possibly more, and an expense any prudent buyer would want to know about before the purchase of the property. Chimney inspections cost from $125 to $175 per chimney.

Chimney companies are usually licensed by the building authority in each state, and their licenses can be verified at the Web site listing contractor's licenses, status, and insurance coverage. All chimney companies should have worker's comp, liability, and errors and omissions coverage.

The Pool and Spa Inspection

The general property inspector normally does not have the equipment necessary to determine whether there definitely is a leak in a pool. Pool and spa leaks can cause excessive yard moisture and undermine the foundation of the adjacent structure, resulting in expensive repairs to the building and the pool. A licensed pool and spa company that conducts pool inspections can inspect the entire pool and spa system and check for pool and spa leaks. These inspections can cost from $100 to $300 or more. All pools and spas should be separately inspected by a licensed and insured pool and spa company.

The Land Survey

Many states require that a land survey be conducted when a property is sold. In those states that do not require land surveys, often no land survey is available to be given to the buyers, and the buyers rely on the real estate agents or the sellers for the size and dimensions of the land.

Many lawsuits result from misinformation regarding property boundaries and easements or right-of-way issues. In states where land surveys are not required, they should be strongly recommended by the sellers and real estate agents. Land surveys can cost from several hundred to several thousand dollars. Land surveyors are licensed by the state. The land surveyor I most frequently work with is also a civil engineer and is very experienced.

The Geologic, Soils, and Structural Engineering Inspections

Geologic, soils, and structural engineering inspections can cost from $500 to several thousand dollars each. In areas with expansive or unstable soils or high moisture levels, or in hillside areas or areas prone to earthquake, these inspections are critical. They should be strongly recommended by real estate agents and the general property inspector. Sometimes the inspectors who conducted prior investigations on the property will update their reports at a somewhat reduced cost. These professionals should also have licenses in good standing and coverage for errors and omissions insurance and liability insurance.

> Wise real estate agents will never tell a buyer that these reports are not necessary and a wasted expenditure, or they will sorely regret hearing those words read back to them in court.

The Plumber, Electrician, Heat and Air Company, and So Forth

Inspections by the plumber, electrician, heat and air company, and so forth may not be necessary; however, sometimes a licensed electrician is called, for example, to quote on a specific defect or further examine a particular problem. The agent representing the buyers might wisely request that while at the property, the electrician check out all the electrical systems. I work with electricians who are willing to do this without charge and to quote on any defects found. It is not uncommon for an electrician to note something the general property inspector may have missed or to find that the severity of a potential problem is less than anticipated. The buyers, in any event, are now given more complete information as to the property condition. This same scenario may happen with a licensed plumber or heat and air company. One of these inspectors may also be asked to quote on an upgrade the buyers may be considering after purchase. For example, the buyers who plan to install central air-conditioning may want to know what it will cost and if it is feasible. A licensed heat and air company can provide a quote.

Environmental Inspectors

Environmental inspectors may be needed to test for lead paint, radon gas, asbestos, bacteria, and mold. Buyers and real estate agents needing these types of environmental inspections should verify contractor licensing within their state and proper OSHA (Occupational Safety and Health Administration) certification for removal of these conditions.

Defer to experts!

DECLINING RECOMMENDED INSPECTIONS

The agent representing the seller normally receives a copy of the buyer's general property inspection and any supplemental inspections either at the discretion of the buyer or according to the terms of the contract. If the seller's agent notes that the buyer has not followed up on recommended inspections by the general property inspector, the seller's agent should send a written memo to the buyer through the buyer's agent recommending that the buyer conduct those omitted inspections and request a reply to this memo from the buyer's agent and the buyer. The memo should be signed as received by the buyer. The seller's agent's memo should state that:

> It is in the best interest of the buyer and seller that the buyer thoroughly conduct all recommended inspections. The seller is making the property available for all inspections of the buyer, within the time frame for inspections indicated in the contract. The seller and the seller's agent request that if the buyer declines to take the advice of their general property inspector to conduct further inspections, the buyer sign a document noting the declined inspections.

Yes, the geological, soils, mold, and structural engineering inspections are expensive, but so is the property purchase. The buyer's agent should note all inspections that were recommended by the seller, the agents, or the general property inspector that the buyer declines to make and similarly prepare a form for the buyer to sign stating the following:

> The buyer's agent notes that the buyer has declined to make the following inspections that were recommended by the seller, the real estate agents, or the buyer's general property inspector. The buyer assumes all liability for defects discovered later that may have been discovered by such inspections.

The buyer should sign and date this document, and copies should be given to the seller and the seller's agent. A copy should be provided to the escrow holder. Real estate agents should be wary of the buyer who says he doesn't care about inspections and just wants the property. In numerous legal cases, I have been told by the real estate agent for the buyer, "I told my buyer client to conduct a geological inspection, but he did not want to spend the money." The buyer then claims, "My real estate agent told me I did not have to spend the money for a geological inspection, since this neighborhood did not have geological problems." Who is telling the truth? Written and signed documents addressing these issues avoid the "he said, she said" claims of the parties. Be sure to add at the bottom of the document above the buyer's signature, "I have read and understood the above and, by signing below, I am indicating receipt of a copy of this document at the date of signing."

If it is necessary for the seller to extend the inspection period of the buyer to allow sufficient time to conduct their inspections, this should be done by mutual agreement and a document extending the inspection period should be signed by the buyer and seller.

It is not in the seller's or the seller's agent's best interest to deter the buyer from making thorough inspections and investigation of the property to be purchased.

Sellers and their agents can be accused by unhappy buyers of "deterring them from making their investigations by the unreasonable limiting of time required to do the investigations and, thereby, attempting to conceal the property's true condition from the buyers." This is often a valid complaint and grounds for legal action later by the buyers.

Note to buyers: This is probably the largest single investment of your life. You are investing, in many cases, your life savings; this is not the time for false economy. You must find out the condition of what you are buying. If the inspections do not find defects, your money is still well spent. The alternative of finding out about a serious problem after the close is more expensive and more stressful.

You do not buy a property with the intent to sue the sellers, agents, inspector, or builder, and you want to avoid the cost, stress, and aggravation of a lawsuit by conducting thorough investigations.

INSPECTIONS OF NEW CONSTRUCTION

Buyers sometimes believe that because a building is "new" and recently inspected by the building department inspector, it is defect-free. The quality of building department inspectors based on their experience and training is not consistent. Building inspectors focus on code compliance and not on quality of construction. In most jurisdictions it is extremely difficult to sue the building department and get any satisfaction. New construction can have many defects and should be as thoroughly inspected as existing structures. If the buyers are purchasing a new home or other building not yet constructed, until the contract is signed, the buyers have some additional inspection options. Buyers should include in their contract the right to enter the property while it is under construction with their own experts to inspect at various stages of construction. Buyer inspections might include a soils engineer or geologist during land preparation and a structural engineer as the foundation is constructed; after framing, with rough electrical, plumbing, and heat and air still exposed; and at the completion of construction before the close of escrow.

Sometimes financial institutions lending funds for new construction will place certain requirements on borrowers for progressive inspections of the property under construction. They may review the contractor's progressive payments to subcontractors before releasing funds to the buyer to pay the contractor or to the contractor to pay the subcontractors. Real estate agents involved with the sale and financing of new construction should review all the lender's required terms regarding inspections prior to submitting any offer to a developer or builder. Qualified, competent builders are proud of their skills. Builders who refuse to allow "in course of construction inspections" or invent obstacles for them may be those of whom buyers should be wary.

A problem found during construction, when it can be more easily repaired, is a benefit to the buyer and the builder. Builders who encourage during-construction inspections are also protecting themselves by being able to point to the fact that they allowed such inspections and that the buyer's concerns were addressed at that time.

Quality builders and developers are willing to provide buyers with land surveys, structural engineering data, soils reports, proximity to hazardous conditions (such as a nearby waste dump), and any other information reasonable and prudent buyers would want to know.

INSPECTIONS OF CONDOMINIUMS AND TOWNHOUSES

Condominiums and townhouses should be inspected in the same way as single-family properties. The focus of the inspections will be the condition of the unit being purchased, rather than the entire building. Buyers should check with their general property inspector regarding how extensively he will examine any other areas of the building or land. Some property inspectors will advise buyers about such things as:

- Cracks in the exterior of the building
- Trip hazards near entrances and exits
- Cracking or settlement of the pool and surrounding decking
- Apparent poor drainage at ground level
- A worn or damaged roof
- Condition of the air-conditioning or heating system if not in individual units

Buyers should ask the general property inspector to view and note any area visible and common that may result in a problem for the buyers with their unit, or a significant repair cost for the building to which the buyers may later have to contribute funds.

In condominium buildings and planned unit developments, it is a good idea to have the general property inspection conducted by an inspector familiar with the development. For example, the inspector may know that a number of houses in the development have soils problems that have caused cracked slabs, or the inspector may know the defects in a prior class action lawsuit against the builder. An inspector familiar with the development would be alert to signs of these conditions and would advise the buyer to have a soils engineer or structural engineer examine the property.

INSPECTIONS OF INVESTMENT PROPERTIES

It is generally assumed by real estate agents that investor buyers are more knowledgeable than typical residential buyers when it comes to thorough investigation and buyer due diligence. From the many cases on which I have consulted, it is apparent that agents overestimate investor savvy when it comes to property investigation. Most investors are not as knowledgeable as they may wish they were. Agents dealing with investors in all property types should still provide the same advice to thoroughly inspect and investigate the property purchase.

Investor buyers, whether dealing with multiunit properties, commercial properties, farm properties, or business sales, need to learn the condition of the property, including the structure and the ground it is sitting on, before the transaction closes. If sellers attempt to limit buyers' inspections claiming that occupants will be disturbed, the buyers should refuse to accept this argument. Tenants, whether residential or commercial, usually have "right of inspection" clauses in their rental agreements and must cooperate with their landlord who is selling the property to allow buyers to inspect it.

Investment buyers should also be present when inspections are conducted. The sellers should be forthcoming in disclosing all aspects of property condition, zoning, maintenance, additions, and permits as well as financial data to the buyers. Buyers and their agents should be wary of sellers who claim not to have this information. The prudent real estate agent will ensure that the requirement for seller disclosure of these facts is enumerated in the purchase contract and that the buyers are advised to make thorough investigations.

What are the occupancy limits? Is there rent control? Will building department upgrades be required for health, safety, and handicap access? Is needed insurance coverage available? If specific licenses are required for operation, what are their costs and the lead time needed to obtain them? When property inspectors know the buyer's intended use of the building, they can gear their inspection to the applicability of that use, such as available gas lines, sewer connections, and adequate plumbing and electrical. If renovations are needed, contractor inspections should be conducted to determine anticipated costs.

Will there be opposition from homeowner associations objecting to noise, traffic, or hours of operation? Should local council members, city supervisors, or building commissions be contacted? The scope of the inspection and investigation can be extensive, and the investigation requires the same adherence to documentation, contract deadlines, and signing by the parties of any alteration in contract terms.

INSPECTIONS OF RAW LAND

Most definitely raw land must be inspected, regardless of its intended use. A land survey must be conducted, if a prior recorded survey is not available.

In one recent lawsuit, the buyer sued the seller and agents for representing the size of the land purchased at 10,000 square feet. The land was adjacent to other undeveloped land and had no available land survey. The buyer did not conduct a land survey and later found out that the land was actually only 4,500 square feet and was worthless because it was too small for development. The real estate agents and seller made an unverified representation of significant magnitude, clearly causing the buyer harm. The buyer should have insisted on the right to a land survey or been advised to conduct a land survey and other inspections. Other issues with land purchases are topography, soil stability, drainage, possible toxic content from illegal or legal prior dumping or agricultural use, access, easements, and zoning.

INSPECTIONS OF MOBILE HOMES

Buyers of mobile homes should have them inspected by general property inspectors familiar with mobile homes. Critical issues are whether the mobile home is considered real property or personal property and which code authority or jurisdiction is responsible for mobile homes. Municipal utilities are often an issue with mobile homes. Is the mobile home accessing utilities in a mobile home park, or is it sitting on a private lot where individual access to utilities is required? In one case on which I consulted, the mobile home was attached to a permanent foundation on a private lot and was regarded as real property. The same issues existed as in conventional single-family construction regarding the disclosure of property defects. The dual agent-seller was sued for nondisclosure by the buyer who won in court.

WHEN SHOULD INSPECTIONS BE DONE AND HOW MUCH TIME SHOULD BE ALLOWED?

The best general property inspectors are in high demand and should be in high demand. Allow at least 10 business days for a general property inspection and additional time for inspections such as land surveys and geological and structural engineering reports. Geologists, soils engineers, and structural engineers typically need several days after an inspection to provide a written report. The general property inspection should be scheduled as soon as possible after the buyer and seller sign the contract.

It is good procedure for the buyer's agent to always ask the seller's agent before an offer is made what problems exist with the property, either observed by that agent or disclosed by the seller. Knowing about property flaws in advance gives the buyer's agent an opportunity to request adequate time for specific inspections in the offer. For example, if the listing agent says that the roof is 20 years old and that the house has a deck with water damage, the buyer's agent can start to line up a roof inspector to check the roof and a contractor to quote on the deck repair.

THE BUYER'S DILEMMA IN A SELLERS' MARKET

In a sellers' market resulting from low inventory and high demand, listings sell quickly. What do buyers do regarding inspections when they are not only being outbid for properties but are also competing with no contingency offers, including a no-inspection contingency? Some desperate buyers are omitting the inspection contingency just to finally be able to make a purchase.

> I strongly advise buyers to never make a no-inspection contingency offer.

Wait to buy or look elsewhere, but never buy without the right to inspect. If you are despondent over losing out to other offers, that will hardly compare to how you will feel when your purchase turns into a property defect disaster!

> The real estate agent for the buyer should strongly recommend that clients never make a no-inspection contingency offer.
>
> The real estate agent for the seller should advise clients to never accept a no-inspection contingency offer.

Accepting a no-inspection contingency offer is a huge mistake for the sellers. In a sellers' market, the sellers will sell, and at a good price. The sellers may not be aware of all the defects in their property and, therefore, may omit disclosures about defects property inspections would have revealed. The coerced buyers who felt that the no-inspection offer was their only way to actually get an offer accepted may reasonably assume that defects discovered after the sale were indeed known to the sellers or their agent who elected not to disclose them. Some buyers' agents are even recommending the no-inspection contingency offer! This is bad advice and not in the buyers' best interest.

The agent who thinks the deal will close faster may be right, but the lawsuit will drag on for years. A sellers' agent may also erroneously think that if buyers do not inspect, that their ability to ask for credits or repairs or a price reduction will be limited because their knowledge of the property will be limited to what the sellers and real estate agents disclose. The sellers and their agent who believe that a no-inspection offer is a benefit to the sellers may be accused of deterring the buyers' ability to investigate, and that accusation will have merit. A variation on this scenario is the sellers' agent who packages various disclosure documents such as a seller's general property inspection, the lead paint disclosure, the Megan's law disclosure, and the termite report. These documents are then given to either prospective buyers or to the buyers when their offer is accepted. The sellers and their agent then tell the buyers, "Mr. and Mrs. Buyer, you have three days to review these documents and accept them, or the deal will be canceled."

> The real estate agent for the sellers should never package disclosure documents for the buyers and give the buyers an unreasonable time for evaluation, resulting in their inability to conduct any inspections and having no opportunity to know the qualifications, if any, of the sellers' chosen inspectors.

There is no fault in the sellers' desire to undertake inspections and produce reports that they turn over to the buyers, but the buyers must always be given a reasonable time frame to conduct their own inspections.

The sellers' real estate agent has no obligation to protect the sellers from the defects in their property. However, the sellers' agent does have a duty to help protect the sellers by strongly advising them to fully disclose all property defects. If the buyers' investigations result in the sellers being newly informed of defects they did not know they had that will result in significant repair costs to the buyers, the sellers may have to provide the buyers with credits or a price reduction. So be it! This is far better at the time of sale than in a lawsuit later.

THE SELLER'S DILEMMA IN A BUYERS' MARKET

The seller who sold his property at the top of the sellers' market (an up market means prices are escalating) may soon find himself in a lawsuit in a buyers' market (a down market means prices are declining), when the buyer finds undisclosed property defects. When the buyer's property is appreciating at $10,000 per month, he is likely to absorb the cost of some repairs. However, the buyer who felt forced to accept little if any time for property inspections and now finds undisclosed defects while she sees her property value declining will be angry and likely to take legal action. Down markets always result in more lawsuits than up markets.

In down markets thorough inspections are even more important. Buyers who would accept some defects in a sellers' market are now in a position to negotiate repairs and credits. They fear a continued decline in values will further erode their equity, and they certainly don't want to pay for the repair of property defects discovered after the close of the transaction.

7

The General Property Inspection

THE GENERAL PROPERTY INSPECTION AND LAWSUITS

If a transaction is going to end up in a lawsuit, it usually starts at the general property inspection.

Buyers and sellers and their real estate agents often underestimate the importance of the general property inspection in keeping everyone out of a future lawsuit. In some areas these inspections are commonplace; in others they are rarely undertaken.

> Every property purchase, whether residential single family, condominium, commercial, or farm, *must be inspected*.

Even in areas where general property inspections are commonplace in transactions, real estate agents, buyers, and sellers sometimes do not understand the importance of obtaining the "best inspection possible." Just any inspection won't do! Inspectors must be *qualified*!

More states in recent years have now required the licensing, qualified registration, or certification of general property inspectors. Some state requirements are genuinely helpful in separating the good inspectors from the unqualified inspectors. Other states' requirements for property inspectors more closely resemble a nonqualifying registration program and require little of the inspector in terms of qualifications. Many states still have no licensing or certification requirement at all for inspectors. In states without any licensing or certification requirements, anyone who decides to become a general property inspector can print up business cards, copy a form from the computer, buy a clipboard, and whoa, become an inspector!

STATES WITH LICENSING OR OTHER REQUIREMENTS FOR GENERAL PROPERTY INSPECTORS

The states that require licenses for general property inspectors are Alabama, Alaska, Connecticut, Illinois, Indiana, Kentucky, Louisiana, Massachusetts, Mississippi, New Jersey, New York, North Carolina, Oklahoma, South Carolina, South Dakota, Tennessee, and Texas.

States that require certification or registration for general property inspectors are Arizona, Arkansas, Nevada, North Dakota, Oregon, Virginia, and Wisconsin.

States that require specific trade practices for general property inspectors are California, Georgia, Maryland, Montana, Pennsylvania, and Rhode Island.

Note that only 30 states are listed above.[1]

The most important recommendation real estate agents can make to their buyer clients is a well-qualified general property inspector.

The strength of a nation is derived from the integrity of its homes.

—Confucius

ADVICE ABOUT INSPECTIONS

Simply telling a buyer to have an inspection does very little to reduce a real estate agent's risk of being sued by a buyer. Inevitably, the roof will

---

[1] American Society of Home Inspectors (ASHI), 2006.

leak and the house will slide. Real estate agents should always include an inspection addendum in standard contracts, specifically advising buyers to have a general property inspection and appropriate specialty inspections, such as a land survey and asbestos or lead testing.

Company addenda are often attached to contracts advising buyers to conduct inspections. They may repeat some of the admonitions already given and add more recommendations, such as the suggestion that buyers inspect for radon, if this is a local issue. Repetition of recommendations for buyer inspections is a very good thing. The more times the buyers are told something and sign receipt of that advisory, the harder it will be for the buyers to claim that they were not told. It also can help to defeat the often-heard explanation of buyers about why they did not conduct an inspection, "We could not read the fine print in the boilerplate of the contract," or "Our agent buried the recommendation in some other forms he did not review with us." Use type that is large enough to be generally readable by the population—a minimum of 11-point type. Include in boldface type above the space for the buyers' signatures and the dates the agreement was signed, "I have read and understood the above."

Repetition also works on plaintiffs' attorneys and juries. An attorney told by disgruntled buyers that they were advised not to have a certain inspection verbally, in spite of written warnings to the contrary, especially a specific memo from the buyers' or sellers' agent, will have a hard time convincing their attorney, let alone a jury.

HOW TO QUALIFY A GENERAL PROPERTY INSPECTOR

With or without state licensing or certification requirements, just how does a prudent real estate agent or buyer qualify a general property inspector?

1. *Experience:* In qualifying any professional, it is always wise to look for experience. How many years has the inspector been doing property inspections, and how many inspections has he done? As experience will vary from one locale to another, check for the most experienced people in your area. Be sure to ask if the inspector is experienced in the type of property being inspected, such as residential or commercial.

2. *No lawsuits:* Has the property inspector ever been sued? Ask if the inspector has been sued; how many times she has been sued, what were the lawsuits about, and what resulted.

3. *Insurance coverage:* A real estate brokerage and its agents should refer to a client only general property inspectors who have current errors and omissions insurance and liability insurance. In states where a surety bond or similar program is available from which a buyer can receive adequate recovery for damages, errors and omissions insurance may not be needed.

   General property inspectors are usually named in every lawsuit in which undisclosed property defects are claimed. Those who have been sued many times cannot get errors and omissions coverage. Liability insurance for property inspectors covers them in the event that they inadvertently damage the property they are inspecting.

   Real estate brokerages, their agents, and buyers should ask the general property inspector for copies of proof of current, active errors and omissions coverage and liability coverage, and they should keep a copy in their files. This information should be reviewed and updated every six months. In lawsuits on which I have consulted, some property inspectors have claimed to have insurance coverage, but they were not asked for proof of coverage. Later the buyers and agent found that the property inspector's insurance had lapsed or had been canceled. General property inspectors who have insurance coverage are glad to show proof of coverage. Ask that proof of coverage be sent directly from the insurance carrier. If the buyers or their agent is dealing with a general property inspection company that employs several inspectors, be sure that the inspector you work with is covered under the company's insurance and has the same high level of experience and other qualifications you desire. The individual who actually does the inspection is the person who must have all the qualifications you seek, not just the inspection company owner.

   Will the general property inspector who has errors and omissions insurance and liability insurance charge more than the inspector who has neither kind of insurance coverage? In all likelihood, yes. Is the added cost worthwhile to the buyers? Absolutely!

4. *General contractor's license:* Another qualification that general property inspectors might have would be a general contractor's

license. The requirements to obtain a general contractor's license will vary from state to state. In states with training, experience, and testing requirements for general contractors, the buyers and their agent can at least know that the inspector has a reasonable understanding of how a building should be constructed.

Recently, I consulted on a lawsuit where the agent told the buyer that the general property inspector was a licensed contractor and had conducted excellent inspections for other buyer clients of the agent. However, the real estate agent made no effort to verify that the property inspector was indeed licensed. A two-minute check on the state Contractors License Board Web site would have revealed that the inspector had had a contractor's license but that it had been suspended a year before this inspection took place. The contractor/inspector hadn't actually used his contractor's license for some 10 years prior to this inspection. He had received only two weeks of training as an inspector from a company that did not even have personnel accompany the new inspector on any inspection. He also had no errors and omissions insurance and no liability insurance. He failed to note the crumbling foundation or charred rafters in the attic. The dual agent, the seller, and the property inspector were successfully sued by the buyer who was awarded $180,000 in arbitration.

Real estate agents who refer unqualified general property inspectors to their buyer clients can be successfully sued for a negligent referral.

---

5. *ICBO inspector:* Another qualification for a general property inspector might be certification as an ICBO (International Conference of Building Officials) inspector. This certification is required for building department inspectors in some states. Although this is certainly a worthwhile credential, it is not adequate as the only credential.

6. *General property inspector professional associations:* Some states have state general property inspector professional

associations. The two most prominent national associations are American Society of Home Inspectors (ASHI) and National Association of Home Inspectors (NAHI). Although "home" is featured in the names of these two national associations, I refer to property inspectors as "general" property inspectors because many inspectors also inspect multifamily and commercial properties as well as residential single-family homes and condominiums.

Most general property inspectors receive their best training in these associations. The associations require their members to:

- Have some experience in inspecting properties
- Use a comprehensive and up-to-date form in their inspections, which covers the major systems of the building and uses adequate verbiage and explanation of conditions observed
- State up front to property buyers what is and what is not covered in the property inspection
- Adhere to a code of ethics and standards of practice
- Take a certain number of hours of education annually to stay current
- Submit copies of inspection reports they have prepared for clients for review and comment
- Have completed a certain number of inspections to receive full membership status (ASHI requires 250 paid professional inspections)
- Pass the National Home Inspectors Exam (required by ASHI; it is a technical exam administered by an independent testing body)

Many general property inspectors become active in their professional associations and become officers in their local chapter associations. These local chapters have meetings of their members to discuss local issues and bring in guest speakers to further educate their members. Just as real estate licensees who belong to the National Association of Realtors, their state association of Realtors, and their local chapter association of Realtors are generally better informed and educated than those real estate licensees who choose not to join these professional associations; the same is also true for property inspectors and their associations.

Some general property inspectors, who do not belong to property inspection professional associations, may claim in their contract forms that they "adhere to the standards of practice of ASHI, or NAHI." These statements are worthless if these inspectors are not actually members who are receiving state-of-the-art updated training. What standards of practice are they referring to? These associations change and update their standards every few years.

Neither buyers nor real estate agents should be reluctant to ask general property inspectors whether they are full members and active in the association(s). Many experienced and capable general property inspectors belong to more that one professional association, usually their state association and a national association.

Real estate agents and buyers can obtain information from these associations about their members, membership requirements, and training, either online at their Web sites www.ASHI.org or www.NAHI.org, for example, or have literature sent to them. These professional associations are pleased to provide real estate agents with pamphlets explaining their association's function, and a copy of their code of ethics and standards of practice. About two minutes on their Web sites, inserting the address of the property to be inspected or its zip code or city, and the members closest to that location are brought up on the screen. Some property inspectors lie about their membership in these organizations. All brokerages and agents should verify association membership for any property inspector they are referring.

All general property inspectors referred to buyer clients by a real estate brokerage or a real estate agent should belong as members in good standing to, at a minimum, ASHI, NAHI, or their state general property inspection association.

In states without any licensing or certification program for general property inspectors, there are individuals calling themselves property inspectors whom I refer to as "handymen with a clipboard and a truck."

The untrained, uninsured, totally unqualified handyman-with-a-clipboard-and-a-truck general property inspector will absolutely guarantee getting all parties into a lawsuit.

HOW NOT TO QUALIFY A GENERAL PROPERTY INSPECTOR

I have often been told by real estate agents who have found themselves in lawsuits that they liked the particular property inspector they referred to their buyer clients because the inspector was "soothing," "not alarmist," "pleasant," "reassuring," "everyone thought he was nice," and so on. It is not the job of the general property inspector to reassure the buyers that the property is really wonderful or that it is so rotten the buyers should not buy it.

The general property inspector's role is to provide the buyers with objective information regarding the condition of the systems and components of the property at the time of the inspection; it is not to play the role of Ms./Mr. Congeniality.

Obviously, in every occupation, a reasonably pleasant personality is desirable. No one wants to work with a nasty, grouchy person, but neither agents nor buyers should place personality over qualifications and a competent inspection. Capable property inspectors will explain the important issues; allow the buyers to accompany them on the inspection, to at least some degree; make helpful maintenance suggestions; produce an easy-to-read report; and take photos to document condition and point out problems. The pizzazz of the report or its speed of delivery is not as important as its thoroughness and accuracy; a one or two day delivery is okay.

INSPECTION TIME, SAMPLE REPORTS, AND REFERENCES

General property inspections of a typical three-bedroom, two-bath home should take two to three hours. Inspectors should be willing to provide a sample report for the buyers' review before the inspection, including their contract. Some inspectors will also provide a list of clients and professional references.

AGENTS PROVIDING INSPECTOR NAMES TO BUYER CLIENTS

Whether the real estate agent provides one name, three names, or more names of general property inspectors to buyer clients, all of these individuals' credentials should be reviewed and verified by the real estate agent or real estate brokerage before they are referred. A real estate agent in a lawsuit said he collected literature that was sent to him by property inspectors or that was dropped off at his office. He handed a pile of these cards and brochures to his buyer clients and said, "Pick one." The two buyers in this case were brothers, a policeman and a flight attendant. How could this real estate agent expect his client to make an intelligent choice with no guidance and no experience with property inspectors?

Remember that three random names given to buyers may include two well-qualified inspectors who have insurance coverage and one unqualified property inspector who does not have insurance coverage. The buyers, without proper guidance from their real estate agent, will likely choose the unqualified property inspector because this person will be cheaper. This is a frustrating situation for the general property inspectors who are well qualified and for their professional associations that try to promote the use of well-qualified general property inspectors in real estate transactions.

There are a few misguided real estate agents who still hold to the belief that general property inspectors who are thorough and find all property defects will "mess up" their transaction. Fortunately, most competent and successful real estate agents have discarded this point of view.

All real estate agents should forever eliminate from their thinking that they want to utilize the services of general property inspectors who do not find too much wrong with the property so as not to complicate the deal. Instead, they want to utilize the services of the most qualified general property inspectors they can find in their market, who will find everything wrong with the property *that is wrong with the property.*

I have sometimes been asked by real estate agents, "If I am legally not required to refer my buyer client to a property inspector or to prequalify a property inspector I do refer to my buyer client, why do I have to do this?" The answer to that question is the basis of this book.

To responsibly refer your buyer clients to a qualified general property inspector is reasonable and prudent and will usually keep the buyers, sellers, and real estate agents out of a lawsuit.

CAN THE PAMPHLET *YOU MUST HAVE INSPECTION PROTECTION* PROTECT ALL PARTIES?

Your buyers' real estate agent has given you three names of recommended general property inspectors. Now what do you do with these names? How do you decide which one to choose? Do you choose on price and availability alone?

There are some real estate agents who fail to provide their buyer clients with sufficient guidance in how to select a property inspector from the several names they may refer to the buyers. Explaining the inspection process can be time-consuming, and the buyers may not understand or remember what is said by their agent. Having faced this situation myself many times when representing buyers, I decided to produce the pamphlet *You Must Have Inspection Protection,* which is a guide to buyers and sellers about the inspection process. This pamphlet is the cheapest additional errors and omissions insurance real estate agents can use to protect their clients and themselves. The pamphlet includes the following information:

- Why inspections are important and necessary
- When inspections should be conducted
- How to find a qualified property inspector
- Why the buyers should consider their real estate agent's advice in selecting an inspector
- How to interview and qualify a general property inspector
- The answers buyers should receive to their questions, which would indicate that they are dealing with a qualified property inspector
- General guidelines on inspection cost
- The people who should attend the inspection
- When additional inspections are needed
- What the buyers should do with the inspector's report when it is received
- Inspections for a condominium or a new home

How long would it take real estate agents to impart all that information to their clients orally? Would the buyers likely remember half of what is said? By giving this information to the buyer clients in written form, the real estate agent is making them more informed and shifting the liability of follow-up in the inspection selection process to the buyers, while giving the buyers adequate guidance to make informed decisions. Isn't this why buyers and sellers hire real estate agents?

Do buyers always read everything they are given by their real estate agent? Probably not. However, the giving of advice, in written form, signed for by the buyers, is still the best protection for the agents, buyers, and sellers. Just in case the buyers forget to read the pamphlet or follow its advice or remember that it was given to them at all, I add to my company addendum to the purchase contract, the following:

> By signing below, the buyer indicates receipt of the pamphlet *You Must Have Inspection Protection*.

The pamphlet *You Must Have Inspection Protection* is available in packages of 20 on the author's Web site, www.BarbaraNichols.net.

SELLER PROTECTION FROM THE BUYERS' SELECTION OF AN UNQUALIFIED GENERAL PROPERTY INSPECTOR

The sellers' agent cannot or should not tell the buyers' agent whom they must hire as a general property inspector. Sellers' agents always seem mystified when they are sued along with the sellers. They frequently claim, "The buyers and their agent picked that lousy property inspector who missed that defect. How can I be responsible?"

The sellers' real estate agent may not be able to select the buyers' property inspector to protect the sellers, but the sellers' agent can give the buyers a copy of *You Must Have Inspection Protection* and have the buyers sign for receipt of it. Now the buyers know how to find a qualified property inspector even if the buyers' agent has not told them.

The sellers' agent can also include as part of the contract, or in a counteroffer, a requirement that the buyers' general property inspector have the following "minimum qualifications"; for example:

- Errors and omissions insurance and liability insurance
- Five years of property inspection experience and no lawsuits against him or her
- Membership in at least one inspection professional association (ASHI, NAHI, or state association)

Real estate agents can add to this list, based upon the qualifications of available general property inspectors in their marketplace. Now the buyers and the buyers' agent have been put on notice that a qualified general property inspector, of the buyers' choice, must be hired. The sellers and the sellers' agent are hiding nothing and want the buyers to have the most competent inspection possible.

CAN THE SELLERS' PROPERTY INSPECTION HELP TO PROTECT THE SELLERS AND THEIR AGENT?

The presale sellers' inspection is excellent for the sellers who want to find out the condition of their property. Some sellers are well informed about their property's condition, while others may have very little information. A presale inspection will alert sellers to repairs they may choose to make before listing the property. When these seller repairs are made, they may increase the property's value or reduce the chance of price concessions or repairs during escrow, when the buyers would have discovered these same defects.

Sellers would now also have in their possession reputable information on their property's condition, thus allowing them to be more precise and accurate in their property defect disclosures. They would now be much less likely to be accused later of failing to disclose fully. Sellers can now attach their sellers' inspection to their property disclosure, along with any receipts for repairs addressed in the report that they have made in advance of listing their property.

If a very serious defect is discovered, such as mold or foundation problems, the sellers can address these issues and remedy them or more fully disclose them. If the defect is repaired by the sellers, this might reduce the likelihood of buyers dropping out of an accepted offer when the buyers discover the problem in their own inspections. In some cases, the sellers who repair the serious defect might avoid losing prospective buyers who would not want to spend the time and money to hire mold inspectors or structural engineers and would just drop out of the transaction. Defects that remain and are not repaired by the sellers can be taken into account when the sellers select the listing price.

THE GENERAL PROPERTY INSPECTOR'S ROLE IN REFERRING ADDITIONAL INSPECTORS

The principal role of referring buyers to additional inspectors is held by the general property inspector. General property inspectors are generalists, not specialists in the systems that comprise a property. It is very important that the general property inspector's contract, which is signed by the buyers before the inspection begins, states exactly what will be inspected and what is excluded from the inspection. The general property inspector should not sign the contract for the clients and should be sure that clients see and approve the contract before the inspection.

Most general property inspections may not cover:

- Detection of pool or spa leaks
- Examination of the interior of a chimney flue
- Detection and analysis of possible mold or mildew
- Geologic issues
- Structural engineering issues
- Soils issues and stability
- Verification the roof is not leaking
- Examination of anything blocked or made inaccessible by the property owner's contents
- Issues related to flood or fire danger
- Issues related to toxic conditions, contaminates, radon, or asbestos
- Conditions related to animals, rodents, insects, or wood-destroying organisms
- Costs to repair, replace, or operate any system
- Compliance with building codes
- Common areas or systems of a common-interest development may be specifically excluded
- Determination of the existence of latent deficiencies or defects
- Obtaining or reviewing any information from third parties
- Researching the history of a property
- Offering any form of warranty or guarantee
- Evaluation of the acoustic properties of any structure
- Operation or evaluation of low-voltage yard lighting or sprinkler systems
- Operation or evaluation of security systems, cable or satellite systems, timers, or intercoms
- Examination or evaluation of fire resistive systems of any structure
- Determination of the age of the structure or installation of any system, or the differentiation between original construction and subsequent additions
- Examination of the stability of trees or any analysis of landscaping unless it affects the dwelling

Wouldn't reasonable buyers want to know what is not included in the inspection at the time of the inspection? As can be seen from the above list, there is a great deal not covered by the general property inspector about which buyers might want information. The general property inspector might recommend an in-depth inspection for an area he has inspected; for example, by an electrician or a plumber. The best inspectors will not hesitate to recommend additional inspections based on their observations, information received from the seller and the real estate agents, as well as concerns expressed by the buyer.

Beware of general property inspectors who also conduct mold inspections, chimney flue inspections, and other technical inspections they may not be qualified to undertake.

THE GENERAL PROPERTY INSPECTOR'S REPORT

The general property inspector's report should generally cover the following:

- Foundations, basements, and under-floor areas
- The exterior of the structure
- Roof coverings and signs of current or past roof leaks if observed
- Attic areas and roof framing
- Plumbing
- Electrical systems
- Heating systems and visible insulation
- Central cooling systems
- Fireplaces and chimneys (but not the flue)
- The building interior
- Built-in appliances and operation of interior spas
- Issues related to property drainage that can be observed
- Exterior pools and spas (but not leak detection), but may be listed as excluded
- Notification of products used on the property that have been recalled, such as furnaces that catch fire or polybutylene plumbing pipes that leak
- Photo documentation of the property

Would reasonable and prudent buyers or their real estate agent risk turning over this analysis to an inexperienced, unknowledgeable, uninsured handyman to inspect one of the largest purchase decisions anyone makes in his or her lifetime? After reading this chapter, I certainly hope not!

CAN AND SHOULD GENERAL PROPERTY INSPECTORS LIMIT THEIR LIABILITY?

In some states, general property inspectors are allowed to place a limit on their liability, usually the cost of the inspection, for errors in detecting property defects. This limitation, however, may not hold up in court. The damage level may be so large relative to the limit of liability that it has the effect of making it seem that the inspector is avoiding responsibility for professional negligence. States that have yet to do away with a limitation of liability for property inspectors probably soon will. Even in states where inspectors can limit their liability, there are inspectors who do not. What point is there in having errors and omissions insurance for $1 million if liability is limited to a few hundred dollars?

Another way to detect out-of-date and incompetent property inspectors is to note items in their contract that have been eliminated by legislation in their state. We still have some inspectors in California limiting their liability to the cost of the inspection, although this was prohibited by law in 1996. Some general property inspectors in California also try to limit the amount of time a buyer has to sue them. However, state law in California gives a buyer four years to sue the general property inspector after the close of the transaction.

The buyer's real estate agent, as well as the buyer, should read the contract form presented by the property inspector and ask questions related to what will or will not be covered in the inspection prior to the start of the inspection.

WHY SOME GENERAL PROPERTY INSPECTORS SHOULDN'T BE INSPECTORS

Even when a state has licensing or certification for general property inspectors, there will always be those who are more qualified than others. This is true in any occupation. Would you want to be operated on by a doctor the first time she was removing an appendix, or by the doctor who graduated last in her class, if a more qualified doctor is available? Of

"I'm here to do your general property inspection."

course you would choose the more qualified doctor. We all have to start out in life as novices. Some prepare better than others, and the wise among us take the time to learn from those more experienced as we move through life and gain our own experience.

The general property inspectors who dismiss professional associations as useless, training as unnecessary, and insurance coverage as not required should find some other way to make a living and spare the property buyers of America from their services. So too should the general property inspectors whose procedures are vague and whose standards are not verifiable. This kind of general property inspector is a lawsuit waiting to happen. The general property inspector should not be making repairs to any property he inspects because this is a direct conflict of interest. Inspecting properties also requires a level of fitness to climb on roofs, in attics, and under houses. The inspector who is too old or too large to handle what is required should not be inspecting properties.

By the way, my favorite general property inspector, in my own area, has been a general property inspector for over 25 years, has completed 26,815 inspections, has errors and omissions and liability insurance, has never been sued, is an expert witness in legal cases involving property inspectors, has a general contractor's license, and belongs to both ASHI and NAHI. In other words, I take my own advice.

8

CHAPTER

Mold, Mildew, Lead Paint, and Other Environmental Hazards

ARE MOLD AND MILDEW LAWSUITS JUSTIFIED OR JUST TODAY'S HOT TOPIC IN REAL ESTATE LAWSUITS?

The U.S. Chamber of Commerce reported in 2003 that there were more than 10,000 mold cases pending nationwide, a 300 percent increase over 1999.[1]

Because of the huge number of claims for mold and mildew damages since the mid–1990s, insurance companies, both property and errors and omissions, have capped their coverage or left the market, leaving property owners and real estate agents unprotected. An E&O insurance carrier may pay for the defense of its insured, but it will not likely cover either settlements between the parties in lawsuits or court financial awards to the injured party.

In one recent case in California on which I consulted, the court awarded the injured party $135,000 in damages in a mold and mildew case. The plaintiff attorney then returned to court, as the prevailing party, to request legal expenses for the plaintiff, which might have totaled

[1] News Release, U.S. Chamber of Commerce, July 17, 2003.

another $50,000. All this to be paid by the dual agent real estate broker and the seller, who was also the broker's mother-in-law!

Insurance companies claim to have lost billions of dollars in mold claims and that they cannot raise premiums enough to cover these losses. They also claim that health issues raised in legal cases have exaggerated health risks. At most, the insurance industry believes that the health effects of mold are allergy symptoms affecting only certain people. They also believe that mold develops in properties because a moisture or water source is allowed to continue to enter the property as a result of poor maintenance by property owners.

Consumer and health groups do not view these issues the same way. They point to devastating health effects. The situation is further complicated by the fact that there are no national standards establishing what levels of various types of indoor molds are unsafe. A particular mold or mold level that may have no adverse health effect on one person may trigger significant health problems for someone else.

ARE BUILDINGS MORE VULNERABLE TO MOLD?

The question arises whether buildings are more vulnerable to mold now than they used to be or is there just more public awareness of the problem of mold? Some of the problem can be attributed to an aging housing stock. Older homes may be more vulnerable to broken or leaking pipes, roof leaks, shower pan leaks, sink leaks, and other deteriorating conditions. However, a good deal of the mold problem is occurring in newer buildings, with the development of sealed, energy efficient structures in the late 1970s.

What has changed is the moisture balance in buildings, according to an article in *Professional Builder* magazine.[2] Properties don't dry out as quickly as they used to because they are better insulated and built tighter. Structures today are built with more moisture-sensitive materials. Mold likes processed wood better than it likes lumber. Paper or high-cellulose products, such as drywall, are a perfect mold food. Construction methods today have increased the ability of buildings to soak up and store some moisture that enters the building shell, because of design flaws, poor workmanship, or construction defects. Buildings today have less masonry and more paper-faced drywall than they did in decades past.

---

[2] Steve Andrews, "Mold a Growing Concern," *Professional Builder*, April 2002.

Mold can be produced by the structural design of a building, the workmanship, materials selection, and maintenance issues. Buildings that may start out with good design to prevent mold development may be altered by nonpermitted additions and modifications. Yard sprinklers may be overwatering or misdirected at walls.

WHAT EXACTLY IS DANGEROUS MOLD?

Mold consists of biological organisms that can grow almost anywhere. Mold is naturally occurring in the environment. Mold produces allergens, substances that can cause allergic reactions, and potentially toxic substances. So-called toxic mold consists of several types of mold called *aspergileus, penicillium*, and *stachybotrys*, which can produce *mycotoxins*. It is estimated that there are over 20,000 different species of mold.[3] Mold is a fungus, which produces microscopic spores that spread the mold.

DO MOLD AND MILDEW HARM PEOPLE?

Numerous health problems have been attributed to toxic mold, including:

- Allergic reactions
- Respiratory problems
- Infections
- Nasal and sinus congestion
- Coughing
- Wheezing
- Skin or eye irritation
- Watery eyes and blurred vision
- Sneezing
- Hair loss
- Fever
- Confusion
- Extreme fatigue
- Migraine-like headaches
- Pulmonary bleeding
- Memory loss
- Brain damage

---

[3] Susan C. Cooper, *The Truth about Mold*, Dearborn Real Estate Education, 2004.

A mold/asthma connection is being studied. Mold can trigger asthma, but it is not yet clear whether exposure to mold can lead to the development of asthma.[4]

WHO IS MOST VULNERABLE TO HEALTH PROBLEMS?

The elderly, asthmatics, infants and young children, and those with weakened immune systems are the most at risk to develop negative reactions to mold. It is estimated that one in three American households suffer from some type of mold problem. In addition, for one in ten households, the mold and mildew levels are high enough to cause environmental allergies and respiratory ailments. There is presently no way to determine how many people have been sickened by mold, because no agency tracks the number of people adversely affected by mold and mildew. There is currently no comprehensive understanding of the scope of symptoms that could possibly be attributed to exposure to mold.

HOW ARE PROPERTIES INVADED BY MOLD?

Mold can enter a property on clothing, pets, building materials, even air through open windows and doors. There are many other ways mold and mildew can infect a property, such as:

- Roof leaks into attics or through ceilings
- Broken or leaking sewer lines under a building
- Backed up sewer lines
- Damp, leaking basements
- Bathroom shower, tub steam, and plumbing leaks
- Toilet and tub overflows
- Leaking shower pans
- Ovens, burner units, showers, and clothes washers and dryers not vented to the outside
- Air duct system contamination
- Humidifiers
- Flooding

---

[4] Andrews, "Mold a Growing Concern."

- Inadequate mechanical ventilation in attics and under buildings in crawl spaces
- Lack of fans or window ventilation in bathrooms
- Lack of hood/fan ventilation in kitchens
- Leaking water heaters
- Windows not properly installed or flashed
- Refrigerator ice maker leaks
- Burst or leaking water pipe
- Blown washing machine hose
- Air conditioner condensate leak
- At the foundation sill plate into the walls and floors
- Through planters or landscaped areas against exterior walls
- At doors not elevated above grade
- Leaks under kitchen or bath sinks, dishwashers, clothes washers, and toilets
- Water damage from fire suppression
- In new homes, wood framing that has become wet or damp (properly dried lumber has a low moisture content of less than 19 percent)
- Improperly installed synthetic stucco [Exterior Insulation Finish Systems (EIFS)]
- No weep screed or the weep screed is covered with stucco (A weep screed is an angled strip, usually metal, located at the base of exterior walls where the foundation and sill plate meet. It is part of the drainage system to carry moisture behind the exterior wall surface to the exterior.)
- Parapets not properly sealed

With all these possible entry points or areas with moisture or water allowing mold growth, it is not surprising that mold has become a great concern in all building types.

ARE THERE RED FLAGS THAT CAN ALERT YOU TO MOLD?

Sometimes property owners don't know that they have mold growing in their buildings. It can be hidden under floors or inside walls and may not show any visible signs or clues. Mold may also hide on the backside of drywall, wallpaper, paneling, under carpet and pads, in roof materials above ceiling tiles, or around pipes. Sometimes mold can hide behind furniture on wall surfaces, or inside closets where condensation forms.

Sellers, the real estate agents involved in the property sale, and the general property inspector should visually inspect the property to look for and note these red flags:

- Moldy smell (musty or earthy)
- Water leaks or moisture
- Cottony, velvety, or granular stain, smudge, or discoloration on a surface; stain may be white, gray, black, brown, yellow, or green; check closet walls, behind furniture, on bathroom walls at showers and tubs, ceilings, around or just under windows, under roof eaves at vent locations
- Condensation on windows and walls
- Warping floors
- Absence of gutters and downspouts
- Obviously sloped yard drainage toward the structure
- Interior floors lower than exterior yard levels
- Damp, wet feel to the air
- Flaking paint near windows or on walls or ceilings
- Patios level with the access door, having no drains, and/or sloped toward the building rather than away from the building
- Tile on shower or tub walls that moves when pressed or feels loose
- Flaking paint inside sink cabinets
- Damp or wet floors or carpets
- Wet basements
- Nails pulling out of drywall

All these red flags should be noted on the general property inspector's report and in the seller's and agents' disclosures. The general property inspector may also note signs of moisture observed under the building in a crawl space or in the attic. The termite inspection company usually tests for leaking shower pans. These disclosures should be in writing and accompanied by a recommendation for a mold inspection.

Real estate agents should be sure to thoroughly question sellers about any prior leaks or water problems that they may have had and repaired. Did the seller test for mold at that time? If some form of testing or remediation did take place, the seller should be asked to provide all available reports and receipts for the buyer's examination. These reports should confirm the proper removal and disposal of any materials that had been contaminated and that mold testing revealed elimination of any dangerous molds. The seller should include any insurance claims submitted and paid, with the date, location of the problem, and amount received.

It is totally inadequate to give buyers a "clue" to the problem, and hope they either catch on and investigate or ignore the clue, to their own detriment. For example:

The seller reports that there was a toilet leak in the master bath, but it was repaired.

A better way to describe the situation is:

The seller reports that last year there was a toilet leak in the master bath. A licensed plumbing contractor was called and made the repair. The plumbing company receipt is attached to this disclosure. The sellers did not test for mold. The seller's agent does not know if the toilet leak could have precipitated a mold problem and strongly recommends that the buyer have a mold inspection.

The second description of the problem may be lengthy, but it is far more useful to the buyer. It may have required some investigation on the part of the listing agent, but it is a description that will much better protect the seller and the agent, as well as the buyer. The buyer's agent should also question the listing agent for more facts. A buyer who refuses to conduct a mold inspection when presented with red flags and a property history that may indicate the wisdom of a mold inspection should be asked to sign a form saying something similar to the following:

The buyer has been put on notice by the seller, real estate agents, and general property inspector that there exist possible red flags for mold and mildew that may be causing physical damage to the property and may cause potential occupant health problems. The buyer has declined to conduct a mold inspection against the best advice of the real estate agents.

Be sure the buyer, who has declined a recommended mold inspection, signs this statement and receives a copy of it. In several recent "mold" lawsuits in which I have consulted, the seller had recently painted the house, covering up the telltale signs of water damage. Did the seller know he was concealing mold, or was he just ignorant of the problem? If a real estate agent notices, or is told, that the building was recently painted, she should ask if any staining or flaking paint was covered up and where it was located, and the buyer should be informed. The buyer's agent should make notes of the answer from the seller or the seller's agent and pass this information to the buyer in writing. For example:

> The seller's agent has told me that the seller recently repainted the building inside and out, leaving the remaining paint cans in the garage for the buyer's later use. There was a stain on the living room ceiling that was covered by the painting. The seller says he does not know if the stain was from a water leak and has not tested for mold. It is recommended that a licensed roofing contractor examine the roof for signs of leaking and that the buyer conduct a mold inspection.

If this sounds like overkill, believe me it is not! Real estate agents have a duty of "reasonable care and diligence" to the party they are representing, and this is reasonable care and diligence.

HOW PHYSICALLY DAMAGING IS MOLD?

Mold can cause structural damage to a building and permeate property contents. Although most infestations are treatable and located in an isolated area of the building, some are so invasive that the building must be taken down and rebuilt. In many lawsuits for mold damage, the personal contents of the buyers, such as upholstered furniture and bedding, became so permeated with the mold that they could not be thoroughly cleaned and had to be disposed of.

All that is required for mold to grow are:[5]

- Mold spores
- High humidity (70 to 80 percent) or liquid water
- A food source, such as organic soil, wood, or paper-based cellulose material
- Oxygen and temperatures from 40 to 100 degrees

---

[5] Ibid.

Wood starts decaying when it reaches 28 percent moisture content by weight and continues decaying until it drops below 20 percent moisture content. Mold is not a surface contamination but rather penetrates deeply, destroying wood. Certain molds are wood destroying organisms.[6]

Builders of new construction, whether original or additions, should be extremely careful to allow exposed framing to thoroughly dry before enclosing it in drywall and stucco or siding so as not to trap the moisture and mold in the walls. Wood framing exposed to rain should be submitted to moisture testing to determine that it is sufficiently dry so that it will not sustain mold growth before it is enclosed.

THE MOLD INSPECTION

If the real estate agents see red flags for moisture intrusion and possibly mold and/or a general property inspector reports signs of possible mold, they should recommend in writing that the buyer obtain a mold inspection, regardless of what other contract document or buyer advisory references mold inspections in a general way. The issue is no longer general; it is now specific to this property.

If mold inspectors or mold remediators are licensed or certified in your state, you will at least have a good starting point from which to qualify these inspectors. In June 2003, Texas became the first state to adopt legislation for the licensing of mold professionals. It is to everyone's advantage to seek out the most qualified mold inspectors based on a reasonable set of credentials. The more highly trained, the more likely the inspection will be done right. Do not hire or recommend a company that offers both inspection and remediation services, which is a conflict of interest. Look for the following list of credentials and try to find an individual, or a company, with as many of these credentials as possible in your area:

- Has specific mold insurance (errors and omissions insurance)
- Council-certified microbial consultant (CMC) [issued by the AIAQC (American Indoor Air Quality Council)]
- Certified indoor environmental consultant (CIEC) (issued by the AIAQC)

---

[6] Ibid.

- Certified residential mold inspector (CRMI) [issued by the IESO (Indoor Environmental Standards Organization)]
- Works with a qualified laboratory to test the samples submitted (the interpretation lab)
- Will take samples inside and outside (the outside sample serves as a baseline)
- Environmental engineer
- Professional engineer
- Provides legal and forensic testimony
- Certification from the Association of Energy Engineers
- At least five or more years of experience; more is better
- Over 500 microbial inspections conducted
- Clear, concise, and comprehensive reports
- Certified Industrial Hygienist (CIH) [issued by the ABIH (American Board of Industrial Hygiene)]
- Ventilation engineering for crawl spaces is also important, and very often overlooked
- Can offer other environmental inspection services such as asbestos, bacteria, lead, radon, and allergens

The mold inspector should be a member of one or preferably more than one of the following:

- American Industrial Hygiene Association (AIHA)
- American Board of Industrial Hygiene (ABIH)
- American Conference of Governmental Industrial Hygienists (ACGIH)
- American Indoor Air Quality Council (AIAQC) [The AIAQC and the IESO merged with the IAQA (Indoor Air Quality Association), but the AIAQC still has its own Web site.]
- Indoor Environmental Standards Organization (IESO)
- Association of Energy Engineers (AEE)

Real estate agents should not refer their buyer clients to any mold inspection company that does not carry a policy of "specific mold insurance."

Mold sampling should require an air sample from outside the building to serve as a reference sample to compare with samples taken from inside the building. The purpose of this reference sample is to determine if interior samples show the presence of molds not in the outside environment or in concentrations far exceeding the outside environment. The sample should be analyzed following methods recommended by the American Industrial Hygiene Association and the American Conference of Governmental Industrial Hygienists. Surface samples may also be required where there appears to be visible mold, for mold type identification and to determine if actual growth is present. The inspector should be able to provide a detailed report, which should include the scope of the problem and the protocol for remediation. Buyers and their agents should ask the inspector for at least one sample of previous reports to check for these features.

The lab report should be easily understood. Results should be clear concerning the location of the problem mold areas and the significance of the findings. Buyers, sellers, and real estate agents should be able to understand the lab's interpretation of the results. The final step in the inspection process is "clearance." The mold inspector must return to the building to retake samples and retest at the lab to determine that the mold has been eliminated by the remediation process.

"I think you are right. We do need a mold inspection."

FINDING A QUALIFIED MOLD REMEDIATOR

Buyers will typically undertake property inspections at their expense, including the mold inspection. If mold is found on the property, the buyers will usually request that the sellers pay the costs of mold remediation, which means that the selection of the mold remediation company is now made by the sellers, with assistance from the sellers' agent. The sellers will undoubtedly ask their real estate agent, "Who should we call to undertake the mold remediation?" This is a reasonable question, since the sellers may have had no prior occasion to contact a mold remediation company and likely have no information regarding qualifications of mold remediation companies.

> Do not let the seller, the seller's handyman, or a general contractor attempt a mold remediation.

Mold remediation must be done correctly to be effective, and this requires a competent, well-qualified, and experienced remediation company, with the following qualifications:

- *A certificate of specific mold insurance:* Most general liability policies exclude mold. Mold-specific insurance should be "state admitted" and full occurrence (not claims made) and should carry the highest A.M. Best rating possible. (A.M. Best is the leading provider of ratings, news, and financial data for the insurance industry.)
- *Certified mold remediator (CMR)* [issued by the AIAQC (American Indoor Air Quality Council)].
- *Applied microbial remediation technician (AMRT)* [issued by the IICRC (Institute of Inspection, Cleaning and Restoration Certification)].
- *Certified microbial remediation supervisor (CMRS)* (issued by the AIAQC).
- *Asbestos abatement license (Fed OSHA 1910.1001):* Mold may have developed above ceiling drywall, and the drywall and sprayed acoustic ceiling now need to be removed. If the sprayed acoustic ceiling (sometimes referred to as a cottage cheese ceiling) contains asbestos, it must be removed by a licensed asbestos contractor. Any unlicensed removal may result in the

building owner and contractor being found guilty of criminal offenses. Asbestos fibers inhaled by occupants can become a serious health issue, and should this occur, subject the remediation company, the seller, and the agents to liability. Samples of the sprayed acoustic ceiling can be scraped into a plastic zip bag and taken to a lab certified to test for asbestos.

- *Lead abatement training certificate (Fed OSHA 1910.1000):* Unlicensed removal of lead-based paints may result in prosecution and/or litigation.
- *Hazardous waste hauler certificate (Fed OSHA 120):* The transport of hazardous materials, such as asbestos and lead-based paint, requires government certification.
- *License to use heat as a disinfectant:* Recent medical literature documents that disease-causing bacteria live synergistically with mold. Heat treatment is one method of killing mold and the insects that spread it, and heat also kills the bacteria that are inaccessible to other forms of abatement. Heat also dries the treated area, making it less vulnerable to mold, insects, and bacterial growth.
- *State structural pest control board operator license:* Recent research indicates that insects transport some mold spores. For complete abatement, you may consider using a contractor that is qualified and certified to eradicate these insects safely. In addition, certain types of fungal contamination require this license for remediation.
- Material data safety sheets, equipment licensed for the jurisdiction, certificate of vehicle insurance, and certificate of worker's compensation insurance.
- Completion of 500 or more indoor air contamination projects.
- In business five or more years.
- Licensed general engineering contractor and general contractor.

The remediation company should be a member of one or more, but preferably all, of the following associations:

- Restoration Industry Association (RIA) [formerly the Association of Specialists in Cleaning and Restoration (ASCR)]
- American Industrial Hygienists Association (AIHA)
- American Indoor Air Quality Council (AIAQC) or Indoor Air Quality Association (IAQA)

Qualified mold remediation companies will be pleased to provide you with documentation demonstrating these qualifications.

MOLD INSPECTION AND MOLD REMEDIATION ASSOCIATIONS AND DESIGNATIONS

The designations, certifications, training, and associations themselves are in a constant state of change in this evolving industry. It is important to check with these associations for the most current information. Designations in addition to the ones noted above are CIEC, CMC, CMI, and CIE. Explanations can be found at www.AIAQC.org and in the Reference section of this book.

HOW IS MOLD REMEDIATION CARRIED OUT?

The first step in mold remediation is for the occupant to remove all personal belongings from the area to be remediated. The contaminated areas must be contained and sealed off from the rest of the structure with a plastic containment barrier. The containment should be placed under negative pressure to prevent cross contamination. Negative air machines with HEPA (high-efficiency particulate air) filtration should be used to manage aerosol (the particulate mass including mold spores that is kicked up into the air when the mold is disturbed during the process). Personnel involved in the remediation work must be dressed in protective clothing and have protective eyewear, gloves, rubber boots, and masks.

The search for the extent of the mold problem begins with the observed mold area or the area that tested high for mold. Drywall is removed at least 24 inches above and below staining or observed mold and around infected window areas. The drywall, carpeting, ceiling material, cabinets, tile, and so on are removed until no further concealed mold is observed. All contaminated materials that are removed must be bagged and disposed of appropriately.

Damaged and weakened building materials are removed, including framing lumber if it is completely permeated. Some framing may be sanded down past the point of permeation and then thoroughly cleaned. Remediation contractors should follow the recommended guidelines of the Environmental Protection Agency's (EPA) mold remediation in schools and commercial buildings, and the guidelines of the American Conference of Governmental Industrial Hygienists. Advanced scrubbing and cleaning techniques are used with HEPA filters and ULPA (ultra-low-penetration air) vacuuming. Cleaning must remove all contamination. If the moisture source is an ongoing problem, it must be identified and corrected to prevent recurrence of the moisture/mold problem.

Clean, dry heat, generated by EPA registered equipment, is then directed into the contaminated area through flexible Mylar ducting, and the inside air is slowly raised to a safe saunalike temperature that is lethal to mold, bacteria, and insects. Once the desired temperature level has been maintained for the specified time, the cool down begins. When no toxic chemicals are used, technicians can enter and monitor the treated area, and there are no harmful residues to contaminate the air or surfaces.

WHAT WILL THE INSPECTION AND REMEDIATION COST?

A thorough inspection with sampling, lab testing, and a detailed report covering the scope of the problem and the recommended protocol for remediation, can average between $500 and $1,500 depending on the number of locations and the number of samples needed. The clearance report from the mold inspector, with resampling and lab tests may cost another $500 to $1,500, again depending on the scope of the problem.

Remediation costs can vary widely depending on the size of the area infected. A bedroom and bath area may cost from $2,500 to $10,000, depending on how much tear out and treatment is needed. The reconstruction costs, including drywall, framing, flooring, carpets, moldings, paint, tile, cabinets, reinstalling sinks, can add up to another $3,000 or more for a bedroom and bath area.

For some buyers, just hearing the word *mold* from their mold inspector may cause them to exit the transaction. If the buyers decide to continue with the transaction, they will usually expect the sellers to pay for the mold remediation, mold reinspection, and any reconstruction needed. The high cost of quality inspections and remediation has led some real estate agents to look for cheaper solutions to save their distraught sellers money. This is a mistake! The sellers have to do "what they have to do" to correct this problem. The buyers and their agent should receive copies of all proposals, analyses, and reports.

SHOULD A GENERAL PROPERTY INSPECTOR OR TERMITE COMPANY INSPECT FOR MOLD?

A few general property inspectors claim that they inspect for mold, and some of these have no doubt been sued. Some general property inspectors have branched out into what they perceive as the lucrative mold inspection business. However, after reading the lengthy list of qualifications mold inspectors should have, I hope by now buyers, sellers, and real estate agents are convinced that the mold inspection business is a separate field of specialization, best left to companies whose focus is on environmental inspections. General property inspectors sometimes do note a suspicious area or stain that they believe might be mold, or they indicate water intrusion and recommend further investigation. This is totally appropriate for them in the course of their inspection.

Mold inspections are not covered by termite companies, although mold is a fungus and wood-destroying organism. Termite companies might also note their observation of mold or moisture intrusion in the course of their inspection and also recommend further investigation. Sometimes an environmental company that does mold remediation will also conduct termite remediation.

HOW LONG WILL THE INSPECTION AND REMEDIATION TAKE?

If the seller indicates that there was a water intrusion problem, that there could be mold, or that there is mold, or the general property inspector sees signs of mold, the buyer or the agent should immediately request an extension of the inspection period, if necessary, to allow for a qualified mold inspector to inspect the property, take samples, and get the report back from the lab. A qualified mold inspector may not be able to get to the property for several days. The lab may take several more days to process the samples and issue a report to the inspector, who then must write a report. My recommendation is to add at least 7 to 10 days to the inspection time allowed, if a mold inspection is to be done. The groaning seller should remember that if he doesn't cooperate with this buyer, he will have to deal with the same issue with the next buyer.

If mold is found in the inspection, the remediation company will take a day or two to come out and provide a quote for the remediation. Once the company is given the go-ahead to proceed, and depending on the scope of the project, it could take two to four days to remediate a bedroom and bath. Another two to five days will be required to have the mold inspector reinspect and sample and have those samples analyzed by the lab. Reconstruction of the ceiling, floor, drywall, framing, and so on might take two to ten days for a bedroom and bath, depending on the scope of the reconstruction required.

   Beware of the mold inspection companies that can inspect and deliver next day reports. Well-qualified companies can do this, but the cost can be higher. Also, _beware of the mold remediation companies that can remediate in two to three days_, unless they have a large crew and two to three days is adequate to accomplish a small remediation. Speed is not as important as quality work. The agents, seller, and buyer want this work to be done right, and if escrow has to be extended, so be it.

HOW CAN REAL ESTATE AGENTS PROTECT BUYERS AND SELLERS FROM A MOLD PROBLEM?

Real estate agents can do the following to protect buyers and sellers from mold problems:

- Conduct a visual inspection of the property looking for mold red flags and note their observations in writing to the buyers and sellers.
- Encourage the sellers to disclose all they know about the history of water intrusion and mold in the property.
- Have the buyers sign for receipt of all mold disclosures, forms, booklets, and agent or general property inspector recommendations for further mold inspections.
- Recommend only well-qualified mold inspectors and mold remediation companies. I have sold properties with mold problems, and the mold inspection and mold remediation companies I have worked with have all of the qualifications on my lists of qualifications.
- Adjust the inspection time period allowed in the contract, by mutual agreement of the parties, to provide sufficient time for a quality mold inspection and quality remediation, reinspection, and reconstruction.
- Be sure that all agreements regarding mold remediation and credit are in writing and signed by the buyers and the sellers.
- If at all possible, schedule the buyers' final walk-through inspection when the sellers have moved out, so that all walls, floors, and ceilings are visible for reinspection.

HOW CAN SELLERS AND THEIR REAL ESTATE AGENTS PROTECT THEMSELVES FROM A POOR MOLD INSPECTION BY BUYERS?

The sellers and their agent may find themselves vulnerable to a lawsuit when an unqualified mold inspector selected by the buyers misses mold in the property or reinspects and finds no mold when mold is still present. The buyers may claim that the sellers and their agent knew more about the mold problem than they disclosed. The buyers' agent may also be vulnerable to a lawsuit for recommending a poor inspector, or not recommending anyone, and letting the unknowledgeable buyers make a selection without any guidance.

Sellers and their agent should provide buyers and their agent with the list of qualifications for mold and mildew inspectors in this book, and request that buyers sign for receipt of this list. The list should be accompanied by a statement from the sellers that says:

> The sellers and their real estate agent are providing the attached list of qualifications for a mold and mildew inspector. It is strongly recommended that the buyers and their agent seek out inspectors that have most or all of these qualifications to ensure a thorough and competent inspection is conducted. The sellers' agent has prequalified several mold inspectors in our area and can provide this list on request from the buyers or their agent. The buyers' mold inspector must have the following minimum qualifications to ensure an adequate inspection:
> * Has specific mold insurance
> * Is a council-certified microbial consultant or council-certified indoor environmental consultant
> * Is a certified industrial hygienist
> * Has five or more years of experience as a mold and mildew inspector

The buyers and sellers should sign and date this agreement as a modification of the contract.

HOW CAN BUYERS AND THEIR REAL ESTATE AGENTS PROTECT THEMSELVES FROM POOR MOLD REMEDIATION BY SELLERS?

Poor mold remediation is a situation similar to poor mold inspection by the buyers. In this case, the buyers and their real estate agent are knowledgeable about mold inspectors and mold remediators' qualifications, and the sellers and their agent may not have this information. A poorly conducted remediation may not eliminate all the mold and may leave mold spores airborne to redevelop elsewhere in the property or be inhaled by the occupants. This situation can clearly lead to a lawsuit by the buyers against the sellers and the sellers' agent as well their own agent for not incorporating appropriate safeguards into the contract.

The buyers and their agent should provide the sellers and their agent with the list of mold and mildew remediator qualifications in this book and request that the sellers sign for receipt of this list. The list should be accompanied by a statement from the buyers that says:

> The buyers and their real estate agent are providing the attached list of qualifications for a mold and mildew remediator. It is strongly recommended that the sellers and their agent seek out mold remediation companies that have most or all of these qualifications to ensure a thorough and competent remediation. The buyers' agent has prequalified several mold remediation companies in our area and can provide this list on request from the sellers or their agent. The sellers' mold remediation company must have the following minimum qualifications to ensure an adequate mold remediation:
>
> * A certificate of specific mold insurance
> * Microbial remediation certificate from the IAQA, AIAQC, or IICRC
> * An asbestos abatement license
> * A lead abatement training certificate
> * In business as a mold remediation company for five or more years
> * Member of the IAQA, IICRC, or ASCR

The buyers and sellers should sign and date this agreement as a modification of the contract.

I am certain that a real estate agent reading the above will be thinking, "Should I provide a list of mold inspectors or mold remediators to the buyer or seller?" The answer is _yes if_ the _buyer or seller does not_ know whom to call and the real estate agent has a prequalified list available. There is much less liability risk in providing a qualified list than in not providing one and having either the buyer or seller hire unqualified inspectors and remediators. Real estate agents should have these lists on hand so that when a mold issue is suspected at a property, an agent knows whom to call.

LEAD PAINT AND OTHER ENVIRONMENTAL HAZARDS

Property sellers and landlords are required by federal law to disclose to buyers or renters whether the property, if built before 1978, has lead paint.

"About 38 million homes, 40 percent of the nation's housing, contain lead paint."[7] A form must be submitted to prospective buyers or tenants with the disclosure, and they must be given 10 days to inspect for lead paint. The sellers or landlords must provide to the buyers or tenants any known available reports, records, or testing they have regarding lead paint on the property. They must also provide a federally mandated pamphlet describing the potential hazards of lead paint. The buyers or tenants should sign for receipt of both the disclosure document and the pamphlet. Should the buyers or tenants once informed about the possibility of lead paint on the property decide not to inspect for it, they should sign a waiver declining to conduct this inspection.

There are a number of potential environmental hazards that might be found at a property; some of these include:

- Asbestos
- Formaldehyde (a bonding agent in particleboard and plywood and also found in kitchen cabinets and blown insulation)
- Radon gas
- Pesticides (on the property or near farmland)
- Carbon monoxide

Real estate agents and buyers should ask sellers about the likely presence of any of these hazards, any testing they may have done, or any documents they may have had provided to them by the sellers from whom they purchased, and any remediation they may have conducted, with applicable receipts and permits. "Because lead has already been removed in many low-income housing projects, much of the remaining threat lies in suburbs where homes are being remodeled, creating a hazard from the poisonous dust stirred up by remodeling."[8] In commercial properties there may be an issue of construction over oil tanks that could leak or possible hazardous waste. Some residential developments have been known to be built over waste disposal sites or adjacent to these sites.

---

[7] "Marla Cone, "Lead Safety Rules May Raise Remodeling Costs," *Los Angeles Times*, June 25, 2006.
[8] Ibid.

NATURAL HAZARDS THAT ARE A FACTOR OF GEOGRAPHY

In California, real estate agents are either required or recommended to provide a natural hazards disclosure to the buyers of residential and commercial properties. This report deals with high fire hazard zones, proximity to earthquake faults, and location in flood zones. In other parts of the country, flood issues, fire, hurricanes, tornadoes, dust storms, and high snow levels may be the environmental issues of greatest concern. Real estate agents and sellers should make full disclosure of these possible conditions to prospective buyers.

The only good is knowledge and the only evil is ignorance.

—Socrates

9 CHAPTER

Material Facts

In almost every real estate transaction the party or parties are accused of failing to disclose "material facts." Unfortunately, some real estate agents, and most buyers and sellers, do not understand the definition of *material facts*.

WHAT IS A MATERIAL FACT?

A *material fact* is any information about the property, on-site or off-site, that would affect the price the buyer is willing to pay or the buyer's decision to buy.

WHY ARE MATERIAL FACTS IMPORTANT IN LAWSUITS?

If it can be proven by the plaintiff that a material fact was known by the seller or the agents, or should have reasonably been known by them, and was not disclosed, the plaintiff will likely win the case. It is the duty of real estate agents and sellers to disclose to the buyer all material facts affecting the property that they know or a court could determine they should have known. Buyers must disclose all material facts concerning their ability to buy the property and complete the transaction. The principal focus of general property inspectors is noting issues that are material facts. Builders and developers are also expected to disclose material facts they know or should have known. Some examples of material facts are:

- This development has a history of foundation problems and soil instability in a number of homes. The buyer is strongly recommended to have a soils engineer and structural engineer examine the property.
- The yard slopes down toward the house, which has no elevation from grade, and this could indicate possible water intrusion. The buyer is advised to have a drainage engineer examine this situation.
- The chimney has a large crack in the brick of the flue as observed from the exterior of the house. The buyer should have the chimney flue scoped by a licensed chimney contractor to check for interior flue cracks.
- Plowing at the adjacent farm can occur 24 hours a day.
- A rehab center for drug users is located one block away on Oak Street.
- The building is on a septic system.
- This area is known to have a history of underground water.
- A well is required on this property because there is no available city water supply.

I am always astonished that some sellers can delude themselves into believing that the buyer will not discover these material facts.

All material facts need to be disclosed.

DO REAL ESTATE AGENTS NEED TO INVESTIGATE MATERIAL FACTS?

Sometimes real estate agents need to investigate material facts or state clearly that they have not investigated material facts and that the buyers are encouraged to investigate for themselves. For example, sellers tell their agent that the master bedroom was built without a permit, but everything else in the structure or on the property had a permit. How would the real estate agent relay this information to the buyers?

> *Wrong way:* "The sellers indicate that the only room without a permit is the master bedroom." As written, that is an affirmative representation of a material fact. The real estate agent has made no effort to support the statement by attaching the permit history of the property or by advising the buyers to check the permit history or to admitting that he has not verified the sellers' representation.

> *Right way:* "The sellers indicate that the only room without a permit is the master bedroom; however, I have not verified whether this information is correct, and I encourage the buyers to check the permit history of the property to verify what is, and what is not, constructed with permits." Or, "The sellers indicate that the only room without a permit is the master bedroom. The permit history of the property is attached to this disclosure document and verifies the sellers' representation." In the second "right way" example, the real estate agent did undertake an "investigation" of a material fact in an appropriate manner.

Real estate agents do need to investigate material facts and/or assist the buyers or sellers in their investigation of material facts.

SHOULD THE BUYERS OR SELLERS INVESTIGATE MATERIAL FACTS?

Both the buyers and sellers should investigate material facts. In the example above, the buyers could also have obtained the building permits.

ARE SELLERS, BUYERS, AND REAL ESTATE AGENTS LIABLE WHEN THEY ARE UNAWARE OF A MATERIAL FACT?

Sellers, buyers, and real estate agents can be found liable without knowledge of a substantial material fact. When all are ignorant but the defect exists, the buyers may have the remedy of rescission of the sale agreement, and the sellers have the same remedy against the agents for the commissions paid.

In a lawsuit the seller, buyer, and agents claimed to have no knowledge that the house was on unstable ground and suffering progressive foundation damage and land movement. After discovering this serious defect, the buyer sued all involved including the bank that was the seller of the foreclosed property. A photo in the listing agent's file showed horizontal cracks along the house foundation, which were inadvertently covered by a fix-up crew before the house was listed for sale. The buyer succeeded in having the transaction rescinded.

10

CHAPTER

Property Stigmas

Stigmas are a thorny issue because they are often unobservable, or unapparent, to the buyer, and therefore, without proper disclosure may be overlooked in the buyer's investigation of the property's condition. The issue of property stigmas is a frequent claim in lawsuits. Real estate agents sometimes are unclear in their understanding of property stigmas. Buyers and sellers may not have even considered the issue at all, or they may have no idea what property stigmas are.

A *stigmatized property* is one with a history that raises intangible fears or perceived future risk on the part of prospective buyers, which can decrease the property's value and its ability to be sold.

WHAT ARE THE TWO TYPES OF STIGMAS?

There are two types of property stigmas. A property where a murder took place or a house that is said to be haunted is called a *psychological stigma*. There are many people in the population who would not buy a property where someone died, committed suicide, or was murdered. There are also people who will not buy a house that is considered haunted. Most states have specific requirements for disclosing this kind of information. The issue of an AIDS-related death or prior occupant with AIDS may be handled differently, and real estate agents should learn the specific requirements within their state for AIDS-related disclosures. Whether a property is haunted is a matter of opinion, depending on whether one believes in ghosts or not. Some properties are notorious as haunted in a neighborhood. If this is a widely accepted condition and the seller believes the property is haunted as well, the real estate agent for the seller should list this as a disclosure. Proving that a property is haunted is unlikely to be substantiated in court, and the unhappy buyer who believes he has unknowingly purchased a haunted house may find himself stuck with the property.

Some properties may have a psychological history a buyer may regard as a stigma, even if the original structure is no longer there. For example, the house where the Sharon Tate/Manson murders took place many years ago has been torn down and rebuilt. Notorious houses may be avoided by some buyers and sought by others. It is probably better to disclose the information to buyers, as the neighbors will quickly inform them of the property's notorious past.

A stigma can also arise from a physical condition. For example, a house with a history of foundation problems may suffer a loss of value, even if there have been repairs, because of a fear that the problems will recur. If a neighbor located above and behind a property had slippage of land onto the property below and caused significant property damage to that property, even if the cause of the slippage has been corrected, the prospective buyers may have a justifiable concern that the problem could recur.

Stigmas can spread to a group of houses or even an entire city. This "guilt by association" might affect every house in a subdivision known to have had foundation problems.

WHAT CRITERIA CAN BE USED FOR CLASSIFYING STIGMAS?

There are some specific criteria for evaluating whether a situation is a potential stigma:

1. A property or its immediate surroundings have suffered major physical damage or have a strong negative psychological connotation, such as the area in Blue Bird Canyon, in Laguna, California, where many houses slipped down the hillside after heavy winter rains in 2005. The neighboring homes that did not slide may still have their value affected.

2. Properties suffering similar problems have sold at discounted prices, compared with similar nonstigmatized properties, or have not sold at all.
3. Real estate agents, lenders, and insurance companies may be wary of this property and discount its value or avoid it.
4. A problem is unlikely to be curable or is likely to recur.

ARE STIGMAS ALWAYS PERMANENT?

Stigmas can be temporary in certain circumstances. For instance, after the 1994 Los Angeles earthquake, home sales slowed and values declined in areas near the earthquake, even in cases where there was no physical damage to a home. Certain areas have become known for weak soil conditions that could lead to severe damage in an earthquake. Many years later, the memory of the earthquake has subsided, and property values have rebounded, even though Los Angeles is just as likely to suffer an earthquake today as it was in 1994. Real estate agents in those areas that suffered damage caused by weak soil conditions should still disclose that situation to the unknowing prospective buyers and recommend that a soils engineer evaluate their purchase.

ARE STIGMAS ALWAYS ON-SITE?

Just as stigmas can be psychological or physical, temporary or permanent, they can also be on-site or off-site. What if sellers said that they absolutely knew for sure that a registered sex offender moved in next door? Real estate agents are told to refer buyers to the Megan's law Web site to check for the presence of registered sex offenders in their area. However, not all sex offenders are registered. If sellers believe they know for sure the next-door neighbor is a registered sex offender, the listing agent should attempt to verify this on the Megan's law Web site and carefully disclose the information to prospective buyers. For example:

> The sellers have disclosed that they believe the neighbor, located to the south of their residence, at 244 Elm Street, is a registered sex offender. I have verified this fact on the Megan's law Web site (or I have not verified this fact on the Megan's law Web site and recommend that the buyers verify this fact).

If the neighbor is not listed on the Megan's law Web site, the real estate agent should say:

> The sellers have disclosed that they believe the neighbor, located to the south of their residence, at 244 Elm Street, is a prior sex offender. I have checked the Megan's law Web site, and the neighbor's name is not listed (or I have not checked the Megan's law Web site and strongly recommend that the buyers check this information).

Would the presence of a registered sex offender next door to the sellers' property be considered a stigma? Yes! Although it is not known if the person would commit this crime again, many buyers would not buy the sellers' property or would buy it only at a steep discount. What if the registered sex offender moves out? This type of stigma would leave with him, making this a "temporary" stigma. Would the sellers' property now be easier to sell and probably at a better price? Definitely!

Stigmas can be psychological and off-site.

WHAT ARE SOME OTHER EXAMPLES OF POSSIBLE STIGMAS?

Here are other types of off-site potential stigmas real estate agents, buyers, and sellers should be aware of and should include in their disclosures:

- The train goes through the middle of town at 3 a.m. and 5 a.m., and the engineer hits his horn several times on each trip, waking up everyone nearby. The buyer looking at a property during daylight or early evening hours might be totally unaware of this situation.
- The property is located in a development that was built next to a former waste dump, which is now covered over and used as a park. The builder-developer would want to be sure to make this disclosure, as should every subsequent seller and listing agent.
- The property is in the flight path of the airport, and flights in and out of the airport continue until 3 a.m. The prospective buyer may be unaware of the noise level during the noise of daylight hours, but would become very aware of this situation at night.
- During fall and winter months, the fog horns sound along the coast, particularly in the early morning and late at night.
- The nearby freeway is scheduled for a major expansion. This might suggest increased noise levels and traffic.

These are all conditions that would reasonably be of concern to buyers that their property inspectors might not be aware of or that would not be included in their reports.

They are the type of necessary disclosures off-site that, overlooked, can lead to a lawsuit.

SHOULD ALL STIGMAS BE DISCLOSED?

If a condition, defect, or situation would impact the price the buyers are willing to pay or the decision to buy, it is a material fact, and it must be disclosed. Real estate agents need to know their state laws regarding psychological stigmas, and if they are uncertain about a disclosure, they should contact their state association of Realtors or a real estate attorney. Agents should separate fact from fiction regarding psychological stigmas. If a stigma is based on rumor and can't be verified, as might be the case with a haunted house, the agent may have no duty to disclose the information. If the buyer asks about a condition, the sellers and their agent should be truthful and accurate in their answer.

If the listing agent concludes that the potential stigma is a material fact, he should discuss it with the sellers. If the sellers refuse to disclose the stigma, they are putting themselves in jeopardy of a lawsuit and are putting their agent in jeopardy as well.

The sellers and the sellers' real estate agent should disclose only facts and avoid making any evaluations, conclusions, or predictions. If the sellers say that the neighbor above them has repaired the cause of the previous landslide and it is unlikely to occur again, they should disclose what happened in writing. They should include all documentation, reports, and permits available.

Documents or other information that suggest a past or potential stigma should be carefully examined to determine whether full disclosure or further investigation is necessary. For example, title company documents might reveal that the property was taken back by the developer because of a history of problems. Real estate agents should know the area where they work and be aware of any off-site stigmas they would be expected to disclose.

11

CHAPTER

Standard of Care

The term *standard of care* is frequently referenced in real estate transactions, but do you really know what it means? Every occupation has a standard of care that's determined by law or that has evolved by custom. Restaurant servers, for example, are legally required to wash their hands after visiting the restroom. As a restaurant customer you also expect hot food to be served hot, cold food to be served cold, and delivery of your meal in a reasonable period of time. You've come to expect this standard of care, even though it may not be required by law.

Real estate agents have a standard of care, as do buyers and sellers. This standard may vary somewhat from state to state, but the sources of the standard of care for real estate agents, buyers, and sellers are generally the same. General property inspectors also have a standard of care, as do builders and developers, mortgage lenders, appraisers, and title companies.

In every lawsuit against a real estate agent or the broker, the plaintiff will claim that the conduct of the real estate agent and the broker fell below the standard of care, causing harm to the plaintiff and financial damages.

WHAT ARE THE SOURCES OF STANDARD OF CARE?

The sources of standard of care for real estate agents, general property inspectors, and builders are the following.

Congress

Real estate agents are required to comply with federal laws applicable to their profession. Such laws include the federal Fair Housing Act and the Residential Lead-Based Paint Hazard Reduction Act. Megan's law is a federal law regarding the development of databases available to the public indicating the location of registered sex offenders. Megan's law is carried out by each state formulating its own procedures. The Real Estate Settlement and Procedures Act of 1974 (RESPA) consists of regulations that also affect the conduct of real estate agents when they are interacting with real estate service providers, such as property inspectors, title companies, and mortgage lenders. Real estate agents have specific forms and disclosures for each transaction, required for compliance with these federal statutes.

Congress has also passed laws affecting the conduct of builders and developers. General property inspectors are not as yet covered under federal regulations, but they may be at some time in the future.

States

State legislatures may add to real estate agents' standard of care. For example, state or local fair housing laws may protect additional classes of individuals.

Many states also define a general standard of care required of real estate agents. Typically, this statement of duty outlines the conduct expected of *a reasonably prudent agent based on the requirements and training necessary to obtain and maintain a real estate license.* Generally, the definition is intentionally vague to allow for the continual evolution of federal and state legislation and case law. Not all states define expectations of conduct in considerable detail. The civil codes or business and professional codes may further define the standard of care as it is applicable to all businesses.

Specific statutes may apply to general property inspectors regarding licensing, registration, or certification and their degree of liability, insurance, and contract requirements. Builders and developers have similar laws specific to their conduct, as do title companies, appraisers, and lenders.

Departments of Real Estate

Real estate agents are usually regulated by a state department of real estate whose interpretations of conduct under the law also create a standard of care. State departments of real estate may publish reference books and quarterly bulletins explaining real estate law. They may also produce publications for consumers and administer license exams and license renewal procedures for real estate agents. Classes taught for real estate license renewal credits for real estate agents are also usually monitored and approved by the department of real estate. They also handle public and real estate association complaints against real estate licensees, establishing complaint procedures and punishment for those found in violation of real estate laws.

Contractors' State License Boards

Builders in all states must have some type of licensing from a state board to function legally as a contractor. These boards require testing and license renewal procedures. They also publish informative guides for licensee conduct and handle complaints by the public against licensees.

Contracts

Contracts are part of the standard of care in real estate transactions. The buyers and sellers sign a contract between them outlining their agreed-to terms and conditions, as well as their truthful representations of information provided. An agent has a contract with sellers when listing their property, or with buyers when agreeing to represent them in a purchase. In each case, the real estate agents and the people they represent agree to perform certain acts in good faith. The general property inspector has the buyers sign a contract for his employment, outlining what he will and will not include in his inspection. Builders and developers have lengthy contracts specifying what they will build in detail and when it will be completed.

Individual Expectations

The standard of care in real estate transactions can also be affected by the experience and skill of the professional and the client or customer. A real estate broker would reasonably be expected to have more knowledge than a real estate salesperson, as a broker's license normally requires greater experience, more course studies, and a longer, more comprehensive exam for licensing. The buyer who has bought and sold many properties may be regarded as more knowledgeable than the first-time buyer.

The Code of Ethics

The National Association of Realtors conduct manual also defines standard of care. Courts often look to the code of ethics of NAR to determine the industry standard, regardless of whether or not a real estate agent is a member of NAR. If a real estate agent fails to adhere to the NAR code of ethics and causes significant harm to her client or customer, she may be sued by the damaged party. To understand the standard of care a real estate agent must meet to prevail in a lawsuit, real estate agents need to be familiar with the current version of the code. The code of ethics is revised regularly to address new issues affecting the real estate industry. The January issue of *REALTOR Magazine,* published by NAR, provides the latest update of the code of ethics. It is strongly recommended that real estate agents read the code in January and tear out the copy provided for continuing reference.[1] The following are some examples of conduct by a real estate agent that might be alleged to have violated the code of ethics.

Article 1 of the code of ethics states:

> When representing a buyer, seller, landlord, tenant, or other client as an agent, REALTORS pledge themselves to protect and promote the interests of their client. This obligation . . . is primary, but it does not relieve REALTORS of their obligation to treat all parties honestly . . .

The following is behavior to avoid:

- A buyer's representative refers a client to a general property inspector without qualifying the inspector's credentials.
- A termite inspection finds extensive dry rot extending into structural beams. The seller's real estate agent gets a repair quote of $250, but does not question the oddly low estimate.

---

[1] The National Association of Realtors code of ethics referenced in this chapter is January 2006.

Article 2 of the code of ethics states:

REALTORS shall avoid exaggeration, misrepresentation, or concealment of pertinent facts relating to the property or transaction . . .

The following is behavior to avoid:

- The listing agent claims a foundation problem was fixed but provides no supporting documentation, such as permits or a current engineer's report.
- The listing agent knows about a prior unfavorable termite inspection and doesn't provide the information to the buyer.

Article 3 of the code of ethics states:

In selling property they own or in which they have an interest, REALTORS shall reveal their ownership or interest in writing to the purchaser or the purchaser's representative.

The following is behavior to avoid:

- Listing agents don't tell the buyers in writing that they have an ownership interest in the property before the buyers are bound by the contract.

Article 4 of the code of ethics states:

REALTORS, for the protection of all parties, shall ensure whenever possible that agreements shall be in writing, and shall be in clear and understandable language expressing the specific terms, conditions, obligations, and commitments of the parties . . .

The following is behavior to avoid:

- The real estate agents fail to get contract changes, such as an extension of the inspection period, in writing and signed by the buyer and the seller, resulting in the expiration of the buyer's inspection period and the buyer later finding defects further inspections might have revealed.

Article 11 of the code of ethics states:

The services which REALTORS provide to their clients and customers shall conform to the standards of practice and competence which are reasonably expected in the specific real estate disciplines in which they engage . . .

The following is behavior to avoid:

- The general property inspector recommends an inspection by a structural engineer, but the buyer's agent makes no written recommendation in regard to a structural engineer's inspection, and tells the buyer a structural engineer's inspection is unnecessary.

A real estate agent's best defense against lawsuits based on code requirements is to know and adhere to the code's tenets. To become ethics experts, real estate agents should:

- Read the code often.
- Attend an ethics class at the local association of Realtors.
- Participate in the state association of Realtors grievance or professional standards committees.
- Read articles in the local association of Realtors publications and *REALTOR Magazine* that interpret the code of ethics and its changes.

Beginning in 2001, Realtors are required to complete two and a half hours of ethics training every four years.

General property inspectors who belong to a reputable professional association for property inspectors will also have their code of ethics and standards of practice to guide their conduct. As with the National Association of Realtors, these associations will periodically update their code and standards of practice. Builders and developers may be held to the code of ethics of the National Association of Home Builders or other associations in the building industry.

State Associations of Realtors

State associations' revisions of purchase contracts and disclosure forms to conform to new laws or events affecting the local area will also evolve professional standards. State associations may also recommend the use of forms or procedures not required by law, such as seller disclosure statements, recognizing that they are a valuable protection for buyers, sellers, and real estate agents. Standardized contract forms developed by the state associations of Realtors are written for the protection of buyers and sellers.

Local Associations of Realtors

Local associations deal with issues of concern at the city and county level. They may provide guidance to their local real estate members concerning these issues and contract addenda or disclosures. For example, these disclosures may concern the property being in the flight path of the local airport or near a planned rapid transit expansion.

Geography

Some West Coast states mandate disclosures regarding seismic zones, while Gulf Coast states may require disclosures of hurricane areas, flood prone areas, or sink hole activity. Some areas are prone to problems with radon gas, while other areas must deal with local regulations regarding snow clearance. It is wise for real estate agents, buyers, and sellers to familiarize themselves with their local geographic issues.

CAN REAL ESTATE AGENTS EXPAND THEIR STANDARD OF CARE?

Real estate agents who advertise that they are the "experts" in their area will be held to what an expert in that area might be expected to know. Real estate agents who claim a certain expertise on the basis of professional designations may also have expanded their standard of care. Real estate agents should watch carefully what they claim or promise to do, because they may be held to those claims and promises in court.

CAN GENERAL PROPERTY INSPECTORS, BUILDERS, AND DEVELOPERS EXPAND THEIR STANDARD OF CARE?

General property inspectors, builders, and developers can also expand their standard of care by making claims regarding their experience and background that give them greater expertise than the standard in their field. Builders who claim they are the expert in a particular area or that their homes exceed all required standards are expanding their standard of

**Real estate agents need to be knowledgeable
about the type of property they represent.**

care and may be expected to prove their claims in court. General property
inspectors who claim that their inspections exceed the standards of practice of one or more of the professional inspection associations and names
these associations may find themselves defending that claim in court.

BUYERS AND SELLERS HAVE A STANDARD OF CARE

Buyers are expected to take the advice of their real estate agent, their inspector, the sellers, and the listing agent regarding a general property inspection
and additional inspections or investigations. Buyers are expected to apply
for their loan in a timely fashion. They should attend the property inspection
or inspections and the walk-through inspection. They are also expected to fill
out and return escrow, title, and other documents in a timely fashion.

Sellers are expected to disclose property defects, neighborhood conditions, and critical routine maintenance items truthfully and completely.
They are expected to make their property available for the buyers' inspections. They should follow through and complete the agreed-to repairs by
appropriately licensed repair people. As for buyers, sellers must fill out
and return escrow, title, and other transaction documents in a timely fashion. It is certainly expected by buyers that sellers leave the property clean
and with all personal property removed that is not included in the sale.

The terms of the contract agreed to by the buyers and sellers create contractual duties and responsibilities. The standard of care of buyers or sellers, though not the same as that of a licensed professional, will still require honesty and good faith in adhering to the terms of the agreement.

A fool and his money are soon parted.

—James Howell

WHY IS STANDARD OF CARE IMPORTANT?

Real estate agents, general property inspectors, builders and developers, buyers and sellers whose conduct falls below their standard of care leave themselves vulnerable to a lawsuit. Parties found in court or an arbitration to have conducted themselves in a manner that falls below their standard of care will likely lose the case.

12 CHAPTER

Fiduciary Duty and Agency Relationships

In almost all lawsuits against real estate agents and their brokerages, the agents and brokers are accused by the plaintiffs of having "violated their fiduciary duty." It is very important for all real estate agents and their brokers to understand their fiduciary duty. It is also important for buyers and sellers of real estate to understand the fiduciary duty they can expect from their real estate agents.

Real estate agents have a fiduciary duty to their "clients," who are also referred to as their "principals." They have the duty of "fair and honest dealing" and of "reasonable care and diligence" to the other party in the transaction, buyer or seller, represented by another real estate agent, and sometimes referred to as their customer. General property inspectors do not have a fiduciary duty to either the buyer or the seller in the real estate transaction. Builders or developers are often the sellers in the transaction and have a standard of care applicable to sellers.

Duties Owed by an Agent to His Principal

A real estate broker who becomes an agent of a seller or buyer, either intentionally through the execution of a written agreement, or unintentionally by a course of conduct, will be deemed to be a *fiduciary*. Fiduciary duties are the highest duties known to the law. Classic examples of fiduciaries are trustees, executors, and guardians. As a fiduciary, a real

133

estate broker will be held under the law to owe certain specific duties to his principal, *in addition* to any duties or obligations set forth in a listing agreement or other contract of employment. These specific fiduciary duties include:

- Loyalty
- Obedience
- Disclosure
- Confidentiality
- Reasonable care and diligence
- Accounting

1. *Loyalty*—This duty obligates a real estate broker to act at *all times solely* in the best interests of his principal to the exclusion of all other interests, *including* the broker's own self interest.

2. *Obedience*—An agent is obligated to obey promptly and efficiently all *lawful* instructions of his principal.

3. *Disclosure*—An agent is obligated to disclose to his principal all relevant and material information that the agent knows and that pertains to the scope of the agency. This duty specifically obligates a real estate broker representing a seller to reveal to the seller:

- All offers to purchase the seller's property
- The identity of all potential purchasers
- Any facts affecting the value of the property
- Information concerning the ability or willingness of the buyer to complete the sale or to offer a higher price
- The broker's relationship to, or interest in, a prospective buyer
- A buyer's intention to subdivide or resell the property for a profit
- Any other information that might affect the seller's ability to obtain the highest price and best terms in the sale of his property

Likewise, a real estate broker representing a buyer is obligated to reveal to the buyer:

- The willingness of the seller to accept a lower price
- Any facts relating to the urgency of the seller's need to dispose of the property
- The broker's relationship to, or interest in, the seller or the property for sale
- Any facts affecting the value of the property

- The length of time the property has been on the market and any other offers or counteroffers that have been made relating to the property
- Any other information that would affect the buyer's ability to obtain the property at the lowest price and on the most favorable terms

CAVEAT: An agent's duty of disclosure to his principal must not be confused with a real estate broker's duty to disclose to non-principals any known material facts concerning the value of the property. The duty to disclose known material facts is based upon a real estate broker's duty to treat all persons honestly and fairly. This duty of honesty and fairness does not depend on the existence of an agency relationship.

4. *Confidentiality*—An agent is obligated to safeguard his principal's confidence and secrets. A real estate broker, therefore, must keep confidential any information that might weaken his principal's bargaining position if it were revealed. This duty of confidentiality precludes a broker representing a seller from disclosing to a buyer that the seller can or must sell his property below the list price. Conversely, a broker representing a buyer is prohibited from disclosing to a seller that the buyer can or will pay more for a property than has been offered.

CAVEAT: This duty of confidentiality plainly does *not* include any obligation on a broker representing a seller to withhold from a buyer known material facts concerning the condition of the seller's property; to do so would constitute misrepresentation and would impose liability on both the broker and the seller.

5. *Reasonable care and diligence*—An agent is obligated to use reasonable care and diligence in pursuing the principal's affairs. The standard of care expected of a real estate broker representing a seller or buyer is that of a competent real estate professional . . . This duty includes an obligation to affirmatively discover facts relating to his principal's affairs that a reasonable and prudent real estate broker would be expected to investigate. Simply put, this is the same duty any professional, such as a doctor or lawyer, owes to his patient or client.

6. *Accounting*—An agent is obligated to account for all money or property belonging to his principal that is entrusted to him . . . [1]

---

[1] "Who Is My Client? A Realtor's Guide to Compliance with the Law of Agency," National Association of Realtors, Legal Series, copyrighted information, reprinted with permission, 1986, pp. 4–7.

In real estate lawsuits, the fiduciary duties of "disclosure" and "reasonable care and diligence" are those most often cited as having been violated by the defendant broker and agent. They are subject to interpretation by the courts based on what is deemed "reasonable and prudent" conduct by real estate agents in the area, laws enacted by the state legislature, and case law evolving from court cases upheld or overturned at the appellate level. Fiduciary duty also includes the duty to verify information known, observed, or believed by an agent to be unreliable.

WHY IS FIDUCIARY DUTY IMPORTANT IN REAL ESTATE LAWSUITS?

If the real estate broker and agent are found to have violated their fiduciary duty to their principal, they will in most all circumstances lose the case.

WHEN IS FIDUCIARY DUTY REQUIRED OF A REAL ESTATE BROKER AND AGENT?

Fiduciary duty is always required of a broker and agent to their principal; it cannot be waived by contract. In one recent case, an agent wrote into his contract that he was a dual agent, but had no fiduciary duty to either buyer or seller and was merely introducing the parties. An agency relationship by its existence creates a fiduciary duty.

ARE THERE EXCEPTIONS TO AN AGENCY RELATIONSHIP ALWAYS REQUIRING ALL THE FIDUCIARY DUTIES?

Some states, such as Florida, have adopted their own form of agency relationship. In Florida an agent in a full fiduciary relationship with a buyer or seller cannot also be a dual agent, representing both buyer and seller. This situation is acceptable, however, in California. Florida law allows a form of representation called a "transaction broker" in which an agent has some, but not all of the fiduciary duties. In this form of representation an agent in Florida is allowed to be a dual agent. Buyers and sellers under this form of "transaction broker" representation are not responsible for any false statements made by their agents, as would be the case in a full fiduciary relationship. "Limited service" brokerages further cloud the issue of agency representation and fiduciary duty, because this form of representation offers a limited number of fee-for-service options. Buyers and sellers should carefully review the available forms of real estate agent representation allowed in their state and select the form of representation that will meet their needs and protect their interests.

WHO IS THE BUYERS' OR SELLERS' AGENT?

Buyers who have visited properties with a real estate agent and then asked that agent to write an offer for them on that property might reasonably assume that the agent is representing them as a "buyers' agent." However, that agent may in fact be a subagent of the sellers. This confusing situation was resolved by the creation of "agency relationship" forms. These forms should be signed by buyers when they have decided which real estate agent they want to work with. It should certainly be signed before preparation of an offer to buy. The agency relationship form will indicate if the agent is representing buyers or sellers, or both, which is called a "dual agency." Some buyer representation agreements also specify that the commission to the agent is to be paid by the buyers and not the sellers. In most cases, the form will indicate that the buyers' agent is sharing the commission the sellers have agreed to pay their listing agent, as a "cooperating agent." Buyers and sellers should carefully read the agency relationship form so that they are totally clear on who is representing whom and who is paying the commission.

A buyers' agent should have the buyers sign a form clarifying the scope of the property search for the buyers. For example: the buyers' agent will search all MLS listings, excluding FSBOs (for sale by owner) for Beverly Hills, Westwood, and Brentwood.

The search criteria can of course be altered at any time. The buyers can then not later claim that the agent failed to show them a better and less expensive FSBO (for sale by owner) in the same area, and therefore failed in his fiduciary duty of utmost care.

The sellers' agent should have the sellers sign an agency relationship form before a listing agreement is written and signed. The listing agreement should clearly indicate how the agent will market the property, including:

- MLS
- Internet
- Advertising (nature and frequency)

- Broker caravans
- Public open houses
- Lockbox entry or not
- Yard sign or not
- Dates of listing (start and end)
- Commission arrangements
- List price

Disputes can sometimes arise when the listing agent is not sufficiently detailed and the agent decides to "pocket the listing" and not expose it to the market. An agent may do this hoping to find his own buyer and not have to share his commission with another cooperating agent. Sellers may feel that this delay results in insufficient marketing of their property. Pocket listings are seldom in the sellers' best interest. The listing agent should place the property promptly in the MLS for maximum exposure according to MLS rules in the area, unless directed otherwise by the sellers.

Agency relationships can sometimes be implied by how an agent acts. The buyers' agent who "assists" a FSBO seller by performing duties or giving advice normally provided by a listing agent may create an unintended dual agency relationship.

WHY ARE FIDUCIARY DUTY AND DUAL AGENCY IN CONFLICT?

In some states, dual agency is not permitted in real estate transactions.

> *Dual agency* is the representation of both the buyer and seller in a real estate transaction by the same brokerage, which can mean one real estate agent or two real estate agents affiliated with the same brokerage firm.

It is not a good idea for a real estate agent to represent the buyer in the sale of his own property, nor is it wise for an agent to buy his own listing. In a dual agency situation, the real estate agent owes a fiduciary duty to both the buyer and the seller. The buyer wants the lowest price, and the seller wants the highest price, and one agent representing both is attempting to make each satisfied with his or her agency representation. It is a tightrope walk at best and difficult for real estate agents to handle well. The possibility that either the buyer or the seller will later believe that the agent favored the other party in the transaction is understandable, and it is sometimes the case. Many lawsuits against real estate agents involve dual agency.

Dual agency should be carefully considered by any buyers. Buyers would be hiring an agent already hired by the sellers. In most cases, the buyers will be better represented by having their own separate representation. Although the sellers' agent may attempt to persuade the buyers that they will give them a discounted sale price based on a typically reduced commission to a dual agent, this should not be the basis of the buyers' decision to use a dual agent. The buyers' own agent might have negotiated just as good a deal on the property, or maybe a better one. In a hot sellers' market, some buyers believe that letting the sellers' agent represent them in a dual agency may give them a better chance of "getting the property." Unfortunately, this may be true in some cases, but it should not be because it is the fiduciary duty of the sellers' agent to get the sellers the highest price, regardless of who represents the buyers.

WHY IS DISCLOSURE IMPORTANT IN AVOIDING REAL ESTATE LAWSUITS?

Because disclosure is a fiduciary duty, it is regarded with great significance in all real estate lawsuits. How much disclosure is enough? The answer is everything a real estate agent knows about the property that a reasonable and prudent buyer would want to know. If the agent is thinking about the item to disclose and debating whether it should be disclosed, the item should be disclosed. The same advice applies to sellers when they are disclosing material facts to buyers. They should disclose fully all facts affecting the value of the property.

CAN THERE BE A CONFLICT BETWEEN DISCLOSURE AND CONFIDENTIALITY?

If a real estate agent is taking a listing and the sellers say, "We added the master bedroom without a permit, but don't tell anyone," the real estate agent is obligated to tell the sellers that a material fact has been disclosed, which must be disclosed to the buyers. If this is not disclosed, the sellers and the agent would be placed in a position of liability. This is a confidence that cannot be kept, if the agent is to take the listing.

CAN THE FAILURE OF "FAIR AND HONEST DEALING" TO THE PARTY NOT IN A FIDUCIARY RELATIONSHIP RESULT IN A SUCCESSFUL LAWSUIT AGAINST A REAL ESTATE AGENT?

A real estate agent can be successfully sued for violating "fair and honest dealing" and lack of "reasonable care and diligence" to the party represented by another real estate agent. A few years ago I consulted on a case in which the buyer sued the seller and the seller's agent, but not his own agent, and won in court.

2 PART

UNDERSTANDING THE PROBLEM AREAS IN TRANSACTIONS

13

C H A P T E R

Contract Modifications and Additions and Mixing Negotiation with Disclosure

CAN REAL ESTATE AGENTS WRITE CONTRACT MODIFICATIONS?

Real estate agents cannot write contracts unless they are also attorneys. Yet real estate agents are often in the position of trying to write contracts reflecting the wishes of the parties involved. Most contract forms and addenda are produced by attorneys working with "form" committees of the state associations of Realtors. Real estate companies often have their own contract and addendum forms prepared by attorneys hired to consult with or work for their companies. Realtor association chapters consult with attorneys who prepare specific addenda applicable to their area, which agents are advised to attach to and make part of their contracts between buyer and seller. In states where attorneys are routinely involved in the escrow function, they may compose documents applicable to the transaction or modify clauses in the standard contract. Some real estate errors and omissions insurers have attorneys compose forms and addenda for real estate agents they insure to use with other contract forms.

Generally, state departments of real estate specify to what degree real estate agents can fill in or modify standard contracts. In most cases, agents are limited to "filling in the blanks," "checking boxes," or adding brief comments, such as, "The escrow will be ABC Company" or "The sale price will be $400,000." Lawsuits can result, however, when real estate agents include a sentence or more of descriptive content in the contract. They may be accused later of engaging in the practice of law without a license. More often, they find themselves in a legal tangle because what they have said was not well worded, was misunderstood, or was wrong.

All the proposed contract verbiage recommended in this book has been reviewed by attorneys. In one case, a walk-through inspection with a written repair list got an agent into trouble. The dual agent wrote the following: "bedroom 1: walls by window to be fixed." Does this mean that there is a hole in a wall of bedroom 1? It is unclear what is meant. She further added: "Front house windows: screens need to be fixed." Does this mean that the screens are missing, or are they in need of being reattached? How many screens are in question?

This property involved several nonpermitted structures. The seller was willing to make any required corrections by the building department, but did not know how to obtain permits and inspections. The listing agent found a buyer and then a buyer for the buyer's home. With three transactions linked together, the dual agent made the following, poorly worded representation at the end of the walk-through inspection checklist of repairs: "Seller guarantees buyer that all work will be completed and all final permits will be given to buyer by close of escrow or thereafter."

The "or thereafter" was her downfall! The buyer moved in, and the seller had barely initiated the inspection and repair process. The lawsuit followed shortly "thereafter." The agent in this transaction needed to learn how to express herself more clearly and to refrain from writing contract language. Agents should not "guess" at the right language. She should have understood the process of inspection, permits, and repair necessary on this property, and she should have advised the seller to complete this process prior to listing the property. The seller also sued the agent for getting him into this difficulty. The agent should have sought help in writing what she was committing the seller to in this agreement. Most real estate offices have an attorney with whom agents can consult. Some E&O insurers will have an attorney available to their insured clients to ask questions or so the attorney can provide assistance in writing some condition into the contract. Some state associations of Realtors provide free legal hotline

"I've made a few additions to the contract."

services for agents to help them avoid this type of problem. Some agents or real estate companies may also subscribe to "Pre-Paid Legal Services" to assist when legal help is needed.

Real estate agents should note in their file whom they talked to when seeking legal advice, the date and time they spoke, the question asked, and what was advised. Should there be a question at a later time, the agent could refer back to these notations.

WHY IS GOOD HANDWRITING ESSENTIAL?

Writing clearly and legibly can keep real estate agents out of a lawsuit, or extricate one from a lawsuit. In many of the cases on which I have consulted, I have been unable to read the agents' handwriting in the terms of the contract, the counteroffer, or the disclosure statement. It is extremely important to develop a clear and readable handwriting or to print if necessary.

THE IMPORTANCE OF CONTRACT CONTINGENCIES

Contract contingencies are usually expressed as, "This contract is contingent upon . . ." or "This contract is subject to . . ." with a remedy for "disapproval" or inability to achieve the contingency. Contract contingencies are important to the buyer and seller. They should be properly worded to be effective. The most common contingencies are loan, inspection, and appraisal. Contingencies usually have a time limit attached to them. The time limit may be achieving the contingency by the close of the transaction, such as a loan contingency; as soon as available, such as an appraisal; or a specific time, such as for the completion of inspections. Some examples of properly worded contingencies are:

- *Loan:* "This contract is contingent upon the buyer obtaining a mortgage loan in the amount of $160,000 at a fixed rate of no more than 6½%, 30-year term, and 1 point by the close of escrow (or by a certain date)." Be specific, just writing "maximum mortgage possible and best terms" is not adequate.

- *Inspection:* "This contract is subject to the buyer's inspection and approval of inspection findings. And should this contingency fail, the contract is void and all deposited funds will be returned to the buyer. All of the buyer's inspections must be completed by May 1, 2007, and the buyer's reply to the seller to accept, reject, or request repairs or credits must be made by May 5, 2007."

- *Appraisal:* "This contract is subject to an appraisal at or above the purchase price. The buyer has 10 days from the date of contract signing to receive the appraisal and notify the seller of acceptance or rejection of this contingency." An appraisal is a very important contingency. This is perhaps the buyer's only chance to learn the actual square footage of the property, as most appraisals require the appraiser to measure the property. The garage is not counted in the square footage. The buyer usually pays for the appraisal but sometimes does not receive a copy of it. The buyer and the buyer's agent should ask the lender for a copy of the appraisal and review it. If a property is appraised for less than the offer price, the buyer may not only be overpaying, but may not be able to finance the amount desired. A loan of 80 percent of $200,000 is $160,000, but if the property is appraised at $180,000, 80 percent of that is $144,000. On a $200,000 sale, the buyer would have to increase the down payment by $16,000.

Other contingencies that might protect the buyer and seller are:

"This contract is subject to the review and approval of the buyer's and seller's attorney." Don't hesitate to refer the buyer and seller to their attorneys.

"This contract is contingent upon mutual cancellation of the first contract of sale and escrow." Be sure that this is stated clearly before entering into a second contract or backup offer.

"This contract is contingent upon the buyer closing on the home of his or her choice within 90 days." Don't make the mistake of saying "finding" a home of his or her choice. The buyer may find it but not get it.

"This contract is contingent upon the buyer receiving delivery and acceptance of all HOA documents requested by the buyer." There is a difference between receiving something and accepting it.

Contingency clauses are also referred to as "out clauses" because they allow the buyer an "out" from the transaction and return of the deposit. Buyers, sellers, and real estate agents must keep a close watch on the clock regarding contingencies. Failure to adhere to the time schedules established for contingencies can result in a loss of that contingency. Buyers and sellers need to be reminded of the time requirements of the transaction and prodded as needed to comply. Escrow officers will sometimes fill this role. Real estate agents should also remind the client of time deadlines and assist the client in meeting them. Agents can be drawn into lawsuits later when the buyer or seller loses a contingency right critical to the transaction or to getting out of the transaction and feels that he or she was not properly advised by the agent.

A verbal contract isn't worth the paper it's written on.

—Samuel Goldwyn

FIXTURES VERSUS PERSONAL PROPERTY

Sometimes the issue of what is taken by the seller and what is left behind can be a source of litigation. Fixtures are to be left by the seller unless otherwise agreed to by the buyer and seller. Personal property can be taken by the seller unless it is agreed between the parties to leave it behind. The person who sold me my home took the smoke detectors with him when he left. Clearly smoke detectors, which are affixed to the property, are fixtures and should have been left. However, he decided to leave many boxes of trash behind, which is personal property and should have been removed. I was able to resolve the problem when I discovered the seller had left eight pairs of shoes behind as well. He returned the smoke detectors, removed the trash, and I gave him back his shoes. Ah, if all disputes could be handled so easily.

Personal property consists of anything not permanently attached to the land or structure, such as a free-standing clothes washer or dryer, refrigerator or range, area rugs, and furniture. Fixtures include sinks, built-in appliances, fireplace inserts, in-ground spas, solar systems, shutters and window coverings, satellite dishes, pool and spa equipment, keys to the property, garage door openers, landscaping, and mailboxes. Chandeliers and light fixtures are also fixtures and seem to create problems when a seller mistakenly takes them. If the seller intends to take a chandelier, this must be included and agreed to in the contract of sale.

E-SIGNING, FAXED SIGNATURES, AND POWER OF ATTORNEY

We live in a high-tech world, and technology can create legal snarls when contract signing is involved. Faxed signatures are acceptable, and it is *not* good practice to have the original documents signed in person later. If a faxed document is unclear, the clear original can be attached. Signing the originals at some later time creates the problem of what date to use—the date on the faxed copy or the date the original was signed. Problems result when items are overlooked thus creating two contracts with different terms. Having two contracts with two dates also will cause confusion about what date the contract clock starts for contingencies.

E-sign signatures can now be used. Both parties, however, have to sign and agree to accept e-sign signatures. Either buyer or seller can withdraw consent to e-sign at any time during the process. Certain documents are exempt from e-sign signatures, such as seller financial addenda and some documents related to landlord and tenant relationships.

I once had a transaction in which the buyer's agent knew the buyer was signing someone else's name to the contract and did not tell me as the listing agent. I found out later through escrow. This is fraud. This contract was voidable because the buyer had no power of attorney or authorization from that party to sign on the true buyer's behalf. The best approach is a limited power of attorney. The party signing should sign his or her name and write under it "signing for John Jones, with power of attorney." The power of attorney document should be attached to the contract. Signing someone else's name is forgery.

> Real estate agents should never sign a client's name to a contract offer based on a phone call, fax, or e-mail, without power of attorney permitting them to do so.

ARBITRATION AND MEDIATION CLAUSES, HOLD HARMLESS CLAUSES, AND OTHER DISCLAIMERS

Most purchase contracts today have clauses that can be signed by the parties agreeing to arbitration or mediation, or both, before filing a lawsuit. Real estate agents should carefully review these clauses with their clients.

I have heard agents who are being sued say, "I just don't understand how they could sue me; the contract had a hold harmless clause." The typical "hold harmless" clause will indicate that the signer will release, "hold harmless," and indemnify the agents and brokers regarding property condition, square footage, and so on. These clauses, also called *exculpatory clauses,* try to negate liability. Many real estate contracts have stopped including these clauses because the courts do not look favorably on them. Sometimes these clauses can be enforceable, but that will depend on the circumstances. If the clause is standard boilerplate in the contract and the buyer and seller have no option but to accept it, in other words it is a take it or leave it situation, the clause might be regarded as unconscionable by a court. A person cannot absolve another of the commission of an unknown error in information supplied to him, an unknown fraud perpetrated on him, and misinformation of which the one absolved is aware and the one releasing him is ignorant.

Interestingly, my attorney buyer and seller clients will always insist on crossing out arbitration and mediation clauses in purchase contracts.

They do not want to limit their legal rights. They will also cross out any "hold harmless" clause in the contact and not sign the contract if that is not agreed to by the brokers and other party. As more than one attorney has said to me, "I'm not holding anyone harmless." Buyers and sellers should review these clauses with their agent and their attorney.

COUNTEROFFERS

Counteroffers must be worded carefully. This is especially true when dealing with multiple offers. Sellers do not want to find that they have two accepted offers. Some transactions have multiple counteroffers. The contract should reference all counteroffers when it is signed. The correct way to counter a counter is to say: All of counteroffer #1, dated June 15, 2005, is accepted with the exception of item #3, price to be $235,000.

Agents are usually writing more contract language in counteroffers than anywhere else in the contract. Again, they shouldn't guess, and they should review what they are trying to do with an attorney.

MIXING NEGOTIATION AND DISCLOSURE

In one case, the agent tried to exclude an in-ground spa from the sale. The seller had told her that in the four years she had lived in the house, she had never used the spa, didn't know if it worked, and didn't want to repair it if it did not work. The listing agent mixed disclosure with negotiation in trying to exclude the spa, a fixture, from the transaction. She further confused the situation by telling the buyer's general property inspector to skip the spa because it was not included in the transaction. The buyer later found out that the spa had leaking pipes underground and had caused serious foundation problems to his two-story home. The seller and the listing agent were sued, and the buyer won in court. The listing agent should have said in her counteroffer that the seller did not know the condition of the spa and would make no repairs or provide any credits toward repair if any repair was needed. She then should have "encouraged" the buyer to fully inspect the spa. Remember to disclose and negotiate, not to negotiate disclosures.

HANDLING TAX-DEFERRED EXCHANGES

As tax-deferred exchanges are becoming more common, there are some key points to remember about when they can be made. Only investment properties or properties owned for use in a business may be exchanged. The exchange must be between like kind properties. The exchange must meet IRS rules for exchanges, and all exchange properties must be located in the United States.

When listing a property for a possible tax-deferred exchange (1031 tax-deferred exchange), the listing agent should not give legal advice about the exchange, but should refer the parties to their tax and legal advisors. A qualified intermediary exchange company may be utilized to hold funds until the second part of the exchange is complete, if the exchange is not simultaneous. The seller is allowed 45 days to find the replacement property and 180 days to close on the property. Real estate agents should add appropriate exchange cooperation language to the purchase and sale contract, such as, "Buyer agrees to cooperate with seller's 1031 exchange, at no expense to the buyer." The qualified intermediary needs to be notified when escrow is opened for the relinquished property. The exchange company should be experienced and have errors and omissions insurance coverage.

WHAT IS "AS IS," AND IS IT NEGOTIATION OR DISCLOSURE?

Most standard real estate contracts for existing construction now have a clause included that states that the property is sold "as is" or in its "present condition." In discussing the expression "as is" with buyers, sellers, and real estate agents, it is apparent that there exists some confusion regarding its meaning.

When a contract is signed by buyers and sellers, which includes the "as is" clause, this means that at the time of the signing it is the sellers' desire not to repair or credit the buyers any funds for any defects the buyers may find in the property through the process of their inspections or investigations, or for any defects the sellers disclose on their disclosure form. The buyers may agree to the "as is" clause, which is a term of negotiation on the part of the sellers. In some cases this clause replaces previous contract clauses that provided a "warranty" on the condition of some, or all, systems of the property. In spite of this "as is" clause, the buyers should have the contingency to inspect the property for defects and the right to withdraw from the transaction if those defects are of a number, type, or cost to repair the buyers deem to be unsatisfactory.

The "as is" clause in no way limits the right of the buyers to determine the condition of the property at the time of the sale.

> The "as is" clause does not reduce or eliminate the duty of the sellers or agents to fully disclose all property defects and other material facts of which they may be aware.

The contract is an agreement between the parties, which can be changed by further agreement between the parties. Should the buyers discover significant defects in their inspection process, either unknown to the sellers or the agents, or more significant and costly to repair than previously believed, they have every right to request credits toward those repairs or that the repairs be made by the sellers.

Because of the "as is" clause, sellers have the right to say that they will not give credits, or make repairs, and that the buyers may withdraw from the transaction if this is not acceptable to the buyers. However sellers may have new information on their property's condition that they did not have before, and this new information must be disclosed to the next prospective buyers. Future buyers may make the same requests as the present buyers for credits or repairs and possibly some additional requests. The sellers may be wise to negotiate with the buyers at hand. The usual result of this situation is that the buyers and sellers agree to some credits or some repairs through further negotiation, and thereby change the agreement, in spite of the prior "as is" clause. In hot sellers' markets, the buyers may have limited negotiation power to request credits and repairs. The buyers may have to accept the property "as is" or cancel the transaction and look for another property. In a slower buyers' market, the buyers may have substantial leverage to negotiate a change in the "as is" clause, winning many concessions from the sellers.

THE ROLE OF ATTORNEYS IN CONTRACT MODIFICATION, NEGOTIATION, AND DISCLOSURE

In states where attorneys are routinely involved in real estate transactions, they should have all the required materials and knowledge to handle all the documents necessary and make any necessary or desired modifications and additions. However, attorneys do not fill the real estate agent's function to inspect the property, make disclosures of observed or known defects, refer property inspectors, investigate important issues, conduct walk-through inspections, assist the buyer with the loan application, or deal directly with follow-up on seller repairs. In states where attorneys are not typically part of most residential transactions, as is the case in California, where escrow and title companies handle documents and funds, attorneys may not have on hand all the current forms and addenda to which real estate agents have continuing access. Attorneys should be contacted, however, when the buyer or seller wishes to change the standard terms of a form contract. Real estate agents should not act as an attorney by making significant changes to a contract, or they may find themselves talking to an attorney later in a lawsuit.

If you don't know where you are going, you will probably end up somewhere else.

—Laurence J. Peter

14

CHAPTER

Seller Repairs and Credits

Dealing with property defects once they are disclosed or discovered can be the cause of lawsuits; for example, repairs not completed at the close or improperly completed, lack of agreement between the buyer and the seller on what was to have been repaired, or inadequate credits for repairs needed. The buyer should be allowed adequate time during the inspection period to obtain cost-to-repair quotes. General property inspectors usually prefer not to provide or are precluded from providing cost estimates.

As the inspection and disclosure process becomes more complex, so does the process of dealing with repairs. The troublesome defects in negotiation are those discovered that are well beyond the expectation of the buyer when first making the offer. Left unresolved with a repair or credit, they will result in a perceived overpayment for the property. The seller desires to obtain the highest price for the property, defects and all, and avoid dealing with repairs and their cost, when the focus is on packing and moving.

Better to repair the pen after the sheep have escaped than not at all.

—Chinese proverb

PROPERTY DEFECTS KNOWN BEFORE THE OFFER

It is generally good policy for the buyers' agent to ask the sellers' agent what defects are known about the property before the buyers submit an offer or have an inspection. Some agents will supply a written seller and listing agent's disclosure of defects at that time or orally point out the known defects of the property to the buyers' agent. If a prelisting inspection was done by the sellers, this can be provided as well. Pointing out the defects at this time can substantially reduce the number of defect repair requests later in the inspection process. Some of the property's defects can then be resolved in the offer/counteroffer process, before contract agreement is reached. If the defect is quite serious, such as a faulty foundation, buyers not interested in dealing with that type of problem will not waste their time or the sellers' time with an offer. If buyers proceed with making an offer in consideration of the known defect, such as a deck that needs replacement, they may not know how much it will cost to fix that defect, and this will be reflected in their offer. Likewise, sellers and their agent may not know the cost to repair the deck, but feel they have taken it into consideration in establishing a list price. Some buyers may choose to bring a contractor with them to view the deck for a rough estimate of replacement cost before they make their offer, and they will attach that estimate to the offer. In the absence of any known cost of repair for the known defect, the buyers might make an offer subject to inspections and determination of cost to repair the known defect and any other defects discovered during inspections.

Sellers and their agent can try to limit the repair cost credit or lowered offer price by countering with an offer of credit "toward the repair," or replacement of the defect. The listing agent might indicate in a counteroffer, "The sellers agree to credit the buyers $5,000 toward the cost of the deck repair to be undertaken by the buyers after the close of the transaction." The sellers might then remain firm on their sale price as the defective deck has already been dealt with both in the list price and in the credit. Should the buyers find out during the inspection that the deck needs replacement at a cost of $20,000, they can drop out of the transaction or submit this information to the sellers and request further credit toward the deck replacement.

HOW TO DEAL WITH THE REPAIR PROCESS

The buyer's real estate agent should review the general property inspector's report with the buyer, and all property defects noted should be separately listed or highlighted. Further inspections should be scheduled as soon as possible, as recommended by the inspector or desired by the client. The principal focus should be on material defects and the major systems of the property. It will not be possible to make a comprehensive accounting to the seller on the property's condition until all the inspections have been made and the quotes for the relevant repairs are received. If there are significant problems with a property requiring numerous inspections and quotes, the buyer's agent should negotiate for more time from the seller for analysis.

WHY HANDYMAN AND SELLER REPAIRS SHOULD BE LIMITED

I have often seen in lawsuits that problems resulted because someone undertook a repair he or she was not qualified to make, and that repair was poorly made or did not resolve the problem. In real estate transactions agents and sellers should limit repairs by the sellers and handyman to only those that are minor repair and maintenance issues, and for which neither a contractor's license nor permit are required. For example, some repairs the sellers or handyman might make, if they are capable, are:

- Replace a fascia board
- Repair a broken tile
- Repair a loose doorknob
- Minor painting
- Repair a window latch
- Replace a door

The problem with seller or handyman repairs is that there is no recourse for a poor repair, except to pursue the sellers. The handyman is an unlicensed, uninsured repair person. I have consulted on lawsuits in which handymen or sellers attempted to repair roof leaks or plumbing leaks with disastrous results.

> Try to avoid seller and handyman repairs in real estate transactions because using them is a false economy that can backfire later.

We all use handymen to make repairs in our homes, and some sellers are truly handy, but handymen and seller repairs made in escrow for a buyer are a different circumstance. Many states release the agents from liability when they have referred the services of licensed professionals. Handymen are cheaper because they are unlicensed and uninsured, but if the uninsured handyman falls off the roof while attempting a repair, the seller who does not have worker's compensation insurance will face still another problem.

A seller should not use unlicensed handymen in making repairs prior to listing the property either. The buyer's general property inspector may find a repair not properly made by a handyman, and the buyer may request that the defect be repaired by the seller for the second time.

> All repairs requiring a licensed contractor must be made by a licensed contractor.

The buyer's request-for-repairs letter should clearly state which repairs are to be made by a licensed contractor. Receipts must be provided verifying the contractor's work, and they should state whether there is a warranty for the work and the length of the warranty. For example:

> The general inspection report indicated that three electrical outlets in the kitchen are faulty. The buyer is requesting that the seller have these outlets repaired by a licensed electrical contractor and that a receipt for this work be provided to the buyer.

In an effort to save time, agents sometimes abbreviate the buyer's list of repairs with such comments as: "Seller to fix 3 faulty outlets in kitchen."

Can you see how less specific the second request example is when compared to the example above and how it could lead to a faulty repair? Should the buyer find a problem three months after the close of the transaction with the three kitchen outlets, whom do you think the buyer will call, if a licensed electrical contractor makes the repair and provides a receipt? The licensed electrical contractor who made the repair will be called first, rather than the seller or the agents. Deferring to experts is always a good idea.

It is important to be specific about exactly how much the seller will pay to get the repairs done. Just attaching a quote from a licensed contractor is not enough. The seller may want to get a quote from another licensed roofer for the same repair, and it may be a lower quote. The final agreement should not say: "The seller will pay to repair the roof," but rather, "The seller will pay to repair the roof, per the quote by the seller's licensed roofing contractor, the Superior Roofing Company, for $500."

HOW SHOULD THE DOCUMENTATION OF THE REPAIR, CREDIT REQUEST, AND FINAL AGREEMENT BE HANDLED?

The repair and/or request-for-credits letter should be typed on the buyer's agent's letterhead and should be signed by the buyer or signed by the buyer's agent and the buyer. Some state associations of Realtors have forms that can be used by the buyer's agent to officially request repairs. If space is not adequate on the form, the agent should write "See attached" and add as many typed pages as necessary. The buyer's letter should also include above the buyer's signature, "By signing below, I am indicating receipt of a copy of this letter [or form]." Often the process of negotiating credits and repairs is handled outside of escrow or without attorney assistance in situations in which attorneys handle escrow. Agents need to be very careful that requests are signed and that copies are received by the buyer at the time of signing. The buyer's agent should prepare several copies of the request. One copy will be sent to the seller's agent, one given to the buyer, and a copy should be retained in the buyer's agent's file.

When the seller's agent receives the buyer's letter for requested repairs or credits with the attached inspections and quotes, the seller's agent should go over this list carefully with the seller. The seller must then decide which repairs to agree to make and what credits to choose to give the buyer. I have seen seller's agents, in an effort to save time, merely place check marks next to items on the buyer's list suggesting that those are the items the seller will agree to do or write "ok" or "no" in the margin next to an item, and then send the list back to the buyer's agent. The seller may later claim he or she never authorized this approval or never received a copy of it. The seller's agent should retype, on company letterhead, the seller's counteroffer to the buyer's requests. Again, some state associations of Realtors may have forms for this purpose or space on the buyer's form for the seller to reply. This letter, or form, should list or relist every item the seller is willing to agree to repair or credit. The seller should sign this letter and receive a copy.

This back and forth process can continue until the buyer and seller have reached agreement, or not, as the case may be. When agreement is reached, the final list of agreed-to repairs and credits should be typed on either agent's letterhead or on an appropriate form, and the list should be signed by both the buyer and the seller. The list should be as specific as possible regarding each repair or credit item. The credit item should say:

> Buyer and seller agree that a seller credit of $3,000 is toward the buyer's repair or replacement of the damaged deck, irrespective of its final cost.

I have seen lawsuits where this process was not followed, and the buyer claimed, "I thought all my requested repairs were going to be made by the seller." The seller replies, "Where do you see my signature agreeing to those repairs?" Above the buyer and seller's signatures the agreement should state, "By signing below I am indicating receipt of a copy of this agreement." Agents may be agreeing between themselves on repairs after consulting with their clients but without a formal, final document, they have not legally changed the contract.

Only by signature of the buyer and seller on any agreement can the terms of a real estate transaction be altered.

Another approach is to forward the final repair and credit agreement to the escrow holder, who can then send copies of the agreement to the buyer and seller to sign. The benefit of handling the agreement this way is that the escrow holder will now also have a signed copy in the file. Typing is recommended over handwriting on these documents so they are easy to read.

HOW DOES THE BUYER'S AGENT KNOW WHAT REPAIRS NEED A LICENSED CONTRACTOR IN THE REQUEST FOR REPAIRS?

Real estate agents and buyers need to have some understanding of what repairs may require a contractor's license and possibly a permit. Normally replacing a water heater or a furnace requires a building permit. What may or may not require a building permit will vary from state to state and even from city to city within a state. The buyer's agent should check with the local building department on any repair request to determine if it will require a licensed contractor and a building permit, before submitting the buyer's request for repairs.

Some major material repairs or credits may have to be quoted or repaired by contractors for whom licenses may not yet be required, such as mold remediators. In this case, it is critical that the most qualified companies be asked to quote on the repair, for the protection of the buyer, seller, and agents. Mold remediation quotes usually cover only the cost to rid the property of mold and not the cost to repair the walls, floors, and ceilings or to reinstall cabinets. A quote from a licensed general contractor will be needed for the reconstruction repair cost.

Some real estate agents may be thinking, "Why do I have to know that? I'm not a contractor." Real estate agents need to understand the issues relevant to the transaction that are of value and benefit to their clients. Real estate agents are hired as professionals to represent the interest of their clients. Typical homeowners are expected by the building department to know what improvements or repairs to their property will need a building permit or when to call the building department to find out what will need a permit or a licensed contractor. The buyer's and seller's agents need to know this information in their local area, or how to investigate and find out this information.

HOW TO AVOID INSUFFICIENT FUNDS CREDITED IN ESCROW FOR A REPAIR

Real estate agents and the buyer and seller should never guess at the amount of a repair, when leaving funds in escrow for a repair to be made later by the buyer, or giving the buyer a credit for a repair. Lawsuits can result when the guess turns out to be far too low to cover the problem, and the unhappy buyer looks to the agent for the difference. The buyer should have a quote from a licensed contractor that addresses the repair, describes in detail what will be done, the materials that will be used, the valid time period for the quote, and any contingent issues related to the quote, such as "a higher cost may result once the wall is opened up." The seller may want to receive his or her own quote from a licensed contractor, and the buyer and seller can then negotiate funds to be left in escrow "toward the cost of the repair or for credit to the buyer."

If the repair cost goes up once work is underway, the agreement should state it is for the "anticipated cost" of repair, and that the seller will not be responsible for unknown circumstances the buyer may find once walls or floors are opened.

HOW TO GET THE REPAIRS COMPLETED BY THE CLOSE OF ESCROW

A major problem can still result after the agreement between buyer and seller is reached on the agreed-to repairs; getting them accomplished before the transaction closes. Lawsuits can result when repairs are not completed by the close date; the buyer takes possession and the seller no longer has access to the property to complete the repairs. These dangling issues at the close are a serious liability concern. Some state associations of Realtors have developed a form for the buyer to send to the seller to remind the seller to perform on agreed-to repairs. In California this form is called "notice to the seller to perform." A similar form can be used when the buyer nears the agreed-to completion date for his or her investigations and the seller has not received the buyer's inspections and repair quotes. This form is called a "notice to the buyer to perform." These forms remind the buyer and seller to accomplish their agreed-to tasks promptly.

There is no substitute for the real estate agents staying on top of the progress of the transaction and reminding the buyer to complete the investigations and the seller to complete the agreed-to repairs. The seller's agent should assist the seller in organizing the repair process, get the process underway as soon as an agreement is reached, and check frequently with the seller on the progress of the repairs. If the seller seems overwhelmed by the repair process because contractors are not showing up or repairs are taking longer than expected, action should be taken. The seller's agent should not wait until a few days before the close of the transaction to find out the status of repairs, but instead should check on what has been done, what is in process, and what has not yet been started at least 10 days before the close. The seller's agent, after consulting with the seller, should call in a general contractor to quote on completing the remaining repairs. The quote should detail exactly what remains to be done and that the contractor agrees to do the work for that sum of money. The buyer and the buyer's agent should then be consulted and presented with this information. An agreement should be signed by the buyer and seller to leave funds in escrow corresponding to the contractor's quote to complete the remaining work.

HOW SHOULD THE FINAL WALK-THROUGH INSPECTION BE CONDUCTED?

Most real estate agents utilize some type of form called a "verification of property condition" or "final walk-through inspection." The buyer's final walk-through of the property is usually conducted a few days before the transaction closes, and preferably after the seller has moved out. The purpose of this inspection is to assure the buyer that the seller has maintained the property in the same condition in which the buyer first saw it, with the exception of verifying that the agreed-to repairs by the seller have been completed. It can also be used to verify that there are no new defects in the property.

In one lawsuit on which I consulted, the buyer and the dual agent walked the property on the final walk-through inspection with the agreed-to list of repairs, and the agent pointed to each item to be fixed and indicated that the seller "told him" it was repaired. The buyer and agent stared at the electrical panel, the water heater, the fireplace, and so on. The agent provided no receipts for the repairs. The buyer moved in and found that many of the repairs had actually not been made.

Improperly made repairs or repairs not made are a frequent cause of lawsuits. The buyer, the seller, and both real estate agents should be present at the final walk-through inspection. The seller's agent should be prepared to review every repair with the buyer and hand the buyer and the buyer's agent a copy of the receipt and applicable warranty by the appropriately licensed contractor who made each repair, with each receipt stamped "paid." In states where funds are put in escrow, contractors can be paid directly from the seller's proceeds. Now there exists substantive evidence the repair was made and that it was made properly. The buyer should also sign a memo or form indicating receipt of the contractor receipts for work completed. The general property inspector may also be asked to reinspect the repairs to ensure that they were properly made for those repairs that can actually be seen, not repairs that are now concealed in a wall or are underground.

SHOULD AN ATTORNEY BE CONSULTED IN THE REPAIR AND CREDIT PROCESS?

The repair and credit process will sometimes result in lengthy written agreements between the buyer and the seller. When repair requests or credit arrangements are complex, it is strongly advised that the agents recommend that their clients have the final agreement reviewed by an attorney before it is signed. An attorney can ensure that the intent and meaning of what is said is clear and not subject to any misinterpretation. If an attorney is handling the escrow function, this person may be able to assist the buyer, seller, and agents in this review. An escrow company or title company handling an escrow will usually not provide any legal advice.

ARE SELLER CREDITS BETTER THAN SELLER REPAIRS?

I would always recommend seller credits to the buyer or leaving funds in escrow for the buyer to make repairs, rather than seller repairs, for a number of reasons.

- Sellers are busy with their own move and possible purchase.
- Sellers notoriously underestimate the time required to make repairs.
- Some repairs are difficult to make with the seller present and in the process of packing and moving.
- Buyers are seldom satisfied with the quality of seller repairs.
- Contractors are not always available to meet the close date.
- There is no pressure on the seller or agents to complete the repairs before the close.
- The responsibility for managing the contractor's progress of making repairs and quality of work is now the buyer's, who would rather monitor a contractor's work on the new home, rather than rely on the departing seller to monitor the work.
- The pressure is reduced on the buyer and the buyer's agent to get the repairs made and verified before the close.
- The likelihood of those unresolved "dangling issues at the close" is reduced.

Some repairs, such as the repairs required for termite or dry rot damage, may need to be completed before the close to satisfy the buyer's lender. Some dry rot repairs should not be done by termite companies, such as structural repairs, and they require a licensed contractor. Termite company repairs should be limited to minor replacement of wood, such as a wood step, railing, or fascia board.

Other repairs the buyer will probably want to be sure are completed before the close are all mold inspections and remediation. The true cost of putting the property back together where drywall, moldings, cabinets, and other materials have been removed will not be accurately known until the remediation process is complete.

ARE SELLER CREDITS BETTER THAN A PRICE REDUCTION?

When seller credits are discussed for repairs, the issue always seems to come up concerning whether the seller should just call the credits a price reduction and advise the escrow holder of the price change. In essence, any seller credit is a price reduction. Reducing the price, however, may have other consequences a credit or merely leaving funds in escrow for repairs may not have. For example:

- A price reduction will affect the price reported to the MLS (multiple listing service). A lower selling price may affect the comparable sales analysis appraisers and other agents may make later for other clients in the area. The other properties may not have the defects found in the subject property.
- A price reduction may affect the commission paid by the seller or buyer. This fact should be discussed among buyer, seller, and agents, and an agreement should be signed so that there are no misunderstandings later.
- A price reduction would affect the seller's net gain on the property and possibly save some funds in taxes paid.
- The final sales price will sometimes affect the tax rate the new buyer will pay.

These issues should be discussed, reviewed with accountants, and resolved in some formal agreement to protect the interests of buyer, seller, and agents. Seller credits of a few thousand dollars will probably not have any substantial impact on any of the above described situations. However, a credit versus a price reduction on a sum of $50,000 might certainly affect these issues.

15 CHAPTER

Building Permits

WHY IS "GETTING THE PERMITS" SO IMPORTANT TO AVOIDING LIABILITY?

In many states, departments of real estate do not require the real estate agent to "get the permits." Many associations of Realtors tell the agents that they are not required to get the permits. However, real estate agents are usually not "prohibited" from getting the permits. I strongly disagree with attorneys who advise real estate agents not to get the permits. In the hundreds of real estate lawsuits on which I have consulted, not one resulted from a real estate agent getting the permits. However, I have consulted on many lawsuits where not getting the permits by anyone involved in the transaction resulted in the lawsuit.

Real estate agents might say, "It isn't my responsibility to get the permits. The buyer is supposed to do that." Unfortunately, few buyers ever get the permits prior to the close of escrow. Sometimes avoiding a lawsuit will entail going beyond what is absolutely required and doing what is in the best interest of all involved in the transaction. I always get the permits in every real estate transaction, regardless of whether I represent the buyer or the seller, and I provide copies to all parties.

Part of the problem in getting the buyer to get the permits is that real estate agents are not always as helpful as they could be in assisting the buyer with this task. For example, agents seldom tell the buyers:

- The address of the closest building department office that would have the permits for the property
- The hours the building department is open
- Which counter to go to, if there are several counters
- What paperwork they may need to fill out with their request
- If there is a charge for the permits
- How long this whole process is likely to take them
- What exactly to ask for

In large cities just getting to the building department can be an ordeal. Once inside the building department, there may be several counters, each with long lines, where one needs to "take a number." Typical buyers are immediately overwhelmed concerning where to get in line and how many lines they may need to tackle to get the information they need. What information do they need? Is this worthwhile? Why did the agent send us here?

If you live in a smaller city with an easy to reach building department and one counter with a friendly clerk who is happy to help you figure out what you need, you are fortunate. In larger cities there is usually the option of hiring a "permit service" to get the permits. Permit services are used by contractors, architects, engineers, and attorneys. I request a "certified copy" of all the documents I receive. A certified copy is what an attorney requests for court. It usually costs me $30 to $40 for the documents I receive, and the cost is well worth it! This is cheap E&O insurance for agents and a blessing for buyers and sellers to keep them out of court.

WHAT IS MEANT BY "GETTING THE PERMITS"?

Permits are sometimes misunderstood by real estate agents, buyers, and sellers. A permit is an approved application to do something to a property and will usually expire in two years if it is not used. Permits for heat and air, plumbing, electrical, and roofing are referred to as *mechanical permits*. In larger permit offices, these permits may be at a separate counter.

In addition to the permits, the buyer should also receive the applicable "certificates of occupancy." The certificate of occupancy, also referred to as the "C of O," indicates that the inspector has inspected the property and approved the work referenced in the permit. Certificates of occupancy are most often used for original construction, but they may also be used for subsequent additions and other remodeling. Room additions may have on file what is sometimes referred to as a *final card*. On this form the building inspector has checked off such items as "foundation, ok; framing, ok; plumbing, ok." In the corner or at the bottom, the inspector signs and dates the form and indicates "finaled." This means that the inspector has checked each phase of the construction and given final approval. More recent permits may be computerized, and the original permit may simply be reproduced with the word *finaled* added and the date of final approval. Sometimes found on the back of building permits is something called a *plot map*. A plot map is a sketch of the outline of the lot, with the building roughly drawn within it. The work to be added or modified by the building permit is shaded in on the building outline. Plot maps can be very useful as a visual tool to follow the progression of work on a building as it is added to or modified through the years. The five items I always request when I get the permits are:

1. General building permits
2. Mechanical permits
3. Certificates of occupancy
4. Final cards or "finaled" permits
5. Plot maps

For those purchasing new construction, the building plans and permits should be requested. There are cities in which permits cannot be obtained without the seller's consent. The consent of the seller for the buyer or the agents to obtain permits should be written into the contract.

WHAT IF SOMETHING IS MISSING IN THE PERMIT RECORDS?

Real estate agents are sometimes reluctant to get the permits because something might be missing in the permit records, and they fear that providing partial permits may be worse with respect to liability than no permits at all. I disagree with this fear, and believe it inhibits obtaining permit records, which is far more beneficial in avoiding lawsuits. In my company addendum, I indicate that I am providing the record of permits available at the building department for the property, that it is what could be found, and that it may not be complete. Permit offices lose records or do not retain older records. Also records could have inadvertently been destroyed in a fire or other event. I then advise the buyer to consult with the building department to check for any additional information. I believe that this is an adequate advisory to the buyer and is far better than avoiding obtaining the permits.

Agents should always ask the sellers for any permits they may have obtained during their ownership of the property and any permits or building plans that may have been given to them by the seller from whom they purchased the property. In some cases, there simply are no permits. The property may be too old, or the building department has no records. In this case, I report this information to the buyer in my agent's disclosure.

IS IT DIFFICULT TO READ A PERMIT?

It really isn't difficult for a real estate agent or a buyer or seller to read a permit. Throughout our lives, if we ever own a property, building permits will be documents we will have to deal with. The heading of the permit tells you what it is—electrical, plumbing, heat and air, pool, building, and so on. Somewhere in the body of the permit, the purpose of the permit is indicated, such as "3 bedroom, 2 bath house" or "20 × 40 swimming pool," or "15 × 15 bedroom addition." That information is all most buyers, sellers, or agents need to focus on in reading the permit.

If a real estate office is one that would prefer its agents avoid touching or reading permits, then the agent or the buyer should hand the permit data to the general property inspector before he or she starts the inspection and ask the inspector to review them. The inspector can then note any visible improvements that do not appear to have permits. Anyone can visually read the plot maps to see the progressive construction to a property. Should you observe a portion of a building that is not reflected on one of these simple drawings, it is certainly a strong clue that the area may have been added without a permit. The first thing I do when I receive a permit file is to put the permits in date sequence, which makes all the records easy to follow and understand.

PERMITS, THE APPRAISER, AND LAWSUITS

There may be some agents, buyers, and sellers who do not know that *appraisers will not count the square footage of any nonpermitted addition to a structure in their analysis of property value. For this reason, agents representing buyers should always make the appraised value at or exceeding the purchase price a contingency of the transaction.*

In one recent legal case, the seller who lived in Connecticut wished to sell her property in Hollywood, California. She had been renting out the property for several years and decided she was too far away to deal with renters and repairs. Her listing agent appropriately asked her if any portions of the property were built without permits. The seller said that the only area built without a permit was the lower-level bath in the two-story house with an upper-level entry. The listing agent dutifully told the buyer and the appraiser that the lower-level bath had been built without a permit. The appraiser valued the property at the purchase price, with the deduction for the nonpermitted bathroom. Because the bathroom represented a small portion of the total square footage, the lender approved the buyer's loan. However, when a considerable portion of the square footage is nonpermitted and thus affecting property value, the lender may refuse to approve the loan because the value of the property may be considerably lower than the purchase price. The buyer in this case closed escrow on his purchase and decided to do some remodeling. He went to the building department and discovered that the entire lower level of the house was constructed without permits. He also discovered that the lower level of the house was not built according to the present building code and, therefore, had to be substantially rebuilt. The buyer contacted his attorney. Some 40 percent of the square footage of the property was nonpermitted, not just one bathroom. The agent's E&O insurer settled with the buyer, as did the seller. The buyer overpaid for the property because the appraisal should have omitted the lower-level square footage. Rarely, if ever, do appraisers obtain the permits. The present property owner is responsible for nonpermitted work regardless of which prior owner constructed the nonpermitted work. The seller of this property should have obtained the property permits when she purchased the house. Can you see how important permit records can be?

Nonpermitted construction is usually faulty construction that may affect not only the area involved but the entire structure.

Homeowners should get permits and inspections for work that requires permits and inspections. Homeowners may think they are saving money on building plans and permits or avoiding reassessments and increased property taxes, but the long-range cost will be much, much higher, not to mention the stress and aggravation.

> Construction work done without permits and inspections is a lawsuit waiting to happen.

PERMITS, THE PROPERTY INSURER, AND LAWSUITS

Nonpermitted additions may also complicate a property owner's claim with the property insurer. After an earthquake, flood, blizzard, or hurricane, the insurer may claim that the portion of the structure that was damaged was not built with approved permits and inspections, not built to code and, therefore, is not covered under the insured's policy. The insurance carrier may also claim that the improperly constructed and nonpermitted addition contributed to the damage to the portion of the structure that was built with appropriate permits and inspections, and the insurer may deny coverage for those portions of the structure as well.

In a rental property when an occupant is injured in some disaster, or from faulty wiring or plumbing in a nonpermitted structure, the tenant may have an additional claim against the property owner resulting from possible faulty and unsafe construction. Liability claims of this type against a property owner by a tenant may also be denied by the property insurer because of the nonpermitted construction.

WHAT WORK ON A PROPERTY WILL PROBABLY REQUIRE A PERMIT?

Buyers, sellers, and real estate agents do not need to become contractors to negotiate real estate transactions, but it is extremely useful to have some basic knowledge of what work may require a building permit or mechanical permit. In most areas the following work will require a permit and, therefore, an appropriately licensed contractor must do the work:

- Room additions
- Expansion of any area that adds square footage
- Reconfiguring interior space, such as moving walls to add a bathroom

- New roof
- Converting a garage to a bedroom
- Converting a carport to a garage
- Kitchen remodel that moves the location of appliances
- New heat and air system
- Replacing a heat and air system
- Bathroom remodel
- New pool
- Repiping the plumbing
- Replacing a furnace or water heater
- Adding skylights
- Property drainage, such as drains, culverts, curbing, and sump pumps
- Replacing a window unit
- Exterior patios

Real estate agents who are informed by sellers that they have done any of the work mentioned above should ask about permits and receipts for that work. A seller who does remodeling work, whether with licensed or unlicensed contractors, is responsible to a subsequent buyer for that work having been done properly. The contractor, or handyman, is an agent of the seller. The excuse, "I wasn't there watching his work," won't cut it in court. If the seller is found at fault in a legal case because a licensed contractor made faulty repairs, the seller can then sue the contractor, but may have no recourse against the unlicensed contractor.

HOW CAN ONE GET NONPERMITTED WORK PERMITTED?

I am always amazed that some agents, buyers, and sellers believe that to get a nonpermitted structure or nonpermitted work permitted, all they have to do is go to the building department, fill out a form, and pay a fee and a fine.

> The seller and the seller's agent should be as detailed as possible in describing what does not have a permit.

"Are you sure this family room has a permit?"

Once the seller and the seller's agent reveal work that was done without a permit, the ball is then in the buyer's court concerning what to do about this situation. If significant work was done to the property without permits, the buyer and the buyer's agent might just choose to look elsewhere for a purchase. If the carport was converted to a garage without a permit or a one-room addition was added without a permit, the buyer may elect to have the general property inspector examine these areas and note any deficiencies. Then the buyer can request repairs or credits from the seller as needed. However, the general property inspector cannot see the framing and foundations that may be faulty, as well as electrical wiring, plumbing pipes, and insulation. Property appraisers will not count the nonpermitted bedroom addition square footage in this sale or in a subsequent sale.

> Nonpermitted additions and work can make the property harder to sell in the future and affect its value.

My recommendation for buyers finding a nonpermitted addition or other significant property modification is to request that as a contingency of the purchase, a permit be obtained and that the structure be inspected by the building department. Any work to repair and bring the addition up to code must be done by the seller and the seller's licensed contractor. The buyer should then be provided a certificate of occupancy, final card, or notice of completion, indicating that the work in total is accepted by the building department. This process will take time and probably money on the part of the seller. However, a lawsuit that drags on for several years is far worse and far more expensive. For sellers who thought they could beat the system, this is when they pay the price for the error of their ways.

> It is wise for sellers with nonpermitted additions to obtain permits, make corrections, and receive final approvals from the building department before listing their property.

This process can take from several days to several months. Waiting until a buyer is found to start this process will probably result in losing the buyer. Some sellers and their agents take the approach that they will just price the property lower to account for the nonpermitted work, but they really do not know how much lower the right number is and may either overly discount value or underestimate the cost of possible repairs.

The result of guessing about what is going on behind walls and underground usually results in a lawsuit, and I am consulting on several of these lawsuits right now.

The building department will likely have the following procedure for obtaining an "as built" permit and providing final approval of the nonpermitted work:

- The seller will have to go to the building department and admit to the nonpermitted work.
- Depending on the scope of what was done, the building department might require:
  - A set of plans from a draftsperson, architect, or engineer
  - A permit and the payment of the normal fee plus a fine
  - An inspection of the property where the inspector marks where the property owner is to open up a wall, expose the foundation, the roof construction, wiring, plumbing, etc., for further inspection; the inspector will then return to inspect

these open areas; and the inspector will tell the seller to close up the openings (if the inspection is approved) and issue a final approval, or the inspector will give the property owner a list of required corrections (if the inspection is not approved) and then once these corrections are made and reinspected, the final approval is issued.

For something as simple as a furnace permit, the inspector can examine the installation, cite any required corrections, reinspect, and sign off on the work. For major additions and remodeling, the process can be more extended. When this process is attempted in escrow, everyone is rushed. If the building inspector finds flaws in construction, the buyer has been put on notice and can withdraw from the transaction, negotiate a credit from the seller, or request repairs, if that is feasible. Any repairs required should be evaluated, and repair costs should be quoted by a licensed general contractor. Any work done with a permit legally obtained but left "not finaled" may need to be altered later to be brought up to current code and receive final building department approval.

THE NONPERMITTED STRUCTURE THAT HAS TO BE REMOVED OR CONVERTED BACK TO ITS PRIOR USE

Even worse than fixing and permitting a nonpermitted addition or other work is the buyer later finding out that the construction must be permanently removed or converted back to its prior legal use. In one lawsuit, a young couple with two children, making their first home purchase, wanted a house with a secondary guest structure for the wife's mother. The property was marketed as having a guest unit. The couple bought the property only to find out later when they were sent a citation by the building department that the guest structure was not permitted in the area, was too close to the rear property line, and had to be removed. Both the dual agent and the seller were sued.

In another case a buyer using an illegal guest unit as a rental, converted from a detached garage, was turned in to "building code enforcement" by disgruntled neighbors. The tenant had to relocate and sued the property owner for damages. The illegal rental unit had to be converted back to a garage. Illegal garage conversions can also cause serious harm to occupants and their property. They may not have adequate means of egress or proper heating or venting. Space heaters improperly used may cause a fire. Eliminating covered parking on the property might also violate building code requirements.

THE BUILDING DEPARTMENT AND WHAT CAN OR CANNOT BE BUILT

In some areas there are restrictions on the ratio of building square footage to lot size, or second story additions are not allowed, as they would obstruct a neighbor's view. Real estate agents, buyers, and sellers need to familiarize themselves with the issues that can substantially affect what a buyer can do with the property purchase. No buyer wants to find out this type of information after the transaction closes. These are material facts that affect property value.

Wise men learn by other men's mistakes, fools by their own.

—H. G. Bohn

16

CHAPTER

Research and Investigation

There are some real estate agents who believe that "research and investigation" are strictly the obligations of the buyer. They think that once the buyer has been notified in writing to investigate and has been given lists of possible issues to investigate, the obligation of the seller and agents to investigate is eliminated. Unfortunately, some agents find out when they are sued, that *their* duty to investigate falls under their fiduciary duty of "reasonable care and diligence."

THE DUTY OF REAL ESTATE AGENTS TO INVESTIGATE

The seller's agent has a duty to question the seller, ask for supporting documentation, and investigate as necessary. Seller's disclosure forms are a first step in this process. After reviewing the seller's disclosures, the listing agent should ask questions that may still not be answered in the disclosure form—or not answered fully.

The listing agent should not wait for the buyer or the buyer's agent to make requests for this information; it should routinely be provided. The buyer's agent needs to assist the buyer in the investigation of the property. Some of the things the buyer's agent may provide to the buyer or investigate are:

- *Provide a property profile from the title company, if this is not provided by the seller's agent.* If the property profile, for example, says that the property has three bedrooms and three bathrooms in 2,788 square feet, but the house now has six bedrooms and four bathrooms, this is clearly a red flag for further investigation. When permits are taken out for additions, and construction is inspected and approved by the building department, the tax assessor is notified and the records of the title company are usually updated to reflect the additions. If the additions are not reflected in the tax database of the title company, it can be reasonably assumed that the additions were made without permits and inspections.

- *Provide the property construction permits, including the certificates of occupancy, final cards, plot maps, and mechanical permits, if these are not provided by the seller or the seller's agent.*

- *Check when the property was sold previously and by whom.* If the buyer's agent or the seller's agent on a prior transaction was in the same office as the present listing or buyer's agent, the knowledge that person has can be attributed to the brokerage and this subsequent transaction. In a lawsuit, the buyer's agent had previously seen the property on an open house. It was later purchased by the party now selling to her buyer. She had firsthand knowledge not only of the property's prior poor condition, but also that the prior listing agent was an agent in her office. She made no effort to ask that agent about the property.

- *Carefully review the preliminary title report for possible red flags.* Unfortunately, buyers are often expected to read documents they are generally unfamiliar with and can easily overlook key information that may need further investigation. Lawsuits regarding encroachments, easements, and road access are all too common. The buyer's agent should carefully review the "prelim" and call the title officer with any questions. Many items reported in the prelim have underlying documents that are available to the buyer and the buyer's agent on request. The buyer should receive a memo from the buyer's agent alerting the buyer to any concern with the preliminary title report, including any discrepancy in ownership, property address, liens, numbers of bedrooms or baths, square footage, and lot size.

- *Carefully review the documents provided by condominium homeowners associations and planned unit developments (PUD) and ask for other documents.* Most states provide for specific disclosures by "required" HOA (homeowners associations). Required homeowner associations, when initially established, require all current and subsequent owners to pay monthly or quarterly dues and abide by certain rules and regulations. Documents usually provided to prospective buyers include:

Rules and regulations

Covenants, conditions, and restrictions (CC&Rs) (originals and all changes)

Minutes from the last 3–12 monthly homeowner association meetings

Financial statements for a certain number of months

Reserve study

Planned special assessments

Recent major repairs or anticipated repairs

Bylaws and changes to bylaws

Pet restrictions (may be regulated, or prohibited by the state)

Allowed floor covering (for example, marble versus carpet)

Insurance coverage

Management company, if any

Association claims against the builder/developer (list of defects)

Any known information on current or anticipated lawsuits either against the association or by the association against another party

A good rule for buyers and their agents is to obtain all the records they can legally obtain. Buyers' agents sometimes do not realize that they have a duty to review these documents and advise their buyer clients regarding issues raised in them; for example, to point out that the association is planning to reroof the building and upgrade the electrical system, which will require each homeowner to pay an extra $2,000 assessment on homeowner dues; the association has not provided for sufficient reserve funds for emergencies; or the builder of the houses in the development is about to be sued for defective construction.

Even if buyers review this information carefully, and they should, the buyers' agents should site any areas of concern or material information in a separate memo to their clients. The buyers' agents may not know the consequences of this information but can recommend that their buyer clients consult with appropriate professionals for further review and recommendation. There is a company in California that provides review of all of these HOA documents and provides a report of its analysis at reasonable cost to buyers—well worth the cost. Other states may have similar companies providing this type of expert document review, or attorneys may perform this function in some states.

In one legal case, the occupants of a huge high-rise condominium building sued the builder and developer for defects that would have required the entire building to be evacuated for some 18 months and residents to be relocated elsewhere. In many other cases, owners of properties in planned unit developments have sued the builder and received funds for repairs to construction defects. Some owners made the necessary repairs, but others did not. Real estate agents should be aware of these situations in PUDs and condo projects. They should ask about any settled lawsuits, if the seller or prior owner received funds for repairs, and what was done to make those repairs. Real estate agents should also:

- *Question the seller regarding any insurance claims paid on damage from fire, hurricane, earthquake, water damage, neighbor disputes, etc.*
- *Carefully review the general property inspector's report and follow up on recommended additional inspections.*
- *Have available lists of various inspectors who may be required for additional inspections.*
- *Request, for investment properties and commercial transactions, all available financial data, repair records, agreements, leases, service providers, inspections, and citations, if any, from local agencies.* The agents should review this information with their clients.
- *Focus on investigating any issue where the buyer has expressed a clear need.* The buyer wants a lot of a specific size for a later subdivision, plans to add a second story, is concerned about the cost of insurance, or wants the home to be in a particular school district. If any of these or other issues stand out as significant concerns to a buyer, the agent should be sure to focus on finding the right information for the buyer or referring him or her to the right sources of information. The agent should give the information

Research and investigation are necessary to provide full disclosure of all relevant information.

to the buyer in written form and cite the source of the information, person spoken with, and the phone number as applicable.

- *Verify neighborhood speculation.* There may be neighborhood speculation concerning drug sales in the area, high crime, constant water intrusion problems, and so on. The agent for the buyer should try to either verify this information or refer the buyer to specific sources to allow the buyer to verify or disprove the information. Further property inspections may also be indicated by neighborhood issues.

THE DUTY OF THE BUYER TO INVESTIGATE

When assisted by their agent, the buyers have a duty to properly follow through on their investigation of the property and take their agent's advice on recommended inspections and document review. The buyers should contact a licensed general contractor to get a quote on known repairs or anticipated renovations and additions. Sometimes buyers may discover that what they wanted to do with the property is prohibited, limited, or cost prohibitive, and this is clearly material to their decision to buy.

THE DUTY OF THE GENERAL PROPERTY INSPECTOR TO INVESTIGATE

General property inspectors should understand the issues in the communities in which they are doing business. These are issues they should be sure to visually investigate at inspections. They should not hesitate to ask questions of the real estate agents and sellers concerning these issues.

If a property inspector has previously inspected this same property, he should pull his report from his records and review it, comparing what he found previously to his present inspection and ask questions of the seller related to his findings. In one legal case the inspector had inspected the property for the seller when he purchased and now, only a few years later, was inspecting it for another buyer. He never mentioned the prior report or searched for it in his files or compared his findings on the first inspection to his later inspection. The first inspection was of a distressed property in very poor condition. The second inspection gave the appearance of a remodeled and a well-decorated home. The inspector never asked the seller what had been done to repair the property defects previously observed. The general property inspector was sued.

The general property inspector should not hesitate to assist the buyer by reviewing property permits handed to him by the buyer or the seller, to examine building plans or receipts for major work done to the property, or to review the seller's and agent's disclosures to assist the buyers in their investigation.

THE DUTY OF THE BUILDER/DEVELOPER TO INVESTIGATE

Builders and developers need to assist buyers by providing research on local community facilities, such as shopping, schools, transportation issues, surrounding zoning matters, and so on. They should be sure to mention any current projects or planned development in the immediate area that may have a potential negative impact on their developments. Buyers will find out at some point, and a lawsuit may result. In one lawsuit against a builder, purchasers were not told about a planned major power transmission facility adjacent to the development. The builder/developer or the salespeople may also be real estate licensees and have all the duties of real estate licensees in the state.

Education is a progressive discovery of our own ignorance.

—Will Durant

17
CHAPTER

Documentation

Whoever said that the computer age would eliminate paper hasn't been involved in a real estate transaction. Even if agents feel the need to make room for the next client's pile of paper, they shouldn't give in to the temptation to toss or thin out old files, or they may be placing themselves at a huge legal disadvantage if a dispute develops later.

Broker managers, and those in brokers' offices who review files before they are put in storage, *please do not throw anything in those files out*, no matter how much space they take up! In many legal cases, it is often that one missing document the agent can remember but cannot find that would have made all the difference in proving what he or she really did in the transaction. Because agents change offices and can lose track of their office files which are out of their hands, it is wise for agents to retain their own file separate from their office on each transaction. This will mean lots of boxes of stored transactions, but it is a necessary fact of life in real estate. Some agents are now scanning their files for storage on disk.

HOW LONG SHOULD AGENTS KEEP THEIR RECORDS?

States vary in how long they require real estate agents to retain transaction records. Sellers and their agents must keep federal lead paint disclosure forms for three years after a transaction closes. Over the years I have seen lawsuits filed as far back as six years after the close of the transaction, but that is rare. Regardless of how long the state may require agents to keep their files, my best advice would be to keep all transaction files for at least five years.

The same advice holds true for buyers and sellers, builders, and developers. General property inspectors should retain the report and any notes, photos, or other documents they were given copies of, such as the seller's disclosure statement and permits, for at least five years. If general property inspectors reinspect a property for a subsequent buyer three years later, they should retain the first report as long as they retain the second one. That would be eight years for the first report and five years for the second one.

THE FILE AND THE LAWSUIT

The first thing an attorney will usually say to an angry buyer or seller who wants to sue is, "Bring me your file." Real estate agents want to be sure that what is in that file will represent their role in the transaction as competent and professional and that their actions represent *what a reasonable and prudent agent would do in the area.* An agent's file should also reflect conduct of *full disclosure, and reasonable care and diligence.* For the buyer and seller, it is equally important to retain all documents in the transaction to prove their case if errors have occurred.

Attorneys, who receive a one-inch-thick file of documents in today's paper-laden real estate transactions, will likely feel that much of what should have been retained was not retained or perhaps never existed. As a real estate broker, I have had residential transactions with files six inches thick or more. I know that my files will stand up to review by an attorney and are complete and in good order.

Keep thy shop, and thy shop will keep thee.

—George Chapman

WHAT SHOULD BE RETAINED IN THE TRANSACTION FILE?

Among the items that should be retained in the transaction file are:

- The principal documents that are part of the transaction, such as the listing agreement, purchase offer, counteroffers, agency relationship disclosures, property defects disclosure, escrow instructions, and repair agreements.

- State- and area-specific addenda recommended by the local and state associations of Realtors, by the real estate agent's franchise or brokerage, and by your errors and omissions insurance carrier.

- Backup documents that demonstrate that the property was priced properly and promoted legally. These include comparable sales data, sales brochures on the property, the MLS listing, property advertisements, caravan sign-in sheets, or business cards for brokers or buyers at open houses.

- Documents that pertain to the physical condition of the property and land, including land surveys, inspections (current and previous, if the seller has kept them), the preliminary title report, permits, receipts from the seller for major repairs or renovations made during the time of ownership, any repairs just made prior to sale, and current repair receipts for agreed-to buyer-requested repairs.

- Signed receipts from buyers that they had received any required or recommended disclosure pamphlets on lead-based paint, mold, earthquake safety, flood warnings, conducting inspections, and so on. Also, signed receipts for any disclosures regarding property condition, seller renovations, and any other document related to property condition.

- All correspondence, e-mails, faxes, and notes of phone calls and conversations between the principals and agents, as well as with third parties, such as with escrow or title agents, inspectors, or repair people.

- Any prior offers and their respective documents and correspondence.

- A log of transaction activities and forms indicating the date that they were signed by the appropriate party or parties. This form should be at the front of each agent's file and carefully reviewed before the transaction closes to be sure everything is signed and in the file. Even if a brokerage office has a "transaction coordinator" whose job it is to check that files are complete, remember that this person is never included in the lawsuit later. Each agent should check his or her own file.

- A conversation log should be kept of important conversations when advice or directives are given to clients, inspectors, repair people, and title officers. Not every conversation is worth noting; the log should relate to conversations for which a record would be helpful later. Would you remember who said what to whom on what day three years from now? What did the inspector say to the buyer when the buyer asked about the water intrusion problem? How did the seller answer the buyer's question about the roof leak at the property inspection? Agents should put these notes in their conversation logs. Buyers and sellers should keep their own conversation logs.

For Real Estate Agents Representing Buyers and for Buyers

The buyer's agent and the buyer should be sure to retain the following documents:

- All, or at least a representative number of, brochure sheets on each property viewed
- Copies of all comparative sales data run by the agent to assist in determining an offer price, signed and dated by the buyer as having been received
- Copies of all offers made by the buyer, even when the buyer lost out to another buyer or the buyer had an accepted offer but later dropped out of the transaction
- All documents received by the buyer or investigations done by the buyer on any property
- A checklist of all forms and disclosures used in the transaction for the buyer, with dates when each form or disclosure was signed

For Real Estate Agents Representing Sellers and for Sellers

The seller's agent and the seller should be sure to retain the following documents:

- Copies of all comparable sales data run by the agent to assist the seller in determining the list price, signed and dated by the seller as having been received
- A copy of the MLS listing, brochure handout sheet, and all advertising, with the seller initialing and dating each as approved by him or her for accuracy and content
- Copies of all open-house and broker caravan open-house sign-in sheets and business cards with each open house dated and the business cards attached
- Copies of all offers received, even though only one is accepted, with each marked with date and time received
- Copies of all accepted offers that fall out of escrow, with all documents generated by the transaction, particularly any investigations and inspections conducted by the buyer and turned over to the seller
- A checklist of all forms and disclosures used in the transaction for the seller, with dates that each form or disclosure was signed

Documentation is important for real estate agents, buyers, and sellers.

WHY ARE DATED AND SIGNED DOCUMENTS IMPORTANT?

During the transaction be sure that all documents, e-mails, faxes, memos, letters, and disclosures—*everything*—are dated. The person signing should write the date when he or she signs. The first thing I do as an expert witness in a lawsuit is to put all the documents I receive (escrow file, brokers' files, agents' files) in date order. Sometimes it is that one document without a date that would have made all the difference in defense of the agent or assisting the buyer or seller with the claim. Buyers and sellers too should be sure everything they generate in terms of correspondence is dated.

Buyers, sellers, and real estate agents should not automatically assume that everything sent by fax and e-mail is received. We have all had others tell us that they have e-mailed or faxed something to us, but we have not received it. Be sure to call the receiving party and verify that the document or correspondence was received. Note the date and time you confirmed receipt for your file.

Be sure that during the transaction all documents are properly signed and dated by all parties, including buyers, sellers, and real estate agents, who are affected by them. For example, the listing agreement is a contract between the seller and the listing agent, so both parties should sign and date it. All disclosure documents, of any kind, should be signed as having been received by buyer and seller. Copies of all disclosure documents, regardless of who generates them, should be made for the buyer, seller, and both real estate agents for their files.

In one recent legal case, the buyer's agent claimed to have questioned the seller and then written and typed a list of all the seller's disclosures of work that the seller made to the property, including jack leveling the house because of sagging floors. For whatever reason, the seller had omitted this material fact from the seller's disclosure statement. The buyer later claimed that he never received the faxed, typed document, and did not know about the jack leveling. The seller's efforts to repair the sagging floors were done without permits and ineffectively, and the buyer had to spend some $200,000 plus to actually make a proper repair. This agent made the following mistakes:

1. She did not request that the seller sign the list as an accurate representation of his disclosure.
2. She never confirmed receipt of the typed list by the buyer.

3. She never had the buyer sign the list as evidence that he had in fact received it and then faxed it back to her.
4. She could not find a copy of the list in her file or her office file, and the seller's agent was never given a copy of the list.
5. She could find only a handwritten copy of the list in the seller's file.
6. She could not find her conversation log, although she claimed to have made one.

This same scenario is repeated over and over in lawsuits.

Remember, excellence in any profession is in the details.

DOCUMENTATION AND FAIR HOUSING CLAIMS

In fair housing lawsuits, buyers will claim that their offer was not replied to or that the seller and the seller's agent said that another offer preceded theirs and was already accepted. Real estate agents and sellers should be sure to date and time-stamp every offer when it is received to be able to later show proof of when each was received.

All counteroffers should be dated and time-stamped when sent and when replies are received so as to keep a complete record.

DOCUMENTATION AND THE REPEAT TRANSACTION

Our culture is always on the move. It is estimated that people sell their homes and move, on average, every three to seven years. Just think of how far ahead the agents and the seller will be when the seller is ready to sell, if they have retained a complete file from when the purchase took place. Disclosure documents and inspection reports will be readily accessible to pass along to a new buyer. The likelihood of missing some significant disclosure will be greatly reduced, and so will the likelihood of a lawsuit.

For agents who have kept the file on a property they sold previously, they will be way ahead of other practitioners, if they are quickly able to pull out all the pertinent data at a listing appointment. Finally, remember, when in doubt, keep it.

DOCUMENTATION AND THE BROKERAGE OFFICE

A brokerage office should have documentation provided to each agent affiliated with its office outlining that office's fair housing policies, recommended procedures for handling multiple offers, and advice on communication with clients and customers, such as promptly returning phone calls, responding to requests, and providing reports on showings. It should advise its agents on requirements for maintaining transaction files, document retention, and working with service providers such as title, escrow, attorneys, inspectors, and lenders.

18

CHAPTER

Injuries and Safety at Properties

A prospective buyer tries to open a jammed window at a vacant property, breaks the glass, and severely cuts her hand; a seller's dog bites a prospective buyer; a child grabs the edge of the bowl on a pedestal cement birdbath, and the bowl falls hitting the child's head and killing him.

Think these accidents can't happen to sellers, buyers, and agents? All these situations describe actual cases that resulted in the real estate agents making frantic calls to their errors and omissions insurance carriers, the sellers placing frantic calls to their property insurers, and the buyers calling their lawyers. All these cases wound up in lawsuits and are only a few examples of what is possible regarding injuries at properties. Other situations I have encountered are buyers or agents tripping on stairs with resulting broken bones and a child receiving severe cuts walking into an unmarked, nontempered sliding glass door. Well, I think after a sigh of, "Please, no more," you have the general idea of what this chapter is about.

Duty of care means taking reasonable care not to cause damage or injury to another and taking reasonable safeguards to prevent such injury. Many of the property injury cases brought against real estate agents focus on negligence and duty of care. A real estate agent is considered a professional, and when showing a property a duty of care is imposed. This duty requires that the real estate agent apply his or her knowledge to be aware of risks and potential hazards and to inform others of those risks in order to prevent injury.

LIABILITY INSURANCE AND PROPERTY INJURIES

A seller's property liability insurance will probably cover injuries suffered on the property before a sale transaction closes, subject to any limitations in the policy. Many carriers are eliminating or severely reducing coverage for some types of incidents. Some insurers no longer cover injuries caused by certain breeds of dogs. In addition, some homeowners carry only fire insurance, which is usually required by their lender, but they may not carry liability coverage. The listing agent should be sure to check with the sellers when taking a listing that they have liability insurance and what it will and will not cover. The sellers' liability policy is the first line of defense in insurance coverage.

The agents' errors and omissions insurance may help to defend them in a personal injury suit, but it may not pay settlements or court awards. In some cases errors and omissions carriers exclude claims for personal injury. Errors and omissions carriers have also eliminated or reduced coverage for health-related injuries attributable to mold. It's vital for real estate agents to check with their errors and omissions carriers to determine exactly what, if any, liability coverage is provided.

All brokerages and independent agents should carry business liability coverage, which would pay claims for all or most personal injury claims. Sellers should have their property covered with liability insurance when listing their property for sale, if it is not already covered.

Early and provident fear is the mother of safety.

—Edmund Burke

WHAT TO DO TO PROTECT AGAINST PROPERTY INJURIES

Agents should be prepared and ask sellers during the listing presentation about any hazardous conditions or any health problems attributable to conditions at the property. Agents should examine the property they are listing for potential safety hazards. The listing agent should post warnings in the property description in the MLS and mark the area with a prominent sign, such as "loose railing on rear stairs." Better yet, agents should

Injuries at properties can result in lawsuits.

encourage the seller to get any hazards fixed or removed before showings begin. If hazards can't be removed or the seller won't remove them, the agent should tie a red flag to the low-hanging branch, put red tape at the front broken step, post a sign not to open the door where a dog is kept, and so on.

Agents showing a prospective buyer a property should check with the listing agent regarding any particular safety hazards before they visit with a buyer. The buyer's agent should also check with the buyer concerning any safety concerns he or she may have. For example, I have had buyers who will not go into a home where pets are not confined in one area, want to avoid a property with a long, winding stairway, or are fearful of properties on hillsides with decks 30 feet above the ground.

Agents should advise buyers to hold their child's hand at all times at showings and not allow the child to touch anything. If there are too many children to keep track of, suggest they stay with one parent in a single room or in the car when the agent shows the property. The parent watching the children can switch places with the other parent to view the property. Better yet, parents should leave young children at home when viewing property, at least until the parents narrow their search to a final one or two properties. Agents should make sure, no matter what, that there are arrangements to confine dogs and other pets during showings. Young children can be fearful and the elderly startled by other people's pets. The listing agent should ask the seller if the pet is covered under the homeowner's liability policy.

Agents should open exterior doors for buyer clients and advise them not to open windows. An agent should also carry a first-aid kit in the car to handle small cuts or bruises, while listing agents should check where the seller keeps first-aid supplies.

Real estate agents should put all disclosures of potential health hazards or dangerous conditions in writing to buyers and tenants. For example, in my area, hillside houses are particularly vulnerable to beehives in the spring, and we are now experiencing killer bee colonies. Any buyer would want to be put on alert to watch for swarming bees in the spring or unusual bee activity at balconies. Agents should not forget to warn buyers and tenants about possibly hazardous wildlife issues in the area. As development encroaches on animal habitats, more communities are seeing wild critters they may not have seen before. In my well-developed neighborhood, we sometimes see packs of coyotes when walking our dogs at night, or we need to be on the alert for rattlesnakes when gardening in the spring and summer. Recently, even bears and mountain lions have been seen in some backyards taking an afternoon dip in the pool or looking for someone's pet as a meal. These suggestions might sound extreme, but only a written disclosure offers absolute proof the agent provided a warning. However, agents will have to weigh their potential liability against scaring off buyers.

WHAT TO DO IF AN EMERGENCY OCCURS

Following is a list of suggestions for what agents should do in case of emergency:

- Call 911 immediately for any serious injury, such as a fall, cut, or dog bite.
- Don't transport the injured person to the emergency room unless there is no other option. The agents risk doing further injury and adding to their liability.
- Record the day and time of an accident, the names and telephone numbers of those involved, what happened, and report this promptly to their office and insurance carrier for agents, and to the homeowner's insurance carrier for sellers.

- Listing agents should report any injury at the property to the owner and to their broker immediately. Buyer's agents should also inform the listing broker and their own broker.
- Follow up with injured parties to check the status of their condition.

Many serious injuries, health problems, and deaths from accidents occur at homes and businesses every year. The best insurance, whether buyer, seller, or agents, is to plan ahead and know what to do when an injury occurs.

WHAT ABOUT INJURY FROM THEFT OR ASSAULT?

Every year hard working real estate agents and unsuspecting sellers are robbed or assaulted while sitting at open houses or showing property to someone who turns out to have motives other than buying or renting. Whenever strangers are given access to a property, just about anything is possible. Some people are perpetual open-house attendees whose real purpose is to either case the property for possessions and access for a later robbery or to steal whatever is immediately accessible. These folks are clever and usually hard to spot. They move from area to area so alert agents have trouble identifying them. Some precautions are advisable:

- Never sit an open house alone; always have someone with you.
- Be sure to notify your office or a neighbor that you are sitting an open house and provide the address.
- I always have a noise alarm or tear gas gun (I have a legal certificate to have one) with me at all times at open houses. Keep car and house keys in your pocket. Park your car in the street, so no one can block your car in a driveway. Better to be safe than sorry.
- Agents should always ask clients to meet them at the office and to provide a driver's license identification before clients get in the car with them to go to an open or vacant house.
- Sellers who try to sell their own homes are inviting in strangers every time they open the door. They should only open the door to someone who has made an advance appointment, and they should not be alone.

- When at a showing, mention that you are expecting your next appointment any minute.
- Explain your home's features, and let the buyers explore it on their own. Do not precede the prospect into bedroom, basements, attics, or garages.
- Do not volunteer too much personal information.
- Don't advertise your own home as secluded or vacant.
- I have a pamphlet, which I wrote, that I give to my seller clients that advises them how to be secure and how to secure their possessions when their property is listed for sale. For example,
  - Remove all calendars from view that show when the family will be away on a trip.
  - Hide all checkbooks, money, keys, credit cards, prescription drugs, wallets, and jewelry Thieves can open drawers, so lock these things up.
  - Identity theft is rampant, so lock up anything an identity thief might take.
  - Lock up small, valuable knickknacks that can fit in a purse or pocket.
  - Put away breakable items on tables that might be easily bumped into and broken.
  - Be sure any security system is working properly, and if you have an emergency code, be sure you know it. Prominently display security signs and security window stickers. Always remember to activate the security system when you're away.
  - Windows should be unobstructed by landscaping and should lock properly.
  - Check that all doors and windows are locked when you're away.
  - Have a porch light or other exterior lights on timers, so they are on in the evening whether you are home or not.
  - Have a few interior lights on timers also, so a prospective thief never knows when you are away.
  - Leave a TV or radio on when you are out, and leave the family dog inside.
  - Put away and lock up handguns and rifles.

LIABILITY WHEN THE SELLER'S PROPERTY IS DAMAGED OR AN INSPECTOR IS INJURED

What if the general property inspector falls off or through the roof? What if a buyer's small child knocks a valuable antique vase off a table? What if an appraiser leans on a railing that gives way and he falls, causing serious injury? The general property inspector, if you have chosen the right one, should have liability insurance to cover damage he may cause to the seller's property. Sellers should either remove valuable items from areas where they might be knocked over and broken or be sure that their homeowners insurance covers specifically listed antiques and other valuables. Most independent, sole proprietor inspectors and appraisers do not have worker's comp insurance to cover injuries in the course of their work at someone's property. Many larger firms may also not carry worker's comp insurance for their employees, or it may have expired. In most states, licensed contractors are required to carry worker's comp insurance on their employees, but this coverage may not cover the owner or contractor—only the employees.

What if an inspector is hired by the seller to conduct a prelisting inspection and is injured? The inspector might sue the seller, who might be covered under his homeowner's liability coverage. What if the buyer's general property inspector causes damage to the seller's property or is injured while inspecting the property? Some real estate contracts may state that the buyer is responsible for any damage to the seller's property caused by her selected inspectors. Most general property inspectors do not or cannot carry worker's compensation insurance on themselves, just on their employees. The buyer's property inspector who is injured at the inspection might sue the seller or the buyer.

An agent called me from New Jersey with an interesting liability situation. He was holding a public open house on a cold winter day. He had the heat on in the vacant house and left it on, he thought, when he closed up the house and left. Apparently, unknown to him, someone who had come into the house had switched off the heat. The seller's pipes froze, and now the agent was being presented with a bill for some $2,000 in damages. If the seller had liability insurance, it would have covered this situation. If the seller did not have liability insurance, the agent, or his broker, hopefully has liability insurance that will cover this claim.

Vacant properties listed for sale are susceptible to damage or unforeseen expense based on the possible lack of care by those who enter on a lockbox. I have seen listings where the party viewing the property turned the air-conditioning way up in the summer and forgot to turn it down before exiting, leaving the seller with a $350 electric bill. In other cases, the agent and client left a door open, and something was stolen, or the child accompanying the client spilled something that stained a sofa. It is very difficult in these situations to determine exactly who the offender is, and the listing agent may take the blame.

It is good policy for all agents to be vigilant when visiting a vacant property unsupervised, locking all doors and windows, returning the air-conditioning and heat to the arrival settings, and watching the client and the client's children to prevent any damage to the seller's property. Any damage that does occur should honorably be reported immediately to the listing agent.

19 CHAPTER

Dealing with Relatives and Friends

Real estate agents want to represent their relatives and friends in real estate transactions. These are the people we are all closest to and know we have their best interest at heart. New real estate agents, who have not yet formed a base of referral clients, tend to look to their relatives and friends for their start-up transactions. Perhaps it is this comfort level that causes some real estate agents to let down their guard or assume that their relative or friend would never sue them if something goes wrong. This same situation would exist for sellers who choose to act as their own agent and sell to a close friend or relative.

WHEN REAL ESTATE AGENTS REPRESENTING THEIR RELATIVE OR FRIEND DIDN'T WORK OUT

A lawsuit referred to earlier had even more dire consequences for the real estate broker, who was a dual agent and represented his mother-in-law, the seller. The buyer sued when extensive mold damage was discovered. The broker had to admit that he had been in the house some 120 times over 20 years, but said he never saw the mold. The mother-in-law repainted the house inside and out just before the sale. The mold started to appear through the paint within six weeks of the transaction closing. The son-in-law, who had been a broker for over 20 years, lost in court, as did the seller. The buyer was awarded $135,000 plus legal expenses from the seller and the broker. The broker's share of this award was not covered by his errors and omissions insurance and the mother-in-law's share of the court award was not covered by her homeowners insurance. The anguish of this lawsuit and the family discord it caused was a factor in the divorce of the broker from the seller's daughter.

An owner of a multiunit apartment building had bought several properties with the assistance of an agent who was his close friend for 30 years. He mentioned that he was considering selling his apartment building because of some gang activity in the area. The real estate agent assumed his friend wanted to list "now" and without taking the time to have his friend sign the appropriate documents, placed a listing in the MLS. Then the agent received two offers and signed an acceptance of one of the offers on behalf of his friend. When he told the property owner what he had done, the seller said he didn't really want to sell "now" and had changed his mind. The befuddled agent insisted he had to sell as the agent had already accepted one offer on his behalf. The agent had the seller sign documents after the fact. Part way through the transaction and before signing a grant deed or escrow instructions, the seller backed out, claiming he was being forced to sell when he didn't want to sell. The seller sued his longtime friend for misrepresentation. The prospective buyer sued the seller for specific performance, and the agent, the seller's friend, for misrepresentation. The agent friend settled the case with both his apartment owner friend and the buyer. The seller and buyer proceeded to court, with the seller defeating the specific performance claims of the buyer. Now an old friendship is ended.

Friendships like marriage are dependent on avoiding the unforgivable.

—John D. MacDonald

WHEN THE AGENT REPRESENTING A RELATIVE OR FRIEND WOULD HAVE WORKED OUT

Sometimes the real estate agent representing a relative or friend is really a good choice. For example, I had a longtime friend who for years promised me I would represent her and her husband in the sale of their home. I had remodeled some parts of the home for them and previously leased it twice. I really knew their home; it's good and bad points, and all of its apparent defects. I was shocked one day when my friend sent me a note telling me that she and her husband had listed their home with a "charming young gentleman" whose office was a little closer to their home than mine, and who was in contact with the "hip young couples" now buying in their area. Anyone who has ever sold real estate will tell you that this scenario is a punch in the stomach every time. The former friend had her house listed six to seven months before it sold to a single man, who promptly sued the charming young gentleman and the sellers. Sometimes sellers make a bad decision to list with a stranger, when the friend who really knows their home has more information to make the full disclosures that are necessary to protect the sellers. I have to believe that in this case my friends were afraid I "knew too much" about their home and would make "full disclosures." I would have made full disclosures and kept them out of the lawsuit. The friendship is over!

> My warning to sellers is not to fear making disclosures, but rather to fear not making them. The buyer always finds out.

No one wants to be in a lawsuit, especially with the people who matter most in our lives. The resulting family and friendship discord may not be resolved long after the lawsuit is ended. So how can real estate agents represent their friends and relatives safely and avoid lawsuits?

TIPS FOR REAL ESTATE AGENTS

Following are tips for real estate agents so that they can avoid lawsuits when they're representing relatives and friends:

- Avoid working in areas you are unfamiliar with and instead refer your relative or friend to an experienced agent in that area.
- Apply the same diligent effort to the transaction with a relative or close friend as you would with any client.
- Never accept any verbal authorization or assumed verbal authorization to sign any document for the relative or friend without an appropriate limited power of attorney.

- Don't hesitate to advise the relative or friend to drop out of a transaction, if this seems right, because their disappointment now is better than a lawsuit later.
- Don't assume more knowledge on the part of your relative or friend in buying or selling than you do for any other client. They require your same good advice.
- If you are listing a property for a relative or friend you have visited many times, the court may reasonably assume you had visual and informational knowledge of that property's condition beyond that of an agent who may have briefly visited once or twice. Disclose all defects you know or observe.
- Do not hesitate to recommend thorough inspections of any potential property defect.
- Sometimes a new licensee's first clients are relatives and friends. Until you are completely comfortable handling transactions on your own, work with a more experienced agent to ensure that all goes smoothly.
- Don't assume that if something goes wrong, your relatives or friends won't sue you. Their attorney may tell the damaged party they have no choice.

TIPS FOR BUYERS AND SELLERS

Following are tips for buyers and sellers who are working with a relative or friend on a transaction:

- Don't forgo working with your relative or friend in favor of a stranger, if the friend or relative is knowledgeable about your property, experienced in real estate, and knows your market area. Everyone appreciates earned loyalty, and ignoring your relative or friend can also result in losing the relationship.
- Do not expect relatives or friends to forget what they know or have observed about the condition of your property. Their knowledge can help to keep you out of a lawsuit.
- Don't encourage relatives or friends to assist you in an area you know is not in their normal working community, but rather ask them to refer you to a competent agent in that area from whom they might request a referral fee.

- Take the advice of your relative or friend agent when he or she recommends inspections and other investigations.
- If you want relatives or friends to act on your behalf, be sure to provide them with a limited power of attorney which clearly defines their responsibilities when they are signing documents for you.

20 CHAPTER

Property History and Future Events

THE IMPORTANCE OF PROPERTY HISTORY

Seller disclosure forms have become commonplace for sellers to disclose what they know about the physical components and condition of the property "at the present time." In some states, written disclosures are also required of the real estate agents documenting what they observe as "present property defects or possible problems." Should disclosures be made of history, such as a hurricane, tornado, or earthquake, that affected a property years ago? Should disclosures be made concerning defects or problems the seller believes have already been fixed? Should the seller or agents have to disclose lawsuits against the original builder or developer of the property that resulted in a settlement of funds to a buyer, perhaps not the current owner, for repairs? Should the seller or agents have to disclose knowledge of prior neighborhood problems, such as gang activity or flooding? Should disclosures be made of prior insurance claims settled with funds provided to the seller for repairs?

The answer to all these questions: *It is advisable to disclose historical property occurrences if the seller or agents have knowledge of them.*

The agents may be expected to have knowledge of some important historical facts that might have had an impact on the property in the area in which they are working. Examples of these issues are a murder at the property or a major landslide. In one current case, the listing agent for a property had been the seller's agent when the seller purchased a distressed property. The seller "fixed up" the property, and the listing agent listed the property as "totally remodeled." The property looked great with new flooring, tile, paint, and landscaping. The listing agent "assumed" that all of the property's previously disclosed problems had been repaired and never asked the seller about them. None of the history about the house was disclosed to the buyer. The buyer inspected the property, but again in this situation, the real problems were concealed beneath a beautiful decor. During heavy winter rains, the buyer experienced flooding into the house and drainage problems around the structure. During the process of repairs, the buyer found undisclosed mold that the prior owner had not remediated in her remodel. The neighbor next door informed the buyer that the property had a long history of flooding and that he had told the seller about this history, which she failed to disclose to the buyer. The buyer had extensive costs to repair and sued his agent, the seller's agent, and the seller.

What should the seller and the seller's agent have done in this transaction to prevent a lawsuit? They should have listed exactly what the seller found regarding the property's condition when she bought the house, exactly what she did and did not do in her remodeling to address these problems, and whether a licensed contractor was used for the work, including the contractor's name and phone number and copies of any permits obtained. Also, they should have disclosed what work, if any that required permits, was done without permits. The listing agent had observed what she thought looked like mold when the seller bought the house and should have asked the seller what she did about the suspected mold. The seller, in this case, did not inspect to confirm mold or conduct any remediation of the mold. The listing agent should have disclosed what she had observed looked like possible mold, pointed out the location, and recommended that the buyer have a mold inspection. If a listing is taken on a property which has been owned less than three years, it is a good idea to request a copy of the property disclosure form from the prior sale. If the property has been listed and taken off the market, request all disclosure documents prepared during that previous listing.

HISTORICAL DISCLOSURES AND INSURANCE CLAIMS

The 1994 earthquake in Los Angeles was a major natural event with billions of dollars in repair costs. Thousands of homeowners and owners of investment properties settled with their insurance companies for payment of repairs. Some of those who received funds for repairs spent only some of the money to make some of the repairs and spent the rest on other things, or they made no repairs at all. I am still asking sellers today if they owned their property during the earthquake, what damage the property sustained, what funds they received, and what repairs they had made. If the property was sold to them after the earthquake, what did the seller tell them about earthquake damage and repairs?

In another lawsuit the seller had experienced a major water intrusion problem. He received $95,000 from his insurance company to make repairs. He carpeted and painted and did other minor repairs, but pocketed most of the money. The buyer moved in, and a few days later the next-door neighbor came by and asked what the buyer thought about the repairs made by the seller after the "big flood." The buyer asked, "What big flood?" and called an attorney. They discovered that a great deal of damage had been covered over and not repaired. The two agents involved were sued along with the seller, who had left the country and left the agents holding the bag. The agents in this case should have questioned the seller regarding insurance claims paid and asked for an itemized list of repairs, along with receipts for work that was done.

In 2005 Los Angeles had a winter with twice the normal rainfall. News reports showed roof collapses, hillside slippage, and flooding. I will be asking sellers for many years to come what water damage they may have experienced during those heavy rains. Real estate agents in Florida will be asking sellers about hurricane damage, along with agents across the Gulf Coast, to be sure that they fully disclose what happened to the property and what was done to repair it.

BUILDER LAWSUITS AND HISTORY

It's a good idea for every brokerage office to have a list of developments, whether planned single-family communities, condominiums, or invest-ment properties, where over time they have come to learn of major prop-erty defects or history that are material facts and should be disclosed to buyers.

In one development in California I have consulted on at least five law-suits. The original builder/developer was sued in a class action lawsuit by the original buyers for water intrusion problems, mold, and poor property drainage. The property owners received funds from the builder/developer in a settlement to allow each homeowner to make his or her own repairs. Some homeowners did make the necessary repairs; others did not. Real estate agents in the area of this development should be well informed of its history. They should be sure that all buyers are informed and encouraged to inspect whether or not these repairs were carried out and check for relevant permits, which would have been required to make the repairs.

DON'T PREDICT FUTURE EVENTS

Buyers sometimes look to their agents for guarantees or assurances of future events, but agents must be careful not to predict the future. Some examples of predictions agents should not make are:

- Houses in this neighborhood do not have land movement and geo problems (a really bad prediction in California!).
- Property values in this area go up by 10 percent a year.
- There is no way that you won't make money on this property.

"I guarantee you that this property will be worth $3,000,000 in no time!"

The better way for an agent to describe any of these situations would be:

- The sellers advise me that no homes in this area have had land movement problems that they know of. However, since the property is on a hillside, I recommend that a structural engineer and geologist inspect the property.
- Property values over the past five years have gone up by 10 percent per year, but I have no way of knowing what future value increases will be.
- The financial data on this investment property indicate a present positive cash flow on the offer terms proposed; however, there is no guarantee concerning future profitability.

The second set of statements removes the future predictions and does not place the real estate agent in a position of guarantor of some situation he or she can't possibly know.

21 CHAPTER

Rental Property Transactions and Property Management

Real estate agents are frequently involved in renting properties as well as property sales. Many property owners may also decide sometime to rent a property they own. Some owners will hire a real estate brokerage firm to manage the rental property for them, while others will choose to manage the rental property themselves. Lawsuits can definitely result from rental property transactions.

THE IMPORTANCE OF RENTAL PROPERTY FORMS AND DOCUMENTATION

The most important document in the rental property transaction is a comprehensive rental agreement. The rental agreement should, at a minimum, include the following:

- The start date and ending dates of the term of the lease
- The means of lease extension and lease termination
- The circumstances under which the owner or property manager may enter the property
- Responsibility for repairs and maintenance
- Penalties for late or nonpayment of rent

- Renovations or alterations to the property allowed or not allowed to be made by the tenant
- Notice for termination or eviction of the tenant
- Numbers and names of persons permitted to reside at the property, other than occasional guests
- Deposits required and their application or circumstances for refunding
- Whether pets are allowed and which kinds of pets and the number of pets
- Insurance coverage and requirements
- Activities that may or may not be carried out at the property, such as a home business or type of business
- Furnishings or contents provided and their required condition when the property is vacated

Having owned rental property myself, I am often amused by the late night infomercial gurus who espouse the ease of owning and managing rental property. You just buy it with nothing down, rent it for a profitable cash flow, and become a millionaire overnight! I regret that my own experiences with rental properties seem more suited to an evening soap opera script. A few tenants did the following:

- Chopped down three 35-foot palm trees in the rear yard with no explanation.
- Had their handyman-boyfriend rewire the house's electrical system and changed light fixtures without my authorization and without grounding the electrical system, nearly burning the house down, and oh, they forgot to pay the rent.
- Dug up my landscaping and took it with them when they left.
- Changed all the wallpaper without my approval to something ugly, which promptly started to peel off.
- Terrified the next-door neighbor with a 160-pound dog that was supposed to be kept restrained.
- Developed a rat problem because of less than sanitary cleaning procedures. I was grateful not to have been asked to dinner by this doctor and his wife.
- Had difficulties with his executive recruiting business and decided to try growing marijuana on my rental property. He

vacated so fast that he left his clothes in the washer and no forwarding address!

- Decided to jump off the roof into the rear swimming pool, severely damaging the roof and nearly breaking their necks.
- Decided to call a plumber on their own to clear the kitchen sink jam. The plumber knocked the fitting off a pipe under the house. They later called about a smell that turned out to be the sink disposal material that was accumulating under the house, which was caused by the separated pipe and fitting.

I think you get the idea. I have wondered how the TV gurus find their perfect tenants. They must be very different from mine. Believe me, I checked references, employment, bank reserves, Social Security numbers, and current and prior landlords. None of which prevented the above list of calamities. I later found out from the local police that the marijuana grower was being pursued by the police with a warrant for his arrest and had a criminal record. From that point on I added "check for criminal record" to my application checklist. What saved me in all these circumstances was thorough paperwork and documentation, which allowed me to pursue the departing tenants in court for damages and rent—all except the one growing marijuana who fled to parts unknown. He did leave me a phone message to keep his security deposit. The TV gurus never seem to discuss the tenants who don't pay the rent or damage the property, and I've always wondered why.

Following are some rental contract items that can help recovery of damages by tenants:

- Never permit the tenant to modify, remodel, repair, redecorate, or change anything without the owner's express written consent for that item, and print this statement in boldface type on the contract.
- Make sure that there is a clause in the contract to allow the owner or the owner's representative to enter the property at least once monthly, even if it is to check the operation of the smoke detectors. If I had done this, I would have seen those marijuana plants!
- Be wary of the tenant who pays in cash. Insist in the contract on a cashier's check or check drawn from the tenant's local bank. This will facilitate collecting on a court order to recover funds, since you will know the bank and the account number of the tenant.

Renters will sometimes do the unpredictable.

- Check in with the neighbors occasionally to ask about the tenant and any problems they have experienced or observations they may have made that you should know about. The next-door neighbor wondered why the tenant was digging up my landscaping and taking it but never called me.
- Be sure the neighbors have the owner's or owner's representative's phone number to call in an emergency. I was very grateful to the neighbor who called me while my tenant was on vacation to tell me that water was pouring out of somewhere on the property and flooding onto the street.
- Be sure that a property condition form is signed by the tenant and that it also references the condition of any owner contents left at the property for the tenant's use, including refrigerators, clothes washers, furniture, and so on. Any existing defects should be noted.

- A walk-through inspection using the property condition form from move-in should be used on move-out and provided to the tenant with documentation of all new damages not considered normal wear and tear.
- Be sure that your insurance policy is written for a "nonowner occupied" situation. I have a case now dealing with a property owner who sold his property on a "lease with option to buy" and never notified his insurance company that he was no longer occupying the property. A mold and water intrusion problem was denied coverage by the insurer based on this change in coverage condition.
- Be sure that the contract requires the tenants to obtain renters insurance on their contents and ask for a copy of the active policy. The 1994 Los Angeles earthquake caused some damage to one of my rental properties and damaged some of the tenant's belongings. The tenant had renters insurance.
- Any pet that is allowed in a rental must be a breed that can be covered under a renter's insurance policy and/or an owner's policy. Note that the tenant should be limited to two pets. Also an additional pet deposit is customary. All damage caused by the pets must be paid for by the tenant.
- Have liability coverage on any rental property and clearly state in the contract what actions that may be hazardous to a tenant are prohibited—though I have to admit I would have never thought about jumping off the roof into the pool!
- Address noise issues, parties, and large group activities, and specify what is and is not permitted.
- Always plan on having adequate reserve funds for repairs and mortgage payments in the event tenants cause damage or there is difficulty with prompt eviction or collecting rents owed.

On numerous occasions I found myself in court, usually small claims court, trying to collect back rent or property damage claims. I am glad to say that with the exception of the marijuana grower, I collected on every one and saved myself considerable money, if not aggravation. On occasion I also found myself in superior court, with the assistance of an attorney, regarding a tenant eviction. Depending on the laws in each state, tenant evictions can be quick or exceedingly slow. In California it can take as long as six months to evict a wily deadbeat tenant. In one case regarding a client's property, I showed up with the sheriff who had to usher the tenant off the property. He was in the act of moving and loading the moving van. I felt compelled to warn the moving company to collect via cash or a cashier's check to avoid getting a bum check from this deadbeat.

I have consulted on numerous cases involving rental property, including a commercial tenant who rented a space to use as a fitness center only to find out later that the premises were not zoned as applicable for that use. Tenants have suffered injuries or assaults called "acts of third parties" at properties and sued the owner. Owners and their property managers must be careful to repair any safety hazard and provide well-lighted and secure premises for tenants. Smoke detectors are routinely required, and carbon monoxide detectors are a good idea. Fireplaces need routine inspections for proper and safe operation. Property management cases involving liability for injuries resulting from adverse conditions in common areas are very common. In one "slip and fall" case at a commercial building, the employee of the tenant slipped in a parking space reserved for the handicapped when he was getting out of his car on his crutches. The downspout from the roof drained directly into the handicap parking space, causing the fall on a rainy day. There are cases of tenants causing excessive damage resulting in constant repairs to plumbing, such as throwing things that are unsuitable into drains or the toilet. These types of issues should be addressed in the "rules and regulations" of the building or property and made a part of the contract. Tenants frequently sue owners who fail to adequately maintain the property, resulting in "uninhabitable" conditions. I had one case in Beverly Hills in which a tenant was paying $10,000 per month to lease a house and found the house infested with black widow spiders and rats. The owner denied any responsibility and was unwilling to correct these conditions.

Property owners and real estate agents involved in property leasing and/or management should be sure to utilize comprehensive and up-to-date rental documents, covering those conditions and situations that could potentially lead to a lawsuit. Learn the requirements in your state and local area regarding leasing certain types of property, and follow those requirements. Check if the property is affected by rent control, requires retrofitting when utilized in a certain way, is compliant with handicap access regulations, and is safe for occupancy. Sometimes when owners are not sure of the condition of their rental property or what may need repair, it is a good idea to have a general property inspection of the property before it is rented. Owners can then make the necessary repairs prior to renting.

It is also a good idea for owners of rental properties to check their permit history to be sure that all areas of the property requiring permits are permitted. A tenant may claim later that nonpermitted work caused their problem and the lawsuit.

AGREEMENTS BETWEEN THE PROPERTY OWNER AND THE PROPERTY MANAGER

If a real estate agent is acting as a property manager for an owner, it is recommended that the agent and property owner have a signed agreement covering the agent's responsibilities. It is common practice to have the property owner sign an indemnity agreement to indemnify, defend, and hold harmless the real estate agent from any lawsuit filed by a tenant. The real estate agent property manager should further require that he or she be named as an additional insured under the property owner's liability policy. It is recommended that an attorney review the agreement. Once the agreement is signed, the real estate agent should request confirmation of the "additional insured" status on the property owner's liability policy. This is a common request and will not usually increase the cost of the insurance to the property owner.

Experience is the worst teacher; it gives the test before presenting the lesson.

—Vernon Law

22

CHAPTER

Title and Encroachments

THE PRELIMINARY TITLE REPORT

The preliminary title report, often referred to as the "prelim," is one of the most important transaction documents and one of the most overlooked and underutilized. Buyers tend to glance at the prelim and often do not understand the significance of what it contains. Some real estate agents may not give the prelim the full attention it deserves. Every for-sale real estate transaction should require title insurance, and a request for title insurance should produce a prelim before the close. In some states real estate agents may be able to access this information from property records and may not receive a prelim. Some states use "title commitments," which are similar to a policy of title insurance, but they list the items that must be cleared prior to the close of the transaction. The prelim will usually include the following, although each state may have its own format of coverage:

- Ownership of subject property
- Manner in which current owners hold title
- Matters of record that specifically affect the subject property or its owners
- Legal description of the property

- An informational plat map
- Type of title insurance offered by the title company
- Exclusions and exceptions in the title insurance
- Coverage
- Recorded deeds of trust or mortgages, or other liens
- Easements
- Agreements
- Covenants, conditions, and restrictions (CC&Rs)
- Present taxes

IS THE SELLER REALLY SIGNING?

The first thing to check in the prelim is who is listed as the owner on title.

> Primary to every real estate transaction is that the seller of the property must have clear title to sell the property.

Sometimes the person signing the contract of sale is only one of two or more owners on title, and the other parties on title may or may not have agreed to the sale. It is important to have all owners sign the contract and agree to the sale in order to have "clear title" transferred to the new owner. In some cases, one owner may be authorized to sign the contract for another owner, or someone not an owner may also be authorized to sign the contract for one or more owners. This situation may occur in a trust sale when there is an executor of an estate, or when the owner on title is out of the area and unable to sign. Improperly signing a contract may later invalidate the contract or result in rescinding of the contract. Real estate agents should always check ownership status before listing a property for sale by requesting a *property profile* from the title company or by checking the county Web site where available.

EASEMENTS AND ENCROACHMENTS

One of the most frequent legal difficulties in real estate transactions involving title insurance is the issue of easements and encroachments.

These types of disputes usually result in neighbor-to-neighbor lawsuits after the sale. Easements are recorded, whereas encroachments are usually not recorded but may or may not be apparent in a visual inspection of the property. It is a good idea to ask the seller what he or she knows about easements and encroachments affecting the property. Just where are the property boundary lines, and does anyone else have a legal right of access? Easements and rights of way are frequently misunderstood by buyers. They are listed in the prelim and usually reference a neighbor's right to cross over a certain part of the property to access his or her own property or refer to the right of way of a utility company for access to poles and lines. Another right of way may be for future construction of an access road. Usually easements may not be constructed upon or fenced so that they obstruct the party who is allowed access from gaining access. Problems result when buyers either do not fully understand where the easement or right of way is on the property or do not understand how it affects their ability to use the property as they had planned to use it.

Currently, I am consulting on three legal cases that are the result of issues in the prelim not fully being understood at the time of sale. Unfortunately fences may not make good neighbors when they extend several feet over the neighbor's property line or into right of way areas and easements. Some states require a land survey when a property is sold, but some do not. Surveys can be quite expensive and if not required, many buyers may decide to avoid the cost. However, the cost later may prove to be much greater.

In the prelim each easement or right of way is listed. Usually a note follows that if further information is needed, the title officer should be contacted. Buyers and their agents should not hesitate to speak to the title officer concerning the nature of the easements and rights of way. If these documents require further interpretation, the buyer should consult with an attorney or land surveyor.

TREES, FENCES, AND TITLE

A property owner has the right to trim vegetation extending or hanging over a boundary line, but not to kill the tree. Neither neighbor has the right to destroy or damage a tree that is on the boundary line without the consent of the other. View protection laws may permit the neighbor whose view is obstructed to reclaim the view by trimming the neighbor's obstructing trees at the expense of the neighbor who is trimming the trees.

"Hi, I'm your new neighbor. There is no easy way to say this, but your living room is on my property."

Some laws protect certain species of trees. If you are planning to cut down the huge tree in the front yard to allow for a room addition, you might want to check whether that ancient oak tree is protected and cannot be removed.

Who owns and maintains a fence is determined by whose land the fence is on. The classic case is the new neighbor who informs the next-door neighbor that he intends to move his side yard fence to reflect "the true property line." His new land survey has found that the true property line cuts through a portion of the neighbor's living room, which had been expanded without a permit. This situation reflects an actual case that resulted in a lawsuit between the neighbors, involving the sellers of both properties and the real estate agents.

WHAT DOES TITLE INSURANCE COVER?

A standard coverage policy of title insurance may cover hidden defects including:

- Lack of a right of access to and from the land
- A forged signature
- Impersonation of the real owner

- Mistakes in interpretation of wills or other legal documents
- Deeds delivered without the consent of the grantor
- Undisclosed or missing heirs
- Deeds and mortgages signed by people of unsound mind, by minors, or by persons supposedly single but who are actually married
- Recording mistakes and missed recorded documents
- Falsification of records
- Errors in copying or indexing
- Fraud
- A document is not properly signed, acknowledged, or delivered

The preliminary title report is an offer to insure under certain circumstances; the title policy is a contract to insure. Every person purchasing a property should get an "owner's title policy." The policy will indemnify the insured against losses resulting from a covered claim and provide for legal fees and defense of the property.

Extended owner's and lender's policies provide broader coverage and are available through the American Land Title Association (ALTA). Additional coverage is extended and might cover:

- Unrecorded liens and encumbrances
- Unrecorded easements
- Unrecorded rights of parties in possession, arising out of leases, contracts, or options
- Encroachments, discrepancies, or conflicts concerning the boundary lines
- Mechanics' lien protection
- Forced removal of the structure under certain circumstances
- Building permit violations committed by prior owners
- Map inconsistencies protection
- Post-policy encroachment, forgery, adverse possession, and prescriptive easement

Real estate agents should not assume that all title policy companies are the same and should question the title company as to what is covered by its policies.

RED FLAGS TO WATCH OUT FOR

There are possible red flags in the prelim that can be transaction problems and are sometimes overlooked until the last minute before the transaction closes. Preliminary title reports also contain requirements that once compiled could also disclose more issues, for example, the "statement of information," which is used to check for liens and judgments against property owners. Some of these red flags might be:

- *Mechanics' liens.*
- *Name of recorded owner different from seller's name on the contract of sale.*
- *Foreclosure.*
- *Notice of action or lis pendens, which is an action filed against a property to delay or impede a transaction.*
- *Bankruptcy.*
- *Uninsured deed requirements.* Title companies are facing more litigation because of their reliance on unescrowed, uninsured transfers of title for little or no value. These transfers are sometimes negotiated by persons in an attempt to commit fraud. The property is deeded to someone by a person who is not the real owner.
- *Access.* Although access to the property (not landlocked) is a covered situation in a title policy, it can be removed by a schedule B exception.
- *Common sense.* This is probably the asset buyers of real estate seem to forget most. If something doesn't make sense, question it until you get an acceptable answer.

TITLE INSURANCE AND THE BUYER'S LENDER

Title insurance is usually, if not always, required if the buyer is taking a mortgage loan on his or her property at the time of purchase. Sometimes the title policy required by the lender will require that a land survey be made, even if this is not a part of the purchase contract between buyer and seller. The buyer will sometimes not receive a copy of the surveyor's report, but can ask for it from the lender.

23

CHAPTER

Discrimination

No one wants to face a discrimination lawsuit—not sellers or their agents. Discrimination goes against the most basic principles of democracy and fair play. We are all considered equal, including situations related to housing, whether renting or purchasing.

I regret that I have had sellers say to me more than once, "I don't want to sell to that [ethnic group]." My answer is always, "Every buyer and every offer must be considered only on its merits and not on any other criteria, or I cannot be your real estate agent." Every member of the National Association of Realtors pledges to avoid discrimination.

> *Each time a man stands up for an ideal, or acts to improve the lot of others, or strikes out against injustice, he sends forth a tiny ripple of hope.*
>
> —Robert F. Kennedy

ADVERTISING THE RIGHT WAY TO AVOID DISCRIMINATION

All advertising for rental and for sale property should avoid any implication of discrimination, and this includes discrimination against families with children, unless the development or building is classified as a "senior citizen residence." Disability and familial status are two protected classes that have been added to the Fair Housing Act. Agents and sellers should avoid language such as:

- No children under age 10
- Perfect for young married couple
- Devout Christians welcome
- No facilities or yard for children
- Close to synagogues

Real estate ads should also avoid including any religious symbols that might imply preference for one group or exclusion of another group.

Advertising should not be discriminatory based on where it is placed, such as only in the publication of a particular religion. Advertising can be placed in such a publication as long as it is also placed in the general media that are open to anyone, and/or placed in the MLS (multiple listing service).

PROPERTY SHOWINGS AND DISCRIMINATION CLAIMS

Agents and sellers must be sure to allow equal and fair access to properties for sale or rent, so that they may be seen by prospective buyers or renters, before an offer is made. For investment properties, such as apartment buildings, all prospective buyers may be told to "drive by only" and view each unit with an accepted offer only. This request places all prospective buyers in the same situation and is not discriminatory. I consulted on a discrimination lawsuit in which the prospective buyer, a member of a Native American group, claimed that the sellers refused access to the MLS listed property, and speaking through a closed door, said they did not want to sell to Indians. The sellers denied the claim. The agent claimed that the property was listed on a Friday but that the sellers did not want any showings until Monday, and the prospective buyer had showed up knocking on the sellers' door on Sunday. The sellers had said, "Please come back Monday." The prospective buyer's agent lived across the street from the listed property and claimed to have seen a prospective buyer enter the listed property for viewing on Sunday.

Agents and their seller clients need to have a clear policy established for showings that will not have any implication of discrimination, and they must apply the criteria to all prospective buyers. Listing agents should indicate when showings will be available and whether there are days or times the seller cannot or will not allow showings, such as:

- No property showings until broker's open house Tuesday, May 23, 11 a.m.–2 p.m., and Sunday public open house, May 28, 2 p.m.–5 p.m.
- Showings not available weekends and evenings

PROCEDURES FOR DEALING FAIRLY WITH OFFERS TO RENT OR BUY

In hot real estate markets, sellers and their agents are often in receipt of many incoming offers and are sometimes unsure of how to handle these offers to avoid any implication of discrimination. Listing agents also have the obligation to try to achieve the highest price and most favorable terms for their clients. Among real estate agents, there may be a concern that the sellers' agents may favor an offer in which they can represent both buyer and seller and thereby receive more commission. Where dual agency is allowed, listing agents must be very careful to consider each offer on its merit, whether or not they represent the buyer, an associate from their office represents the buyer, or the buyer is represented by another real estate firm. Such discrimination is a violation of the National Association of Realtors code of ethics and may also be perceived as an act of discrimination, exposing an agent to a possible charge of discrimination from a buyer or renter.

When an agent or a seller acting on his or her own behalf anticipates receiving multiple offers on a property or many applications to rent, the following guidelines can reduce the possibility of a lawsuit for discrimination:

1. A listing agent should review with the seller what procedure the seller wants to follow regarding multiple offers before the receipt of any offers. For example, does the seller want to reply to each offer as it is received, or does the seller want to set a date to review all offers and then reply to the offers?

2. A listing agent or seller should not verbally claim he or she is or expects to be in a multiple-offer situation or check the multiple-offer box on a counteroffer form, if the agent or seller is not expecting or has not received multiple offers.

3. If a listing agent has been notified by more than one buyer's agent that they are writing an offer, the listing agent should:
   a. Notify each buyer's agent of this fact and the seller's desired procedure for replying to multiple offers.
   b. Give each offer a fair chance to be reviewed by the seller:
      i. Such as request that all offers be presented by a certain date and time.
      ii. Indicate that the seller will review all offers and counter each if he or she chooses, allowing each offer the same time interval for a response.
      iii. Seller counters should be based on the specific offer and may not be the same to each offer, but they will be based solely on the merits of each offer.
      iv. If additional offers are received by the seller or the seller's agent, the seller or the agent will inform all agents representing buyers allowing all to respond with their best and final offers.
      v. If the seller is countering more than one offer, the counteroffer should say that the seller has the "right of final decision" on any counter accepted by a buyer to avoid selling the property to more than one buyer at the same time.

4. All offers should be given equal consideration, regardless of the real estate office or agent. The listing agent owes a fiduciary duty to the seller to help him or her obtain the best price.

5. The listing agent should not reveal the existence of any one offer to another agent or buyer unless the listing agent is revealing this fact to all agents making offers. An agent should carefully consider whether to reveal the price and terms of any offer, because this may result in offers being submitted with the buyer indicating that the offer is confidential. If the price and terms of an offer are revealed to an agent making an offer, they should be revealed to all others making offers. Agents should check whether revealing the price of an offer to another prospective buyer is permitted in their state.

6. Another approach rather than revealing any one offer's price or terms would be to indicate to all offers being countered that the

seller has rejected, or will reject, for example, offers under $400,000 and with more than a 60-day escrow.

7. If the listing agent is a dual agent representing one of several buyers making offers, the listing agent should obtain a signed acknowledgment from the seller that he or she cannot reveal the buyer's price or terms to other agents submitting offers without breaching the fiduciary duty to that buyer. This will help to clarify the nature of dual agency to the seller.

8. At no time should the listing agent indicate to any agent or buyer what he believes his seller client will accept in regard to price and terms. This could be regarded as a breach of fiduciary duty to the seller, as well as lead to a possible discrimination lawsuit. The appropriate reply of the listing agent to the buyer or buyer's agent who asks, "What do you think the seller will accept?" would be, "Please put your offer in writing for my seller's consideration."

The listing agent has a duty to present all offers to the seller. To tell all agents representing buyers presenting offers of the existence of other offers may, for example, cause all buyers to back out leaving the seller with no offers. The policy reviewed and agreed to by the seller and the seller's agent must not be discriminatory in any way and should be documented for the transaction file.

If offers start to arrive by fax or in person, the listing agent or seller should be sure to date and time stamp the arrival of each offer. Each offer will indicate a date and time during which the offer is effective and will then expire. The agent, or seller not represented by an agent, should then contact each prospective buyer or renter, preferably in writing, and indicate when the seller or landlord will reply to offers that are received. If the seller chooses to reply with acceptance or a counter to a specific offer as it is received, the agent or seller should be sure to date and time stamp the counter or acceptance and promptly notify any other offers that may be forthcoming. The seller may reply to an offer with a counteroffer that indicates, even if signed by the buyer, that the seller reserves the right to final acceptance. The seller may elect to place a similar or better offer in backup position to the accepted offer, if this is acceptable to the prospective buyer. The backup offer should be truthfully in backup status if the accepted offer falls out for any reason. The seller and the seller's agent should be very careful to treat the accepted offer fairly, regardless of whether the backup offer is similar or better. Agents, buyers, and sellers should consult with legal counsel when there is a question in dealing with discrimination issues.

The real estate agent should not disclose the racial composition or ethnic diversity of a neighborhood to a prospective buyer, even if asked to do so by the buyer. This information given to a buyer could result in a discrimination claim of unlawful "steering" or suggesting that a buyer avoid a neighborhood because of its racial or ethnic composition. Providing general information, such as that found in a property profile, is not discriminatory. This report will summarize price ranges of properties, education and income levels of residents, and location of public services, such as schools, stores, restaurants, and religious facilities. Real estate agents should handle all transactions in a similar manner regarding any issue related to discrimination to prove a policy of nondiscriminatory conduct.

Discrimination can happen whether the market is a hot sellers' market or a buyers' market. Careful and fair practices in dealing with offers, counteroffers, and offers to rent are the right policy for any brokerage or property owner. Sellers and their agents should review both federal and state regulations regarding fair housing to be sure that their actions are in full compliance with the law.

Integrity has no need of rules.

—Albert Camus

24

CHAPTER

New Construction

According to the National Association of Home Builders (NAHB), in 2004 home builder liability was calculated to add to the cost of new construction by between $2,700 and $15,000 per housing unit. NAHB estimated that for every $1,000 price increase, 260,000 households are being priced out of the market.[1] Lawsuits have led to rising or limited liability insurance for builders. Coverage for builders on mold has also been excluded by the insurance carriers. Amid rising defect litigation and soaring insurance costs, major builders and their insurers are requiring third-party reviews throughout the building process. Builders owe buyers an implied warranty of habitability and quality workmanship and materials.

SOME OF THE CAUSES OF BUILDER LAWSUITS

Among the causes of the increased number of builder lawsuits are:

- Only marginal land is still available, thus increasing the cost to prepare the land
- A lack of skilled workers

---

[1] Rhonda Jackson, "To Repair or Not to Repair," *Professional Builder*, April 2006, pp. 39–40.

- Substandard material selection and poor design
- Not completing the project
- Mishandling of deposits

WHAT CAN BUILDERS DO TO REDUCE THE NUMBER OF LAWSUITS?

There are many improvements builders can and are making to improve the quality of construction and reduce the number of lawsuits. These include:

- Investing in worker training
- Conducting inspections at crucial stages of construction.
- Promptly responding to customer complaints
- Initiating tougher quality standards
- Exercising caution in adopting new and unproven products and technology
- Allowing buyer's inspections and heeding inspection results
- Making all prudent disclosures to buyers regarding on-site and off-site issues

THE PROBLEM WITH EXTERIOR INSULATION FINISH SYSTEMS

Exterior insulation finish systems (EIFS) also called *synthetic stucco* have been used in certain parts of the country and have resulted in numerous cases of water intrusion and rotted framing. Applying EIFS correctly is expensive and complicated. In some areas EIFS has been banned. Any property with EIFS needs to disclose this fact, and property inspectors need to be on the alert for it. There are possible tests that can be conducted to determine high moisture readings in walls. The seller of a house with EIFS that has been repaired must describe in detail how it was repaired. There is debate on what constitutes an adequate EIFS repair, short of its total removal from the entire house. A structural engineer should be called to inspect a property with EIFS.

WHAT CAN BUYERS DO TO PROTECT THEMSELVES AND CHOOSE THE RIGHT BUILDER?

First of all the buyer should make sure that the builder is licensed. Check complaints, if any, against the builder with the state contractors license board and the Better Business Bureau. Talk to the local building inspector about the builder. Call homeowner advocacy groups, the county district attorney, and the state attorney general's office. Inquire about past defect litigation claims and insurance coverage. Some builders do learn from their past mistakes and correct them. Read the annual survey conducted by *Professional Builder* magazine that ranks major home builders on customer satisfaction. Check state laws regarding builder warranty programs and the statute of limitations on construction defect claims. Check what is and is not covered in the builder's warranty. Seek the advice of a local real estate agent familiar with the builder. A qualified real estate agent will have a reasonably good idea of how satisfied buyers are with the builder's product and the resale and appreciation history of the builder's developments. Ask an attorney for assistance in reviewing the developer or builder's contract before you sign away rights or release the builder from further liability for specific flaws or future defects. Ask the builder for a copy of all permit records on the property. Have an engineer evaluate the builder's soils report and structural calculations.

A buyer who visits the building site on a regular basis and talks to the builder and the crew, and takes notes and photos, will likely end up with a better-constructed home. Any property problem should be documented with photos, and a certified letter should be sent to the builder requesting prompt corrective action. Ask builders for a list of developments or other homes they have built, and drive by them. Ask homeowners you see how satisfied they are with their homes and how the builder handled any problems they may have had.

25 CHAPTER

Appraisals

Appraisals are an important part of any real estate transaction. Appraisers are frequently involved in lawsuits, either resulting from an inaccurate appraisal or as an expert witness for the plaintiff or defendant. The appraisal contingency is vital whether the buyer is obtaining financing to purchase or paying all cash. A properly conducted appraisal will inform the buyer of whether he or she is paying market value, below market value, or above market value for the property. An appraisal will help the buyer accurately assess or confirm the amount of equity he or she has in the property at the time of purchase. In a market with values climbing monthly, buyers may not be concerned with the true value of their purchase. However, an economic downturn or job loss may make this a critical piece of information. An appraisal can also assist the seller in deciding on a list price.

For most buyers the appraisal is the only opportunity to verify the square footage of the structure or structures. Few real estate agents will measure a building and are often counseled by their office not to measure the building for fear of liability resulting from an inaccurate measurement. Some structures are difficult to measure, such as two-story buildings and those that overhang a hillside. Real estate agents will sometimes include assessor data on square footage in their listings. Assessor data will usually

"I don't think this property is 3,000 square feet."

reflect permitted square footage. Appraisers measure structures with an exterior, perimeter measurement, unless this is impossible to do. If the appraiser finds that the actual square footage is greater than what is reported by the tax assessor, the additional square footage might indicate that something was constructed without a permit and be a red flag for further investigation.

Most buyers' only concern about their property appraisal is that the property appraises at or above the purchase price, but few buyers ever ask to see the appraisal, which is usually conducted for the lender. Buyers are paying for the appraisal in most transactions. Under the Federal Equal Credit Opportunity Act home buyers have the right to request a copy of the appraisal used by a lender to value the property.

> Buyers should always ask the lender for a copy of the property appraisal if they are not hiring their own appraiser.

The buyer should find out what *type of appraisal* is being conducted for determining valuation and should request a *full appraisal.* In some cases buyers may be charged for a full appraisal and receive something less. Other types of appraisals are:

- Automated appraisals—pulled electronically from databases
- Broker price opinions (BPOs)—based on the broker's opinion of value
- Exterior-only appraisals—known as a "drive-by appraisal"
- Condition and marketability reports
- Short-form appraisals

IS THE APPRAISER SOMETIMES A PROPERTY INSPECTOR?

The subject of the appraiser as an inspector is an issue in discussing FHA (Federal Housing Administration), HUD (Housing and Urban Development), and VA (Department of Veterans Affairs) property sales. These organizations may or may not disclose defects in their property sales. Buyers are often under the misguided impression that the appraiser for these agencies is also a general property inspector.

> Appraisers for the FHA, HUD, and VA are not general property inspectors.

Appraisers for these agencies report "observations" using a checklist of readily observable items and write a yes or no as to whether the item appears functional. Sometimes this form is not given to the buyer until five days before the closing. The appraiser's main function is to observe if, in his or her opinion, the property appears to be worth the money the buyer is borrowing so that the lender can recover the money it has loaned in case of foreclosure. The buyer receives a one-page summary report of a more detailed four-page report the appraiser gives to the lender. A buyer can and should ask for a copy of the four-page report.

> Buyers of an FHA, HUD, or VA property should always conduct their own general property inspection as a contingency of the purchase.

It is extremely difficult to pursue these agencies on legal grounds for failing to disclose defects or for an inadequate and faulty inspection by the appraiser.

THE IN-HOUSE LENDER AND THE PROPERTY APPRAISER

The buyer who is using the lender affiliated with her real estate agent's brokerage would be wise to verify the lender's appraisal with an independent appraisal of her own and make that verification a contingency of the transaction.

In a recent case the buyers were told that their purchase was appraised at the purchase price by the appraiser for the in-house lender of the dual agent broker. A second independent appraisal found that the buyers were paying some $75,000 more than market value. Because the first appraisal met the contingency to appraise at or above market value, the buyers could not use that contingency to pull out of the transaction, and they feared they would lose their deposit. The transaction closed, and the buyers sued their brokerage for the $75,000 they believed they had overpaid. Brokerages with in-house lenders must be careful that the lender's appraiser accurately reflects the true market value of the property irrespective of the purchase price.

THE REAL ESTATE AGENT'S ROLE IN WORKING WITH THE APPRAISER

The listing agent will normally meet the buyer's lender's appraiser at the property. Appraisers will usually ask the listing agent for the following information:

- Significant defects or characteristics of the property
- Structural additions built without permits
- Knowledge the agent may have about the interior condition of comparable sales in the area
- Neighborhood inventory of properties for sale
- Days-on-market average for sales
- Whether multiple offers have been made on this property or other nearby sales
- Public or neighborhood improvements that may affect value
- Price reductions on current listings

The agent may have seen the sold properties inside when they were listed and be able to provide information concerning quality of amenities, special features, or problems the appraiser could not know. The agent could also know of seller's concessions, such as contributions toward the buyer's closing costs or credits for repairs, that would not appear in public records listing property sales. The buyer's agent should also have information on comparable sales.

> The real estate agents should never demand or coerce an appraiser to come up with a particular value for the property.

"The Federal Bureau of Investigation's Suspicious Activity Reports concerning mortgage and appraisal related fraud increased by 28% in 2005, and estimated losses due to such fraud rose to more than one billion dollars, according to the U.S. Department of Justice Statistics."[1] Real estate agents must take care not to be drawn into mortgage and appraisal fraud. The current availability of zero down payment loans combined with a possibly inflated appraisal may further exacerbate loan fraud.

STIGMA ISSUES AND THE APPRAISER

Appraisers will sometimes need to deal with issues of stigma in developing their appraisals. Did a notorious murder occur at the property? Did the neighbor next door experience a major landslide in last winter's heavy rain? Real estate agents should also be sure to inform the appraiser about any on-site or off-site stigma issue that could affect the appraisal. If they know of similarly affected properties in their area that sold for less because of these conditions, the appraiser should be told about them.

PROBLEMS WITH RAPIDLY CLIMBING OR DECLINING MARKETS

The appraiser's job is even more difficult when prices are appreciating at $20,000 a month or declining just as rapidly. Real estate is a cyclical

---

[1] Francois K. Gregoire, "Appraisal, Oh No! It's Low!" *REALTOR Magazine*, June 2006, pp. 32–33.

market, and the appraisal can describe value only at a particular point in time. Clearly lenders worry more about declining markets than advancing markets, and appraisers must be careful not to place the lender at risk when market values are falling.

26
CHAPTER

Escrow

Escrow, also referred to as the *conveyancer,* coordinates all the pieces of paper and money exchanged in a real estate transaction. A party who handles the escrow function is required to be a neutral intermediary in the transaction. Lawsuits can sometimes result when one party or the other believes that the escrow holder is neither neutral nor competently handling escrow matters. How escrow is handled and who acts as escrow varies widely through out the United States. In northern California, for example, the escrow function is handled principally by the escrow division of title companies. In southern California the escrow function is handled principally by escrow companies. In many parts of the United States only lawyers are permitted to conduct escrows.

Escrow agents have limited duties and responsibilities to the parties, and those are usually outlined in the escrow instructions. Escrow agents have a fiduciary duty to the principals in a transaction. They act as a trustee responsible for the safekeeping of money, documents, and other items of value deposited with the escrow holder.

SOME OF THE DUTIES OF THE ESCROW AGENT

The escrow agent's usual duties include:

- Placing a demand with the seller's lender for a statement of funds owed
- Distribution of documents to the parties and real estate agents and having these documents properly filled out and signed by the parties
- Calculating adjusted payments and interest owed as of the date of closing
- Obtaining or ordering reconveyances
- Computing property tax, water stock, and other prorations
- Ordering the fire insurance policy
- Providing data sheets to the title company and tax assessor
- Dealing with the assignment of leases and rent statements, where applicable
- Handling power-of-attorney documents properly
- Distributing the preliminary title policy in states where this is done
- Distributing documents with changes in terms agreed to by the parties for their signatures
- Distributing the termite report and termite clearance
- Sending reminder memos to the parties regarding deadlines of contingencies in the contract and calling for the return of signed documents
- Payments to some service providers from buyer's or seller's funds
- Preparation of the grant deed
- Calling for the buyer's funds for the closing
- Calling for the buyer's lender's funds for the closing
- Preparation of a settlement sheet of all costs for the buyer and seller
- Handling the final signing of documents at the closing, where this function is not handled by an attorney, which will transfer ownership from seller to buyer
- Submitting the documents for recording the sale with the recorder's office

- Holding funds for the buyer's repairs after the close, as agreed to between the parties
- Notary services

This list of important services in the transaction places the escrow agent in a position of significant responsibility to the buyer and seller. The escrow file becomes an important file of documents in any lawsuit between the parties and can involve the escrow agent in the lawsuit.

NEUTRALITY AND THE IN-HOUSE ESCROW COMPANY, OR ESCROW HOLDER

Escrow agents must remain neutral in any conflict between the parties. The buyer may wish to cancel the transaction and demand the deposit back, but the seller may refuse to sign a cancellation instruction returning the buyer's funds. The escrow agent must hold the funds until buyer and seller settle their dispute.

Problems can sometimes occur when the escrow agent is an affiliated company of one of the brokerages involved in the transaction. The other side in the transaction may not view that escrow agent as neutral.

In one case the in-house escrow agent for the dual agent broker, who was also the seller, failed to heed the buyer's instructions to stop the close of the transaction until the issue of uncompleted seller repairs could be resolved. This escrow agent also failed to send some critical documents to the buyer, such as the termite report. The buyer in this lawsuit sued the seller, the dual agent brokerage, and the escrow company owned by the seller.

As real estate brokerages become increasingly integrated into other services and functions of a real estate transaction, they will also be placing themselves at a greater risk of accusation for lack of neutrality. For this reason, the buyer and seller should always be presented with a list of non-affiliated escrow agents and given the opportunity to decide whether to work with either the affiliated or nonaffiliated service provider.

THE ESCROW AGENT AND UNCLEAR CONTRACT INSTRUCTIONS

Escrow agents are required to follow instructions of the buyer and seller exactly, unless the instructions are unclear. When this occurs, the escrow agent must stop and wait for a resolution of the matter before proceeding. In another case involving a dual agent who was also one of the buyers of a nine-unit apartment building, the real estate agent altered the draft escrow instructions eliminating a carryback loan late payment penalty for the buyers. The seller did not notice the change, which was not pointed out to her by the dual agent buyer and was not questioned by the in-house escrow agent of the brokerage. The contract failed to specify which party was to pay transfer taxes. The dual agent buyer decided that the seller should pay, and so informed the escrow agent, who did not request confirmation of the unresolved matter by the seller. The dual agent buyer further instructed the escrow agent to withhold funds from the seller past the close of escrow without any prior signed agreement of the parties. The in-house escrow holder in this case was clearly biased toward the brokerage and not acting in the neutral interest of buyer and seller. The seller sued the brokerage and the dual agent.

Unclear contract language must always be resolved by signed agreements between the parties specifically addressing the unclear issues.

THE ESCROW AGENT AND THE UNLICENSED REAL ESTATE AGENT

Laws relating to the conduct of escrow agents will vary from state to state and are always evolving as cases come before courts. Recently in California an escrow company and escrow agent were found at fault in a lawsuit that was upheld on appeal. The buyer sued the escrow company claiming he had paid a commission on the sale to a real estate agent representing the buyer, who did not have a valid real estate license at the time of the transaction. The escrow company had not checked the license status of the agent. It is a violation of the California business and professional code to pay anyone compensation for performing any act for which a real estate license is required, if that individual does not have a real estate license. The escrow company and the escrow agent were found to have violated their fiduciary duty to the parties.

TIME IS OF THE ESSENCE

Escrow agents must be well organized individuals, who must shuffle many documents, transfer buyer and seller funds, and stay on time with the terms of the contract. They need to return calls promptly and heed the directions of the parties in a neutral function. Handling many transactions at one time is an organizational nightmare the best escrow agents can handle with ease. Whether escrow is performed by an escrow company, title company, or attorney, there are numerous pitfalls that can lead to a lawsuit. Real estate agents need to understand the neutral function of escrow when in-house escrow affiliates are utilized and exercise care. Truly competent escrow agents will keep the parties informed and on time throughout the transaction.

Real estate agents should be sure that their clients have adequate time to read and review the escrow instructions and documents. One of the most common complaints of "suing" buyers is that they were not given sufficient time to read and understand the escrow documents. Real estate agents should review documents with a client but should avoid commenting that a particular document is "just boilerplate."

27
CHAPTER

Termites and Other Pests

Most lenders will require a "termite clearance" on a property before they will give final loan approval. They want to be sure that these ravenous little bugs aren't chewing up the building. Termite and pest control operators are either licensed or registered professionals. They frequently deal with poisonous chemicals that can be hazardous to those using the chemicals and to the property owners as well. Termites have survived for millions of years and are found in every state except Alaska. Termite problems are somewhat less frequent in colder northern states, but can be a major headache in California and the southern states.

Builders can utilize a number of different methods to reduce termite entry into new construction. Among the methods they use are:[1]

- Pretreatments that are applied to the soil before the foundation is poured and are poisonous to termites
- Baiting systems that are stakes or stations placed in the ground around a house and are installed after the house is built

---

[1] Meghan Stromberg, "Termite Tech," *Professional Builder*, July 2003, pp. 63–64.

- Physical barriers such as a steel mesh or polymer sheet placed over the soil before the slab is poured
- Wood treatments that are sprayed on the wood framing to repel termites

Property owners and real estate agents are frequently baffled by the variation in termite reports. One report might indicate the need for whole house tenting and fumigation, and another for the same property might indicate that only localized treatment is needed. Clearly consistency in termite inspections is not always the case, leaving the property owner and the agent wondering who is right. If two reports from termite companies differ in their analysis and proposed treatment, the buyer must receive both and can request the more extensive treatment proposed. A seller or an agent should never get one report that recommends tenting and withhold that from a buyer, giving him or her only the report that recommends minor treatment, because that is a sure way to get sued.

Who conducts the termite inspection, who pays for the inspection, and who pays for repairs are usually negotiable between the parties, although custom may dictate who usually pays. The seller might pay for the inspection covering areas of evident infestation and conditions likely to lead to infestation. However, the buyer might pay for correction of conditions that could possibly lead to infestation. Termite inspections and repairs of condominiums and attached common interest developments will usually cover only the interior and exterior of the particular unit involved in the transaction and not any common areas.

WHAT IS COVERED IN THE TERMITE INSPECTION IN ADDITION TO TERMITES?

What is and is not covered in termite inspections can be confusing to property owners and real estate agents. Termite inspectors will frequently conduct a test to determine if the shower pan is leaking. They will also note any areas of apparent dry rot, such as at a fascia board or on wood siding. Dry rot is caused by wood-destroying fungi, not termites. However, termite inspectors usually will not inspect for mold and mildew, which are also fungi; although some inspectors might point out a suspicious condition and recommend to the buyer that a mold inspection be conducted. Sometimes the termite inspector will note a lack of adequate ventilation in either the attic or the crawl space under the building.

In a legal case the listing agent had a copy of a prior termite report that said the crawl space lacked adequate ventilation and could develop moisture problems leading to mold and dry rot. He failed to provide the report to the buyer until after the close of the transaction. He was a dual agent and also failed to attend the current termite inspection where he would have easily seen that the termite inspector, who weighed around 300 pounds, could not have climbed into the attic or under the house to do a thorough inspection. The inspector missed several serious conditions. The agent never reviewed the termite report with the buyer. The agent lost in court.

In yet another case, extensive structural dry rot was noted by the termite company on beams supporting balconies at an apartment building. Termite companies usually do not make structural repairs unless they have a general contractor's license. The quote from the company making the structural repairs was $250, which should have been a red flag for the agents that the repairs would likely be inadequate. It turns out they were inadequate. The termite company clearance report did not give a clearance on the structural repairs and was limited to verification of termite eradication. Termite companies making repairs of wood materials should be limited to minor repairs such as a broken step or a fascia board; structural repairs should be completed by a licensed contractor and inspected by the building department.

Sometimes dry-rot damage can go undetected inside walls. Repeated moisture damage can eventually turn wood framing to dust. I have remodeled buildings where the removal of an old window merely required the workman to lean on it; it fell out along with disintegrating framing. Thorough inspection of any area previously experiencing moisture damage is important and should be pointed out to the termite inspector.

HOW CAN YOU FIND A QUALITY TERMITE INSPECTION COMPANY?

Real estate agents, buyers, and sellers should first verify that a termite inspection company is properly registered or licensed in their state and has not had frequent complaints filed against them by unhappy consumers or been involved in lawsuits. The most frequent complaints are usually that the company missed an infestation or misapplied pesticide. They might also be members of the National Pest Control Association. This association will help keep them up to date on the latest information and continuing education. They should also have errors and omissions and liability insurance. Other questions that should be asked are:

- What techniques will be used to eradicate the termites, and what type of warranty will be provided?
- What pesticides will be used, and what problems might they cause, such as damage to exterior landscaping or interior contents?

Frequently used treatments include chemical fumigation, heat treatment, baits, and spot treatment.

WHAT OTHER PESTS CAN CAUSE PROBLEMS?

Termites aren't the only pest problem faced by property owners. Rodents, spiders, and roaches are other annoying, expensive, and sometimes hazardous pests. Termite companies may or may not deal with these other types of pests. A general service pest control company or specialized rodent control company might be needed. Rats or mice on roofs and in walls, attics, crawl spaces, or inside the building can be an expensive and offensive problem. In one legal case several years ago, the renter of a huge estate in Beverly Hills sued her landlord because of a rat and black widow spider infestation inside the house. She was paying $10,000 a month in rent! Yes, they do have rats in Beverly Hills.

In one transaction where I represented the buyer, rats were discovered in the attic by the termite company. The insulation was soaked with their urine and other matter. A rat control company was brought in and had to remove all the attic insulation, seal all the openings that allowed the rats to get into the attic, and then set traps to catch the rats still in the attic. This process took several weeks, as traps were set and removed, and until there were no more rats in traps. An insulation company then had to replace the roof insulation. The seller paid the cost which amounted to several thousands of dollars.

Roach infestations require traps to be set with frequent follow-up visits by pest control companies. Growing up in Florida, we had a scheduled visit every two weeks by a pest control company, and our home was immaculate. I recall one night glancing down on the living room carpet and to my surprise seeing a scorpion! We scooped it into a jar and called the pest control company who advised us that scorpions usually travel in pairs. I didn't sleep for a week. I'm happy to report that this scorpion was a loner.

Those annoying pests can chew up your investment.

It is next to impossible to keep tiny roaches, ants, and spiders out of buildings no matter how tightly they are sealed. Rats and mice can squeeze through an opening the size of a quarter, and doggie doors can also provide easy access. Rats and mice can gnaw on wiring, drywall, wood, and insulation. I recently had a $450 bill from my alarm company to repair chewed wiring under my house, and rodents have damaged my telephone wires on several occasions.

Agents and sellers need to be aware of these problems and be sure to make full disclosure to buyers. A careful review and follow-up on termite report findings and further recommendations are essential.

28

Excuses That Won't Work in Court

I'M NOT A CONTRACTOR

Real estate agents, buyers, sellers, and even general property inspectors are not required to be licensed contractors. Buyers will reasonably claim that they relied on their agent and their professional inspectors to inform them about the condition of the property, along with the disclosures of the seller. Real estate agents are not selling a dress or a pair of shoes, but rather a big-ticket purchase sometimes requiring the buyer's life savings. They need to know something about what they are selling, and they should be familiar with construction issues or problems prevalent in their area. Do homes have synthetic stucco? Have fireplace flues possibly been damaged by a recent earthquake? Have roofs been damaged by an especially heavy snow-fall the past winter? Did flooding from heavy rains cause an increase in mold problems? Real estate agents and general property inspectors will not find a sympathetic jury for the excuse, "I'm not a contractor," when there are issues they should have known about in their work area.

IT'S THE OTHER AGENT'S FAULT

Two real estate agents, one representing the buyer and the other representing the seller, may not have the same training and experience. Each agent needs to focus on his or her own responsibilities and duties regardless of the other agent. If the other agent seems to be less attentive to the transaction than it requires, that agent's office manager or office broker should be notified, and that agent should be directed to get back on the transaction with appropriate follow-up. Believe me, claiming in court later that, "It was the other agent's fault," just won't work.

THE SELLER LIED TO ME

Do sellers sometimes lie? Yes, they do. This is a fact of life for real estate agents. Sellers may be justifiably concerned that telling everything they know about their property would significantly lower its sale price, or perhaps even make it not salable. The seller who lies is asking for a lawsuit. The buyer will find out. The real estate agents can reduce the likelihood of the seller getting through the transaction with a lie if they follow what is discussed in this book. By requesting full and complete disclosure of the seller, advising the seller of the potential consequences of failing to disclose, and allowing the buyer to conduct thorough inspections with well-qualified inspectors, the buyer will in most cases discover the truth before the transaction closes.

I DIDN'T KNOW

I have actually heard real estate agents say in court "I didn't know," when asked about something they failed to do or did wrong. Unfortunately, "I didn't know" will not work in court. Ignorance of what a real estate agent should have known is not an acceptable excuse. Real estate agents must be sure they keep up to date and are fully aware of their responsibilities.

I HAD 10 DEALS GOING WHEN I SOLD THAT HOUSE

Congratulations! Every real estate agent works toward success, which is reflected in completing many transactions. Balancing the workload with adequate attention and follow-up to each transaction requires good organizational skills. Real estate agents should never take on more than they can handle well. They must also be careful not to delegate more to unlicensed assistants than they can handle or activities not allowed to be handled by unlicensed assistants. Sales success will not be an acceptable excuse in court. Buyers and sellers should be sure to ask agents with many listings and transactions how much time they will have for their property. Will the buyer or seller be dealing with assistants? Has the agent ever been sued, and what was the lawsuit about?

EVERYONE ELSE DOES IT

Believing that it's okay to do something because everyone else does it is not going to save an agent from a lawsuit. I've heard this excuse a lot from agents being sued. "Everyone uses that inspector," or "Everyone writes long contract clauses." "Agents here don't attend the inspections." Sometimes the "everyone else does it" excuse is like spinning a roulette wheel, and your number came up, just not the way you hoped it would. Each real estate agent owes each client thorough and knowledgeable service regardless of what everyone else does or doesn't do. Agents need to be sure they help buyers find the most qualified general property inspectors. They should never guess at the wording of contract language but should seek assistance from attorneys. Attending the property inspections should be a part of every real estate agent's responsibilities. The agents are witnesses for each other and the buyer and seller as to what transpired at the inspections and who said what to whom.

THE SELLER (OR THE SELLER'S AGENT) SAID IT WAS FIXED

The buyer's agent should insist on documentation from the seller or the seller's agent from an appropriately licensed contractor that the problem, whether it occurred before escrow opened or was to be fixed during escrow, was fixed. Neither the seller's agent nor the buyer's agent should accept a spoken, "It was fixed," from the seller as adequate verification. The agents should also not assume that some problem was fixed because the seller had contractors doing work on the property. Any seller representation without documentation should be carefully disclosed to a buyer with the agents either verifying the information or stating that it has not been verified.

3 PART

ADDITIONAL IDEAS TO REDUCE RISK

29 CHAPTER

Understanding Your Duties—If You Want to Stay Out of a Lawsuit

Duties of buyers, sellers, real estate agents/brokers, general property inspectors, and builders/developers may vary somewhat from the following list state by state. All are advised to check the specific requirements in their state.

UNDERSTANDING YOUR DUTIES AS A BUYER

The following is what buyers should do to avoid getting involved in a lawsuit:

- Carefully select your real estate agent
- Undertake all of the inspections recommended by your agent, the seller's agent, the seller, and the general property inspector
- Read all transaction documents and disclosures, and do not hesitate to ask questions

- Adhere to contract deadlines and request reasonable extensions for additional inspections or investigations
- Attend the general property inspection and inspections by the structural engineer, geologist, soils engineer, mold inspector, or drainage engineer if any of these inspections are recommended

UNDERSTANDING YOUR DUTIES AS A SELLER

The following is what sellers should do to avoid getting involved in a lawsuit:

- *Fully disclose,* in writing, all known material facts affecting the property on-site and off-site
- Allow the buyer adequate time and property access to complete his or her own inspections and evaluation of the condition of the property
- Provide receipts, permits, and any other documentation available for recent and significant repairs or alterations to the property
- Provide prior inspection reports prepared by geologists, soils engineers, structural engineers, mold inspectors, land surveyors, and drainage engineers, which the seller has retained
- Attend the buyer's general property inspection and honestly reply to all questions regarding property condition or neighborhood issues

UNDERSTANDING YOUR DUTIES AS A REAL ESTATE AGENT/BROKER

The following is what real estate agents/brokers should do to avoid getting involved in a lawsuit:

- Provide the utmost care, integrity, honesty, and loyalty to the client
- Disclose all known material defects:
  - Question the seller about property condition, and disclose all facts and related documents
  - Be aware of and disclose on-site and area off-site material defects and history, especially those facts not readily apparent

"This is the sixth one this month. I don't remember this on the sellers' disclosure."

or observable to the buyer, but which the agent would reasonably be expected to know about

- ○ Conduct a reasonably competent and diligent visual inspection and disclose *all* visual red flags that would be expected to be seen by a real estate agent, in writing, whether or not already disclosed by the seller

- Exercise reasonable care and diligence:
  - ○ Negotiate the best possible transaction for your client
  - ○ Encourage the use of experts and defer to them
  - ○ Monitor the transaction deadlines, documents, and terms
  - ○ Make only those statements of fact that have been verified, and confirm them in writing to the buyer or seller
  - ○ Read and review all documents with the client, note and investigate red flags in documents, and advise the client, in writing, to investigate red flags
  - ○ Advise and counsel the client on his or her duties, preferably in writing
  - ○ Refer the client to publications and official sources to assist his or her investigation

- Act with honesty and fair dealing to all parties
- Verify material facts received from the seller or buyer or state that they have not been verified
- Explain and counsel the client about what has been disclosed, thereby helping the client to make an informed and considered decision to buy or sell
- Attend the general property inspection and other inspections that may be needed
- Maintain current errors and omissions and liability insurance
- Sell only property types with which you are familiar
- Sell only in a market area you know well
- Do not give legal advice; and be sure to encourage the buyer and seller to obtain legal advice

As a broker/manager, your duties are to:

- Provide reasonable supervision and training for agents
- Monitor transactions

UNDERSTANDING YOUR DUTIES AS A PROPERTY INSPECTOR

The following is what property inspectors should do to avoid getting involved in a lawsuit:

- Prepare a comprehensive report covering all systems of the property and include adequate information to explain any defects
- Include photos of the property, particularly defective areas
- Maintain records for each inspection for at least four years
- Provide advice to the buyer on recommended additional inspections
- Clearly indicate in the contract what is and what is not included in the inspection
- Maintain current errors and omissions coverage and liability insurance
- Get comprehensive training as a property inspector and continue to update that training

- Provide for time at the inspection to point out to the buyer any areas or issues of concern and to review key findings
- Provide a thorough and comprehensive report, even if this means sending it to the buyer and the buyer's agent a few days after the inspection

UNDERSTANDING YOUR DUTIES AS A BUILDER/DEVELOPER

The following is what builders/developers should do to avoid getting involved in a lawsuit:

- Allow the buyer to inspect the construction of the building periodically as it is being built
- Allow the buyer to thoroughly inspect the completed building and property before the close of escrow, and make all required repairs
- Provide copies of all reports (soils, geologic, etc.) to the buyer as disclosure documents with a time period allowed for buyer review as a contingency of the purchase
- Make any analysis and repair of subsequent buyer complaints after the close with appropriately licensed subcontractors

30

Keep Up with Changing Laws, and Do Not Assume Buyer/Seller Knowledge

KEEP UP WITH CHANGING LAWS AND FORMS

I always shake my head with surprise when I read a purchase contract from a lawsuit and find that it was not up to date when it was used or that forms routinely used at that time were not included in the transaction. Agents should use the standard sales contract forms, addenda, and disclosures recommended by their state association of Realtors unless the specifics of the transaction require other forms, and these should be prepared only by attorneys.

Real estate agents have many sources to keep them updated on recent changes in the law and on the forms and contracts they use. Some of these sources include:

- State departments of real estate
- The National Association of Realtors
- State associations of Realtors
- Local chapter associations of Realtors

- Various real estate publications produced by NAR, specifically *REALTOR Magazine*
- National, state, and local real estate association publications, bookstores, and catalogs (for example, the book recently published by the National Association of Realtors, *Broker to Broker*, to which I was a contributing author)
- National, state, and local real estate association conventions, meetings, special speakers, and training sessions
- Continuing education training required to maintain a real estate license
- Participation in national, state, and local real estate association committees (for example, I serve on the professional standards committee of the Southland Regional Association of Realtors in California, and have served on the grievance committee as well)

January issues of real estate magazines usually highlight the significant changes in real estate laws that may affect real estate licensees. Forms used in transactions are changed or added as necessary throughout the year. All licensed real estate agents and their brokers must keep up to date on legal changes affecting their conduct and maintain the most current transaction documents for their use with clients. The real estate profession is that: a profession. As professionals, real estate agents should acquire a library of professional reference materials including not only those aimed at increasing their productivity, but also those developed to elevate their professional service to their clients and customers, such as this book.

General property inspectors are also professionals who should focus on maintaining a current knowledge of real estate laws and civil codes that could affect their conduct. Membership in their professional associations is an excellent way to keep up to date. Real estate agents who are up to date on real estate laws and civil code changes are also informed of these changes as they affect general property inspectors, and agents should be able to recognize in the general property inspector's contract with buyers clauses or content that does not meet current requirements.

Builders and developers are also subject to numerous regulations and civil code changes through their state legislatures and state contractors' licensing boards. Local schools that offer training for contractors and subcontractors for taking contractors' license exams frequently have bookstores with current contract forms and reference books. There are many builder magazines and trade associations that also keep builders and developers up to date on construction methods, national and state legislation affecting conduct, issues that are coming up in lawsuits against builders and developers, and many ideas to improve their quality of production and service to their customers. Among the best of these educational sources are the National Association of Home Builders and *Professional Builder* magazine.

Buyers and sellers have equal access to bookstores that contain racks of books dealing with buying and selling real estate, and now they have this book, which covers issues on how to avoid lawsuits in real estate transactions. Chapter associations of Realtors frequently have bookstores that allow sales of current real estate forms to nonmembers. Numerous pamphlets are produced by government agencies to inform buyers and sellers. These are available to the public and are often provided by real estate agents to their clients. The local real estate sections of newspapers produce many special articles of local and national interest, and they carry syndicated writers' columns, dealing with issues related to inspections, remodeling, financing, and leasing. Those who own real estate or plan to buy real estate should read this readily available information.

Ignorance of the law excuses no man.

—John Selden

DO NOT ASSUME BUYER/SELLER KNOWLEDGE

There is an old expression that a little knowledge can be dangerous. This is certainly the case in real estate transactions. Sometimes buyers or sellers believe they know more than they really do. Many real estate agents have encountered the buyer or seller who believes that all real estate agents do is put up a sign, have an open house, or show property. What an easy job, and they get a commission too. I would hope after buyers and sellers have read this book that their impression of what real estate agents really need to know and what they really do will have expanded to something more realistic.

Real estate agents know that the first-time buyer needs a total education on real estate buying. However, some agents can assume that people who have already purchased a property, regardless of when that occurred, know more about the process than they really do. The seller who made a purchase 10 years ago is not up to date on current requirements for contracts or disclosures for selling now. Laws, regulations, disclosures, and forms are constantly changing. Buyers and sellers are rarely current on their knowledge of real estate. The smart real estate agent will regard every buyer or seller as a novice and cover all aspects of the transaction thoroughly. A frequent complaint of buyers and sellers caught up in a lawsuit is, "I didn't know, my real estate agent didn't tell me, and I looked to her for advice."

Agents should explain to sellers that the long arm of a plaintiff attorney can find them almost anywhere to pursue a lawsuit. Moving out of state after the sale will not free them from legal exposure. The advice in this book will go a long way to helping to protect sellers from themselves, and buyers from the uninformed sellers. It will also help the real estate agents protect themselves from buyers and sellers who will not take their good advice and who suffer a loss later that could have been avoided.

Sellers need to understand the importance of their decision to sell. Once they have accepted an offer, should they back out of the transaction without cause as referenced in the contract (sometimes called *seller's remorse*), they may face a buyer claim of "specific performance." They may owe real estate commissions even if they won't sell, and a buyer may force them to sell through the legal process. Buyers who back out of a transaction for reasons not covered in a contract contingency (*buyer's remorse*) may risk losing their deposit to the seller.

General property inspectors need to also understand that they should treat every buyer as a novice as they review and detail property defects, their possible cause, and the need for follow-up inspections. Few buyers have sufficient technical knowledge to understand the significance of a property defect if it is not adequately explained.

Builders and developers must also regard buyers as novice buyers and take the time to educate them with knowledgeable and patient people, who realize that their job involves not just selling, but also educating. Builders must be sure that they have covered all the details of what is included, the cost of extras or upgrades, how firm the completion date is, what happens if the completion date is delayed, and when and how buyer inspections are allowed.

The art of teaching is the art of assisting discovery.

—Mark Van Doren

31 CHAPTER

Home Warranties, Seller Protection Plans, and General Property Inspector Warranty Plans

HOME WARRANTY POLICIES

Property warranties that will cover some routine repairs are now as common in real estate transactions as are property inspections. The Murphy's law of buying any property could be that the day after escrow closes and the buyer takes possession, something breaks. Regardless of how thorough the inspections, investigations, and repairs, buildings are in a constant state of change. Systems continuously age and deteriorate over time. Almost any property owner has a "to-do list" of repairs or anticipated repairs and upgrades.

Home warranty plans provide property owners with a contract that states that if something were to break after the transaction closes, the repair cost will be fixed at a small service fee, usually $35 to $50 for all covered systems and appliances. Home warranties are taken out during escrow or at the close of the transaction. The cost for a one-year policy runs from approximately $250 to $600. Sometimes as added peace of mind to a buyer, the seller or the real estate agent will offer to pay for the one-year policy. Buyer's agents will generally request that the seller pay for the policy, although who pays is negotiable.

Any real estate agent can report a phone call from a client who has recently moved into a home, turned on some appliance or the air-conditioning, and found that it did not work. The buyer called the home warranty company, and a few hours later someone showed up who made the repair. The call to the agent was to report the buyer's satisfaction and appreciation for the home warranty policy. I had a client call me once to report that the air-conditioning failed and that the home warranty company service technician replaced the broken compressor for $45. It had worked just fine when it had been inspected during escrow. The client was very impressed. These are the kind of calls real estate agents love to get from their clients.

All the companies offering these policies will provide real estate agents with brochures that describe what is covered in the policy, the cost of each type of coverage, and limits and exclusions. The agents can pass the brochure along to the seller and the buyer for their review. The basic policy may cover heating, plumbing, stoppages, garbage disposal, built-in microwave, water heater, oven/range/cooktop, dishwasher, attic and exhaust fans, ceiling fans, trash compactor, whirlpool bath motor and pump, doorbells, electrical system, telephone wiring, duct work, garage door openers, instant hot water dispensers, circulating pumps, pressure regulators, toilet tanks, sump pumps, central vacuum system, and pest control service.

Homes over 5,000 square feet may have additional charges. Multiunit residential properties would require buyers' individual coverage for their units in most cases, although some policies will cover multiunit residential properties.

Additional charges would cover air-conditioning, evaporative cooler, washer/dryer, refrigerator, well pump, sewage ejector pump, septic tank pumping, limited roof leakage, and swimming pool/spa equipment.

Some policies will cover "structural" problems, which are a major source of lawsuits against agents and sellers, however, this coverage may require a preclosing inspection by the warranty company's approved inspector, and inspected items found to be nonfunctional would have to be repaired prior to close of escrow or would be excluded from coverage.

Coverage can also be obtained with some warranty companies for guest units and mobile homes.

All these policies have "limits of liability" that should be carefully reviewed by buyers and real estate agents. Usually these policies cover normal wear and tear and do not cover damage as a result of flood, earthquake, hurricane, riot, storm, mud, vandalism, and misuse. Most of these policies will not cover defects found during general property inspections that the seller would not agree to repair. They also will not cover defects that could have been discoverable during a general property inspection, visual inspection of agents and the buyer, or through reasonable mechanical testing, such as turning on a faucet. Most of these policies are renewable at the option of the home warranty company by the buyer at the buyer's expense, after the one-year initial policy expires.

Some real estate agents may have home warranty policies recommended or endorsed by their errors and omissions insurance carrier that offer some additional negotiated coverage, such as structural coverage. Some real estate trade associations may offer endorsed programs with a certain home warranty company that will agree to give association members and their clients a reduced price.

Real estate agents and buyers need to have a realistic understanding of what home warranty policies will and will not cover. Making statements to the buyer such as, "Don't worry, this broken dishwasher will be covered by your home warranty even if the seller won't repair it," won't necessarily work, if the home warranty company reasonably concludes that the problem existed before the effective date of the policy. The real estate agent should always remain at arm's length from the home warranty company and not accept any referral fee or payment in return for recommending any particular company. The best approach for a real estate agent is to present information on several warranty companies, explain their similarities and differences, and let the buyer follow up in the selection process. Sometimes the seller who is paying for the home warranty selects which company to use and what is to be covered. In this situation the seller's agent should also present the seller with several options and review the policies and costs. The buyer would still have the option, at his or her expense, to add any extra coverage.

It is important to deal with warranty companies that are well established, are financially sound, and have a good reputation for providing quality service with few consumer complaints. The company should provide information on the dollar limits of the warranty, and whether there are dollar limits on individual repairs. The repair people should all be insured and licensed contractors. Response time to make repairs should be the same day or next day in most cases. The property owner should be told how long the warranty period will be on any repair or replacement.

SELLER PROTECTION PLANS

Some errors and omissions companies will offer "seller protection plans" to their insured real estate agents. These plans may cover $25,000 (over a deductible of, for example, $2,500, which the seller would be obligated to pay) to apply to legal defense and other costs should the seller be sued by the buyer for alleged undisclosed defects in a residential property that was the seller's primary residence. These plans would apply to costs of a lawsuit, arbitration, or mediation. There are certain situations and exclusions that are not covered, such as intentional, dishonest, or fraudulent acts; covered circumstances the seller had knowledge of before closing but did not disclose; claims by the seller against the seller's real estate broker or agent; or claims against the seller for damages that occurred to the property after closing.

The real estate agent for the seller will usually pay for this coverage for the seller client for 180 days after the close of the transaction. The seller has the option to extend the coverage for an additional 180 days for $100 to $200. This type of policy provides some additional protection for the seller in the event of a claim by the buyer.

GENERAL PROPERTY INSPECTOR WARRANTY PLANS

General property inspectors who carry errors and omissions insurance sometimes have policies that will cover the buyer's real estate agent up to a certain amount should the buyer have a later claim against the agent for property defects that should have been discovered in the property inspection and were missed by the inspector. This type of coverage affords the real estate agent another level of insurance coverage. Real estate agents should ask for a copy of the general property inspector's policy on this additional agent coverage.

BUILDER HOME WARRANTIES

Many builders also provide a "home warranty," which is a 10-year policy that covers the structure and foundation of new-home construction. Builder home warranty policies are different from existing home warranties discussed above. Some home warranty companies that cover existing properties are now also covering new construction. Some of the builder home warranties are backed only by the builder, rather than by an independent warrantor, and are subject to the continued strength of the builder. If the builder files for bankruptcy, the homeowner's warranty from the builder would be worthless. Even if new-home warranties are backed by national warrantors, homeowners can still experience delays and dissatisfaction with repairs. New-home warranties are usually paid for by the builders and may cost from $300 to $500 or more.

New homes still under builder warranty when they are resold by a real estate agent may create a whole new area of concern for real estate agents and sellers. Did the seller retain a copy of the policy? What is still covered under the policy? Is it transferable to a subsequent buyer? Did the builder make any repairs under the policy, and were these repairs satisfactorily made? In one legal case on which I consulted, the buyer purchased the home from the original owner while the builder's warranty was still in effect. The buyer discovered some undisclosed defects in the original construction and sued the seller, the real estate agents, and the original custom home builder. The builder pursued his subcontractors for faulty work, and the outcome involved settlements with several parties. New-home warranties should be put in a safe place by new-home buyers and should be provided to any subsequent buyer if they are still in effect. Records should be kept of any repairs requested and completed by the builder under the warranty and any repairs not made, or not satisfactorily completed; this information should be turned over to a subsequent buyer. If the original buyer received funds from the builder to make repairs, the information on what needed repair and receipts on what was repaired should be provided to the next purchaser.

I have consulted on legal cases in which the builder sent a handyman to make a plumbing repair. The handyman caulked around the shower. The problem was not the caulking, but rather a shower pan leak that continued and eventually developed into a mold problem. Builder repairs under warranty should always be made by an appropriately licensed subcontractor.

32 CHAPTER

Select Your Real Estate Agent the Way You Would Select Your Brain Surgeon!

TO GET AN AGENT OR NOT TO GET AN AGENT

After reading Chapters 1 through 31, if any sellers or buyers still believe, "I can do this myself, I don't need a real estate agent," perhaps they should reread Chapters 1 through 31. Real estate representation clearly involves a great deal of knowledge, a lot of hard work, and considerable liability. When buyers or sellers act on their own behalf, they assume all the liability for errors they may make, and some of these can be life-threatening and financially devastating.

Real estate agents can not only help buyers and sellers avoid health and financial risks, but they have a much better grasp of how to realistically price a property. They can give it maximum exposure in the marketplace which results in more offers and a higher sale price. Real estate agents spend many hundreds of hours from start to finish on any transaction, including listing, preparation of advertising and sales brochures, showings, open houses, broker caravans, and the transaction itself. Sometimes there is personal risk in showing property. Every year real estate agents are robbed or assaulted at open houses and showings, and some have even lost their lives. "Between 2001 and 2004, the latest figures available, 25 real estate agents died as a result of assaults and violent acts, according to the Bureau of Labor Statistics."[1] When people open their door to strangers, anyone can walk in. Buyers and sellers need to be knowledgeable and understand the issues discussed in this book, and then they should turn the work of finding the property they want to purchase or sell over to a competent real estate agent.

I have a file drawer of some 50 or more forms and disclosure documents that could possibly be used in various real estate transactions. How could a buyer or seller reasonably know what forms to use or when? Would a buyer be able to keep the forms current? Even in areas in which attorneys perform the escrow function rather than title or independent escrow companies, much of the content of the transaction, particularly inspections and disclosures, is handled by real estate agents. The Internet has become a wonderful tool for buyers and sellers to check what properties are available or selling, but it cannot take the place of a real estate agent.

When I decided that the time was right for me to write this book, I was contacted by book publishers and contacted others myself. When I started to read the lengthy contracts I was sent, I quickly realized that this was a field of knowledge about which I had no experience and very little information. I spoke with several literary agents and selected one who was experienced and well qualified. The resulting contract was far better than what I could have achieved on my own. Her assistance and guidance were well worth the commission she will receive. The same is true for going it alone or utilizing the services of a real estate agent. The literary agent reads publisher contracts frequently; she knew what could be asked for and what constituted a good offer. She knew how to negotiate the best contract. Real estate agents apply their experience and knowledge in advising buyers and sellers. The 2005 National Association of Realtors (NAR) profile of home buyers and sellers found that only 17 percent of FSBOs (for sale by owner) used the Internet to market their home, while 77 percent of all home buyers used the Internet to look for a home. Real estate agents have access to list properties on the Internet on the most frequently used sites by buyers searching for properties. Real estate agents can access Web sites to list or search for properties that may or may not be accessible to buyers searching for properties on the Internet. For example, through the

---

[1] G. M. Filisko, "Keep Associates Protected," *REALTOR Magazine*, September 2006.

Multiple Listing Alliance, I have access to listings for my buyer clients throughout southern California.

Most people would not consider acting as their own attorney, and yet there are those who would choose to represent themselves on perhaps the most important financial decision of their lives. Most real estate agents have errors and omissions insurance and liability insurance to protect their clients. Buyers and sellers have no professional insurance to fall back on should they make a serious mistake in handling their own transaction.

DO FSBOs REALLY SAVE THE SELLER MONEY?

The 2005 NAR profile mentioned above found that 13 percent of sellers conducted their transactions without the assistance of licensed real estate agents. The median sale price of an agent-represented home was $230,000 versus $198,200 for the FSBO. This is a difference of $32,000 or 16 percent. Even at a 6 percent commission (almost $13,800) to the buyer's and seller's agents ($230,000 − $13,800 = $216,200), the seller using a real estate agent came out ahead by $18,000. And this doesn't take into account the time spent by FSBO sellers on the transaction and their liability exposure.

ALL REAL ESTATE AGENTS ARE NOT CREATED EQUAL

Just as all general property inspectors are not equally competent, so too for real estate agents. I have found it interesting to ask plaintiffs in lawsuits how they happened to select the real estate agent they were suing. The one characteristic of the agent that is at the top of the list in the plaintiff's selection process is charm. That's right, charm! Charm is a wonderful personal quality to have, but it should clearly be lower on the list of criteria for selecting a real estate agent. No one would select an attorney or a doctor on the basis of charm. I would strongly prefer competence and experience to charm in an attorney or a doctor. One plaintiff told me he selected the agent who was the first person he saw when he entered the real estate office! Others have said that they just could not say no to their relative who is a real estate agent. Some called a name on a sign and never asked anything about the agent's background. Selecting an agent because the buyer walked into an open house they liked and the agent was the listing agent is also mentioned.

Perhaps as real estate agents we have not educated the public enough about our qualifications. To some buyers and sellers we are all alike as long as we have a license. The National Association of Realtors has conducted a national advertising campaign in recent years trying to educate the public regarding the services that real estate agents provide and to distinguish Realtors who are members of the National Association of Realtors from real estate licensees who hold a real estate license but do not belong to this professional association. There are now approximately 1.2 million members of the National Association of Realtors, and it is the largest professional association in the world. Professional association membership is a worthy credential for real estate agents for many of the same reasons it is a worthy credential for general property inspectors. The National Association of Realtors provides the following to its members and the public:

- A code of ethics and standards of practice that each member pledges to follow
- A monthly magazine that advises agents on their conduct and has as its goal to inform, educate, and create an ever-more professional real estate agent
- Pamphlets and books providing real estate agents with information on specific subjects of interest
- A national annual convention where members hear speakers on diverse subjects and add to their base of knowledge
- An informative and up-to-date Web site
- State chapter associations of Realtors that hold state conventions and provide publications, contract forms, and other services to their members
- Local chapter associations of Realtors that provide services similar to those of the state associations but at the local level

There are other professional real estate associations that deal with specialized areas of real estate to which real estate licensees may belong. Clearly association membership affords real estate agents with a greater opportunity to stay current, to learn new information, and to better protect the public they serve.

Other qualifications of real estate agents that should surely precede "charm" are:

- *Experience, there is no substitute for it:* We all have to start somewhere as beginners. Most real estate agents would greatly benefit from apprenticing with a more experienced agent when they start out.

> *The best substitute for experience is being sixteen.*
>
> —Raymond Duncan

- *Risk management training:* How much and what kind of training has the agent had in risk management to protect clients and all parties from a lawsuit? In some states risk management training is now mandated. Smart real estate agents will take every class offered (and read this book) to be sure they are prepared to properly represent their clients and avoid liability issues.

- *Insurance coverage:* Be sure the real estate agent has active errors and omissions and liability insurance coverage. Some real estate agents operate without this coverage. Some states require real estate agents to have errors and omissions coverage.

- *A clear track record:* If general property inspectors are asked, "Have you ever been sued?" real estate agents should be asked the same question. Why were they sued? What were the issues in the lawsuit? How was the lawsuit resolved?

- *Education:* There are still states in which a person with a high school education who passes a two-hour exam can obtain a real estate license. If you as a buyer or seller had to choose between that person and someone with a college degree or possibly a master's degree in business, whom would you choose? Education and intelligence are key factors in dealing with the complexity of today's real estate transactions.

- *Community involvement:* Real estate agents who are active in their community will have more information and knowledge about the issues that will affect that community and a real estate transaction than those with no community involvement.

- *Involvement in professional associations:* Real estate agents who are actively involved in their local association of Realtors will learn from other agents and may gain special insights by participating in committees.
- *Credentials in related fields or activities:* The real estate agent who has a degree in real estate from a university, is a licensed general contractor, is an expert witness in real estate, is a real estate attorney, or is a teacher of real estate classes will undoubtedly have a greater degree of knowledge as a real estate agent. Some real estate agents also acquire additional certifications from NAR, such as GRI or CRS designations that indicate further educational training.
- *The broker's license versus a sales license:* The real estate broker's license in most states requires considerably more training and a more comprehensive exam than does the sales license.

Make the most of yourself, for that is all there is of you.

—Ralph Waldo Emerson

- *Courses in related subjects:* Wouldn't a real estate agent who has taken courses in negotiation techniques, finance, or title issues be able to add significantly to the outcome of a real estate transaction?
- *Personal service versus the group/team agent:* Buyers and sellers need to understand *whom they will really be working with on a transaction.* When the listing agent takes the listing, is that the last time that agent will be seen? Will the details of showings, offers, and escrows be handled by less experienced agents or unlicensed assistants? Working with an experienced real estate agent or licensed real estate broker throughout the listing and sale, or search and purchase, who is always available, might be preferable.
- *The agent who has time for full service:* We have all seen the glitzy ads and self promotion of real estate agents who have 40 listings, 20 deals in escrow, and another 15 that just closed. Do

you really believe that such an agent will have time to focus on selling your property or taking you to 25 houses before you select the right one? The real estate agent with fewer listings not only would be more motivated, but also would have the time to focus on your property and all the necessary details this entails. The agents who have dozens of listings may not mention how many didn't sell or were canceled or how minimal was their personal involvement in each transaction.

- *Full-time versus part-time agents:* You wouldn't want to get a diagnosis from a part-time doctor, would you? Deal with a real estate agent or broker who is committed full time to the profession. Beware the mortgage broker who has a real estate license and suddenly decides to also represent buyers and sellers. This person needs to have the necessary experience and knowledge to represent buyers and sellers, and that is far more important than a reduced fee on the loan transaction.

- *Get references from satisfied clients:* Always ask for references from satisfied clients who are not the agents' relatives. Read the references carefully and look for words like "knowledgeable," "available," "professional," "thorough," and "smart."

HOW TO AVOID THE CHARM SYNDROME

I see it every day in legal cases; the buyer who picked that handsome or beautiful smiling agent's face from the sign or was overwhelmed by an impressive ad. The sellers who were snowed by a presentation that claimed the agent would advertise their 1,200-square-foot home to the world, or who select an agent who has reached near celebrity status and deems their dwelling worthy of a listing.

If you think these real estate agents don't get sued, they do. One such hot agent has been sued twice on the same block in my area. Several others who have been sued are known to me when, as an expert witness, I am called by attorneys either suing them for clients or trying to defend them.

Never select a real estate agent for only the following reasons:

- You've seen the agent's name on a sign, on a billboard, or on a bench ad.
- A friend told you he or she has heard of the agent.

- The agent is the friend, cousin, sister, or whatever of a friend or relative.
- This person is the "big name" agent in the area.
- The agent listed the house across the street or next door.
- You met the agent at an open house.
- The agent has deluged you with slick advertising.
- You haven't talked to anyone else.
- This is the first person you see at a real estate office.
- The agent is charming, so your good sense and reason are somehow repressed.

Many very successful real estate agents are well qualified and competent. They are not, however, one's only choice. There are many exceptional agents with large and small companies or who are self-employed and who may not have the flashy ads or name recognition but who have labored for many years to hone their skills and who can perform exceptionally for a buyer or a seller. Who your real estate agent was will not be what you want to rave about later, but rather how well the agent performed in your best interest. It costs no more to use the services of the most qualified real estate agent than it does to use someone less qualified.

Beware the real estate agent who is not prepared to say more about his or her background than, "Here's the list of properties I sold last year." Clearly getting the job done is important, but it is not the whole story. Many of those properties may have been sold in collaboration with other agents. Interview several real estate agents before making a decision. Remember, you are hiring the individual representing you, not just the brokerage company.

Be sure that substance prevails over pizzazz, in selecting a real estate agent to assist you with buying or selling. Your life savings and your mental health are at stake.

ARE INTEGRATED SERVICE BROKERAGE COMPANIES A GOOD IDEA?

Many of the large real estate companies are now integrating other real estate services with their offerings to the public. They may own or have an

"He has a nice smile. Maybe we should pick him as our real estate agent."

affiliation with an escrow company, title company, home warranty company, or lender. If you combine these services along with dual agency, there might be an increased liability risk. I am consulting on a case now involving a dual agent who referred the buyer to his "in-house" lender. The lender's appraiser valued the house at the accepted offer price. The buyer decided to also apply through another lender whose appraiser valued the home some $75,000 lower. The buyer felt he could not back out of the deal for fear of losing the deposit. When the transaction closed, the buyer sued the brokerage and agent. Buyers and sellers should be sure to verify that if they agree to these in-house services, they will not be paying more than they would with independent companies that offer the same service.

A buyer may not want to use and pay for all the affiliated services of the seller's listing agent. Normally, who provides affiliated services and the fees for the services are negotiable between buyer and seller. All affiliated services and fees received by companies from their affiliates must be disclosed to buyers and sellers according to RESPA (Real Estate Settlement Procedures Act) requirements.

ARE LIMITED SERVICE BROKERAGES RIGHT FOR YOU?

Sellers should carefully consider their choice of a limited service real estate company. These companies are sometimes called "MLS entry-only brokers." They offer a limited number of service options. They seem like a good way for the seller to reduce the commission paid to the listing agent to a few hundred dollars, but the savings may not be worth the limited service. These companies also place the buyer and the buyer's agent in a difficult position. The seller has representation, but the limited service provided often leads the seller to lean on the buyer's agent for help, which clouds agency relationships. It is recommended that the buyer's agent give written and signed notice to the seller that he or she does not represent the seller; some state associations of Realtors have forms for this purpose. The buyer's agent must then be careful not to act as the seller's agent. In limited service real estate representation, is the real estate agent providing real estate agency or marketing?

Because each state has its requirements for agency representation by a licensed real estate agent, is the limited service agent complying with a state's minimum agency requirements? Some states are enacting minimum service rules as a critical consumer protection. Sellers should have a very clear understanding of what services will and will not be provided by their limited service agents. Few cases have come before the courts to date involving limited service real estate companies, and their role will be tested as lawsuits are resolved.

BEWARE THE UNLICENSED REAL ESTATE AGENT

Most buyers, sellers, and real estate agents take it for granted that people who say they are real estate agents and have a business card are real estate agents. Unfortunately, this is not always the case. If someone is unlicensed and is involved in real estate activity that requires a license, this person is committing a crime. Some states may require agents to include their license number on a business card or contract form, or the state association of Realtors may recommend doing so.

To avoid any potential problems by unknowingly transacting business with an unlicensed real estate agent, it is recommended that you check the agent's license status at the earliest opportunity. Most states have Web sites that enable users to check agents by name or license number. The Web site might also include information on whether a licensed real estate agent has had any complaints against his or her license or has had the license suspended.

If buyers or sellers discover they have entered into a contract of sale with an unlicensed real estate agent, or the agent representing one party discovers the other agent is unlicensed, the person making the discovery should consult with an attorney. A licensed real estate agent working with an unlicensed agent may be exposed to criminal and licensing sanctions. The person who is unlicensed and is acting in the capacity of a licensed agent should be reported to the state agency that handles real estate agent licensing. Brokers and office managers need to keep track of the licensing status of their agents to be sure that licenses are valid and are renewed as required.

33
CHAPTER

Summary

By no means could I hope to cover all possible legal pitfalls for all property types in this book. I have, however, covered the issues most frequently encountered that result in real estate transaction lawsuits. Any real estate agent, broker, buyer, seller, inspector, or builder reading and absorbing the advice in this book will significantly reduce the likelihood of being involved in a dreaded lawsuit. There are approximately 2.5 million real estate licenses in the United States. It is estimated one in five agents will likely be involved in a transaction lawsuit with 40 to 60 percent of the cost of the claim involving defense costs that are paid by the agent's E&O insurance carrier, if the agent is insured.[1]

"Sales of new and existing homes, including town homes and condominiums, topped 7,000,000 units annually (2002–2005). The top 100 real estate companies, however, hold only a 17% share of real estate sales."[2] Real estate is a field open to qualified professionals who help people achieve their dream of property ownership, a cherished dream that should

---

[1] Lisa Robinson, "Top 10 Myths of Errors and Omissions Insurance," *Arizona Journal of Real Estate*, 2004.

[2] Robert Freedman, "Is Real Estate Anticompetitive?" *REALTOR Magazine*, February 2006.

not be marred by avoidable lawsuits and their accompanying high costs and high stress.

Real estate has become a complex profession with complex transactions. I am sometimes told by real estate agents, "I've had some difficult deals I thought might lead to trouble, but this transaction was so smooth I am shocked about the lawsuit." Following the same methodical and thorough procedures with every transaction is the best policy for real estate agents, general property inspectors, and builders.

In a recent survey of home buyer satisfaction with builders of new homes in the United States and Canada, *Professional Builder* magazine found that buyers want to deal with builders who genuinely care about the buyer and who want to build a quality home. The most satisfied buyers were those whose builders met with them at different stages of construction, provided a homeowner's manual covering what to expect throughout the entire home buying process, and scheduled visits to the home to inspect for problems before and after the buyer had moved in.[3]

It is my sincere desire that this book will help advance the professionalism of those involved in the real estate and construction industry, which has been an important part of my life for many years. It is also my hope that it will be of great assistance in educating the millions of buyers and sellers of real estate who need to be better informed before investing their life savings.

Treat people as if they were what they ought to be and you help them to become what they are capable of being.

—Johann W. von Goethe

---

[3] "Home Buyer Builder Satisfaction Survey," *Professional Builder*, November 2005.

Glossary

appraisal   The property appraisal will assess the value of the property as determined by a licensed appraiser. The appraiser is frequently assisted in his or her analysis of value by data provided by local real estate agents. The appraiser is not a property inspector, but should be informed of any major defects in the property or any area of the building that does not have a permit, in order to give an accurate appraisal.

arbitration   Parties in dispute can elect to arbitrate the dispute by mutually agreeing that the dispute be heard and decided on by a party they select. Arbitration can be either "binding," where the parties agree to accept the decision of the arbitrator, or "nonbinding," where the parties can reject the decision of the arbitrator.

as is   The seller wishes to sell the property in its present condition and chooses not to give the buyer either credits or make repairs for defects the buyer may discover or that are disclosed to the buyer. By mutual written agreement of the buyer and seller, the "as is" clause can be altered and often is altered.

association of Realtors   Real estate agents are licensed in each state. They may choose to join their local chapter association of Realtors, which will also give them membership in their state association of Realtors, and the National Association of Realtors.

balanced market   A balanced market is when approximately a six-month supply of homes is available in the area, and neither the buyer nor the seller has any advantage over the other in negotiation.

bankruptcy   Being or becoming insolvent and unable to pay creditors; filing with a court that administers debtor repayment or division of existing assets to repay creditors.

bench trial   A trial with a judge only and no jury. Both parties to the lawsuit must agree to waive a jury trial.

broker   In all states, agents are licensed as "sales agents" or as "brokers." A sales agent must work under the auspices and license of a broker. A licensed broker may operate alone.

brokerage   A term used to describe the real estate company that may or may not employ, under their license, numerous real estate salespeople.

business and professional codes   Codes developed in each state to define the conduct of those engaged in business and various professions.

buyers' market   A market in which the inventory of homes for sale exceeds a six-month supply in that area. The advantage in negotiation may then be greater for the buyer than the seller.

caveat emptor   Latin for, "Let the buyer beware." Suggests that a seller, the seller's agent, and the broker have no obligation to provide any information including known defects. Fortunately, real estate is no longer sold under these conditions.

CC&Rs   Covenants, conditions, and restrictions; typically establishes the rights, responsibilities, and restrictions applied to owners in a homeowners association (HOA) or subdivision. Any requirement of CC&Rs that conflicts with more recent state and federal laws is ineffective, such as those that restricted homeownership to members of certain ethnic groups or nationalities.

civil codes   Codes developed by states that relate to conduct in particular professions or between individuals and/or businesses in various matters.

CLUE report   The Comprehensive Loss Underwriting Exchange (CLUE) is used by insurers to check on the insurance claim history of a property. If the property has a recent history of major claims, insurance coverage may be denied, or the cost for insurance may be substantially increased.

complaint The papers filed with the court that state what the parties are being sued for and the reasons justifying the lawsuit.

condominiums and PUDs Condominiums or cooperatives are also referred to as planned unit developments (PUDs) or common interest developments (CIDs) and are real estate holdings that function under a homeowners association (HOA). PUDs can be multiunit buildings, townhouses, or single-family homes.

contingency clauses Contract conditions that must be fulfilled to allow the contract to proceed. (See Chapter 14.)

cooperating agent The agent who cooperates with a listing agent in bringing a buyer to the transaction. This agent may be considered an agent of the seller or exclusively representing the buyer.

cross complaint A complaint filed by a defendant in a civil action against the plaintiff or other defendants.

CRS A designation of the National Association of Realtors that stands for certified residential specialist.

defendant The person or company against whom a complaint or lawsuit is brought.

deposition The parties to the lawsuit—plaintiff and defendant—are questioned under oath by the other side regarding the circumstances of the transaction. Depositions usually take place after a complaint is filed and interrogatories are replied to but before a trial. Others may be questioned in depositions who are either general witnesses or expert witnesses.

dual agent A real estate agent or brokerage who represents both the buyer and the seller in a real estate transaction and, therefore, has a fiduciary duty to both parties.

easement The permission granted by a property owner to another property owner to use a portion of the property for a specific purpose, such as a road access.

encroachment Any structure or portion of a structure that extends into the property owned by another party, or use of the property owned by another without that party's consent.

errors and omissions insurance   Insurance that covers certain errors and omissions, mistakes, or negligence of the professional, such as the real estate agent. Commonly called *E&O insurance.*

escrow agent   The escrow agent, or settlement agent, is the intermediary who receives, holds, and distributes funds and documents between the buyer, seller, real estate agents, and some others, including termite companies, title companies, insurance companies, and lenders. In some areas independent firms act as escrow agents. In other areas this function may be handled by title companies with an escrow division or by attorneys.

expert witness   Someone who is regarded as an expert and is hired by either the plaintiff or the defendant in a lawsuit. The expert witness will review the circumstances of the lawsuit and agree to testify on behalf of one side or the other.

foreclosed property   A property that has been taken back by a lender when the buyer has failed to make required payments. When banks foreclose, the property is referred to as an REO, or real estate owned by the bank.

FSBO (for sale by owner)   Refers to properties that are being sold directly by the owner without the assistance of a real estate agent or other professional.

general property inspector   The professional who conducts an overall inspection of a property's condition. Sometimes referred to as *home inspectors,* these inspectors also inspect other types of buildings.

GRI (Graduate Realtors Institute)   A designation of the National Association of Realtors. Agents attending this advanced program of classes are required to have a certain number of years of prior experience and sales volume. Upon completion of a series of classes the agent is given the GRI designation.

interrogatories   Lists of questions that are posed to a plaintiff by a defendant and by a defendant to a plaintiff in the course of a lawsuit.

latent defects   Defects in a property that are concealed or not visually apparent.

liability insurance   Insurance for injury to third parties at a company office or at a property; it may also cover theft or damage at the property.

lis pendens   A Latin term that refers to a pending lawsuit or claim filed with a court against a property that clouds title and negatively affects the ability of a sale to be completed or the desirability of a sale.

listing agent   The real estate agent who has a signed listing contract with the seller of a property for sale.

material fact   Any fact that affects the buyer's decision to buy or the price the buyer is willing to pay.

mediation   A legal approach used to facilitate a discussion between disputing parties to assist them in resolving their dispute. See also *arbitration*.

MLS (multiple listing service)   A service used by real estate agents to list properties for rent or sale, giving the property wide exposure through the Internet and Realtor association listing sites to possibly thousands of other agents who may have buyer clients.

parapet   Any low protective barrier at the edge of a balcony or roof.

plaintiff   The party bringing a complaint or lawsuit against another party.

pocket listing   A real estate listing that a real estate agent does not list in the MLS, with the permission of the client.

preliminary title report (prelim)   A report delivered during escrow that indicates to the buyer the willingness of the title insurer to insure title and under what conditions. The prelim will disclose liens and easements of record, a property description, the present title holders, and any title issues that must be resolved prior to closing.

professional standards committee   A committee that is part of most chapter associations of Realtors. The committee is made up of member volunteers who sit on panels and hear complaints of one agent about another or complaints of a member of the public about an agent or broker. These committees usually have the authority to suspend membership, levy fines, require courses for members found at fault, and refer members to the state department of real estate for disciplinary action. Commission disputes between brokers can also be heard and mediated. These committees cannot award any funds to the public.

property profile   A report supplied to real estate agents through title companies. It usually provides information concerning present ownership, certain characteristics of the property, recent recorded loans and loan payoffs, some neighborhood information, a plot map location, and some comparable sales figures.

quitclaim deed   A deed in which one owner relinquishes his or her ownership interest in a property to another owner. A quitclaim deed should always be recorded with the public recorder's office of the appropriate city or county.

real estate agent   A person who holds a real estate license and works under the real estate license of a real estate broker and who may not conduct real estate transactions on his or her own. Also called a *sales agent* or *salesperson*.

real estate broker   A person or company that is licensed by the state and is allowed to hire real estate agents to work under his or her license, management, and direction, or the broker can operate independently in representing buyers and sellers in real estate transactions.

Realtors   Real estate agents and real estate brokers who are members of the National Association of Realtors. In addition to calling themselves licensed real estate agents or brokers, they may also refer to themselves as Realtors, a trademarked designation of the National Association of Realtors.

rescission   The revoking of the purchase of a property after the transaction has closed with the seller taking back the property.

RESPA (Real Estate Settlement and Procedures Act)   A federal law enacted in 1974 to ensure that buyers are provided with sufficient information about the nature and costs of financing and closing escrow on a home. To protect buyers from unnecessarily high closing costs, buyers must receive a "good faith estimate" of all costs required to close the transaction. RESPA section 8 prohibits a person from giving or accepting a fee, kickback, article, or service of value for referring business to settlement services. The existence of affiliated service providers must be disclosed at or before the time of referral, and the buyer cannot be required to use the service. RESPA section 9 prohibits a seller from requiring the buyer to buy title insurance from a specific title company.

sales agent   A person with a real estate sales license. The agent must work under the auspices and license of a real estate broker. Also called *real estate agent* or *salesperson*.

sellers' market   A market in which there is less than a six-month supply of homes on the market in an area; this provides the seller with an advantage in the negotiation.

selling agent   A real estate agent who brings in the buyer for a transaction. Also called *cooperating agent* or *buyer's agent.*

specific performance   A situation in which the seller is forced to go through with the transaction and sale.

title policy   The contract that ensures title under certain circumstances. A document usually delivered to the buyer after the close.

transaction broker   A form of representation used in some areas that does not require a real estate agent to fulfill all the fiduciary duties that might be required elsewhere.

walk-through inspection   An inspection for the purpose of determining whether agreed-to repairs have been made by the seller and that the property has been maintained as it was at the time the contract was signed. Buyers of new and existing properties usually write into their contracts the right to have a walk-through inspection a day or two before the closing.

weep screed   A device placed at the upper edge of a foundation footing to allow proper drainage and prevent water intrusion. It should not be buried under soil or covered by stucco.

References

GENERAL SOURCES

Web Sites

Appraisal Institute, www.appraisalinstitute.org.

Better Business Bureau, www.bbb.org.

Comprehensive Loss Underwriting Exchange (CLUE), www.choicetrust.com.

Department of Housing and Urban Development (HUD), federal fair housing information, www.hud.gov/offices/fheo.

Megan's law, www.meganslaw.org. To search for registered sex offenders in all 50 states, www.registeredoffenderlist.org.

National Association of Realtors, www.realtor.com, www.realtor.org.

Recommended Readings

Coit, Charles, S., *Introduction to Real Estate Law,* 3rd ed. (Chicago, IL: Real Estate Education Company, 1989).

de Heer, Robert, *Realty Bluebook,* 32nd ed. (Chicago, IL: Real Estate Education Company, 1998).

Freedman, Robert, ed., "Management Lessons from America's Most Successful Companies" in *Broker to Broker* (Hoboken, NJ: John Wiley & Sons, 2006).

Nichols, Barbara, "Home Inspection Risk Reduction," *REALTOR Magazine,* August 2000.

———, "Put Stigmas in Their Place," *REALTOR Magazine,* December 2000.

———, "Red Flags: Find and Conquer," *REALTOR Magazine,* May 2001.

———, "Ten Ways to Land in Court," *REALTOR Magazine,* March 2002.

———, "Commit to the Code," *REALTOR Magazine,* July 2002.

———, "Standard of Care, Measuring Up," *REALTOR Magazine,* April 2003.

———, "Don't Ignore Flaws," *REALTOR Magazine,* April 2004.

———, "Keep It or Weep," *REALTOR Magazine,* November 2004.

———, "Watch out for That #*!@* Tree!" *REALTOR Magazine,* February 2005.

———, "Don't Get in a Fix," *REALTOR Magazine,* September 2005.

———, "Don't Get Sued by Uncle Joe," *REALTOR Magazine,* August 2006.

"Property Disclosures: What You Need to Know," a Sales Associate Guide, Legal Liability Series (Chicago, IL: National Association of Realtors, 2000).

Reilly, John, *Agency Relationships in Real Estate* (Chicago, IL: Real Estate Education Company, 1987).

"Who Is My Client? A Realtors Guide to Compliance with the Law of Agency," Legal Liability Series (Chicago, IL: National Association of Realtors, 1986).

RESOURCES ON MOLD, MILDEW, AND OTHER ENVIRONMENTAL ISSUES

Web Sites

American Board of Industrial Hygiene (ABIH), www.abih.org.

American Conference of Governmental Industrial Hygienists (ACGIH), www.acgih.org.

American Indoor Air Quality Council (AIAQC), mold, www.iaqcouncil.org. This organization issues:

- CIEC, certified indoor environmental consultant
- CMC, certified microbial consultant
- CMI, certified microbial investigator
- CIE, certified indoor environmentalist
- CMR, certified microbial remediator
- CMRS, certified microbial remediation supervisor

American Industrial Hygiene Association (AIHA), www.aiha.org.

Center for Environmental Research and Technology, Inc. (CERTI), Radon measurement and mitigation courses, www.certi.us.

Environmental Protection Agency (EPA), www.epa.gov/mold/moldresources.html, www.epa.gov/mold/moldguide.html, www.epa.gov/lead, and www.epa.gov/asbestos.

"FAQs About Mold," by Michele Lind, www.aaronline.com (search: FAQs about mold).

Indoor Air Quality Association (IAQA), www.iaqa.org. The American Indoor Air Quality Council (AIAQC) and the Indoor Environmental Standards Organization (IESO) merged with this association.

Indoor Environmental Standards Organization (IESO), www.iestandards. org. This organization issues: CRMI, certified residential mold inspector.

Institute of Inspection, Cleaning and Restoration Certification (IICRC), www.iicrc.org. This organization issues: AMRT, applied microbial remediation technician.

Restoration Industry Association (RIA) [formerly the Association of Specialists in Cleaning and Restoration (ASCR), www.ascr.org].

Recommended Readings

Cooper, Susan S., *The Truth About Mold*, (Dearborn, MI: Dearborn Real Estate Education, 2004).

"Fighting Mold in Your Home or Office: Controlling Moisture through Better Building Practices," Responsible Solutions to Mold Coalition (RSMC), 12-page brochure, available at www.responsible moldsolutions.org (members represent industry associations, government agencies, and academia).

RESOURCES FOR PROPERTY INSPECTIONS
Web Sites

American Society of Home Inspectors (ASHI), www.ashi.org.

National Association of Home Inspectors (NAHI), www.nahi.org.

RESOURCES IN THE BUILDING INDUSTRY
Web Sites

EIFS Legal Network, www.stuccolaw.com, deals with EIFS (synthetic stucco legal issues) and mold.

Energy and Environmental Building Association (EEBA), www.eeba.org, dedicated to providing awareness, education, and development of better building principles and practices.

Homeowners Against Deficient Dwellings, www.hadd.com, deals with home builder ratings and builder complaints.

National Association of Home Builders (NAHB), www.nahb.org, check "pre-settlement walk through tips" in the site's search area.

J. D. Powers & Associates, National Home Builder Ratings, www.jdpower.com/cc/homes/index.jsp.

Professional Builder magazine, www.probuilder.com.

Recommended Readings

Fields, Alan, and Denise Fields, *Your New House: The Alert Consumer's Guide to Buying and Building a New Home* (Boulder, CO: Windsor Peak Press, 2002).

Miller, Thomas E., and Rachel Miller, *Home and Condo Defects: A Homeowner's Guide to Faulty Construction* (Santa Ana, CA: Seven Locks Press, 2001).

INDEX

ABOUT THE AUTHOR

Barbara Nichols is a real estate broker, a licensed general contractor, a real estate risk management educator, an author and expert witness, and a national expert in real estate risk management and liability. She is the owner of Nichols Real Estate and General Contracting. She has a bachelor's degree from Simmons College in Boston and a master's degree in business from Cornell University, and she is a member of the Cornell University Real Estate Council. Since 1994 she has served as an expert witness in hundreds of real estate–related lawsuits involving real estate agents, their brokers, buyers, sellers, general property inspectors, and builders.

Barbara has authored 11 articles over the past six years for the National Association of Realtors' monthly publication *REALTOR Magazine*, which is distributed to over 1.2 million real estate agents. Her articles have appeared in the law section of the magazine and advise agents how to better serve their clients and customers and avoid lawsuits. She is a continuing writer for *REALTOR Magazine*. Barbara has also written *You Must Have Inspection Protection*, an informative pamphlet advising buyers and sellers why property inspections are so important and assisting buyers in finding qualified general property inspectors. She is a contributing author to the recently published National Association of Realtors' book *Broker to Broker*, which contains management lessons from America's most successful real estate companies. She was also a contributing author to the *Guide to Construction Marketing Research*.

In addition, Barbara served on the grievance committee of the Southland Regional Association of Realtors in Los Angeles, and she currently serves on this organization's professional standards committee. She has appeared as a featured speaker at the National Association of Realtors' annual convention where she spoke on risk management.

She has taught classes for the American Marketing Association and the American Management Association. Thousands of real estate agents have benefited from her three-hour class titled, "How to Stay Out of Court." She has produced an accompanying four-hour, four-CD audio series that covers a great deal of additional information on major risk management topics and a review of the live class.

Barbara has been interviewed by the *Los Angeles Times* concerning property disclosures; the ABC news program *20/20, MarketWatch/Dow Jones*, and Fox News on property stigmas; and her local ABC network in Los Angeles on property inspections.

To request Barbara as a speaker or to order the audio CD series "How to Stay Out of Court," please call 760–753–4066, or visit Barbara's Web site at www.BarbaraNichols.net. To contact Barbara as an expert witness or broker representing buyers and sellers in West Los Angeles and the San Fernando Valley, please call her at 310–273–6369.